INTERNATIONAL COURTS AND THE PERFORMANCE OF INTERNATIONAL AGREEMENTS

Nations often turn to international courts to help overcome collective action problems associated with international relations. However, these courts generally cannot enforce their rulings, which raises the question: how effective are international courts?

This book proposes a general theory of international courts that assumes a court has no direct power over national governments. Member states are free to ignore both the international agreement and the rulings by the court created to enforce that agreement. The theory demonstrates that such a court can, in fact, facilitate cooperation with international law, but only within important political constraints. The authors examine the theoretical argument in the context of the European Union. Using an original data set of rulings by the European Court of Justice, they find that the disposition of court rulings and government compliance with those rulings comport with the theory's predictions.

Clifford J. Carrubba is a professor of political science, chair of the Political Science department, and professor of law, by courtesy, at Emory University. He also founded and is currently serving as the director of the Institute for Quantitative Theory and Methods at Emory University. Carrubba has published in *American Political Science Review*, *American Journal of Political Science*, *Journal of Politics*, *International Organizations*, *Political Analysis*, *Legislative Studies Quarterly*, *Comparative Political Studies*, and *Journal of Law, Economics, and Organization*.

Matthew J. Gabel is a professor in the Department of Political Science at Washington University in St. Louis, where he also serves as the associate chair of the department. In 2010, he was a John Simon Guggenheim Foundation Fellow. He is the author of *Interests and Integration* (1998) and has written articles for *American Political Science Review*, *American Journal of Political Science*, *Journal of Politics*, *Legislative Studies Quarterly*, *Journal of Common Market Studies*, and *Comparative Political Studies*. Gabel is a founding associate editor of *European Union Politics*.

COMPARATIVE CONSTITUTIONAL LAW AND POLICY

Series Editors:

Tom Ginsburg
University of Chicago

Zachary Elkins
University of Texas at Austin

Ran Hirschl
University of Toronto

Comparative constitutional law is an intellectually vibrant field that encompasses an increasingly broad array of approaches and methodologies. This series collects analytically innovative and empirically grounded work from scholars of comparative constitutionalism across academic disciplines. Books in the series include theoretically informed studies of single constitutional jurisdictions, comparative studies of constitutional law and institutions, and edited collections of original essays that respond to challenging theoretical and empirical questions in the field.

Volumes in the Series:

Comparative Constitutional Design edited by Tom Ginsburg (2012)

Consequential Courts: Judicial Roles in Global Perspective edited by Diana Kapiszewski, Gordon Silverstein, and Robert A. Kagan (2013)

Social and Political Foundations of Constitutions edited by Denis J. Galligan and Mila Versteeg (2013)

Presidential Legislation in India: The Law and Practice of Ordinances by Shubhankar Dam (2014)

Constitutions in Authoritarian Regimes edited by Tom Ginsburg and Alberto Simpser (2014)

Social Difference and Constitutionalism in Pan-Asia edited by Susan H. Williams (2014)

Constitutionalism in Asia in the Early Twenty-First Century edited by Albert Chen (2014)

Constitutions and Religious Freedom Frank Cross (2015)

Reputation and Judicial Tactics: A Theory of National and International Courts by Shai Dothan (2015)

International Courts and the Performance of International Agreements: A General Theory with Evidence from the European Union by Clifford Carrubba and Matthew Gabel (2015)

International Courts and the Performance of International Agreements

A GENERAL THEORY WITH EVIDENCE
FROM THE EUROPEAN UNION

CLIFFORD J. CARRUBBA

Emory University

MATTHEW J. GABEL

Washington University, St. Louis

CAMBRIDGE
UNIVERSITY PRESS

University Printing House, Cambridge CB2 8BS, United Kingdom

One Liberty Plaza, 20th Floor, New York, NY 10006, USA

477 Williamstown Road, Port Melbourne, VIC 3207, Australia

4843/24, 2nd Floor, Ansari Road, Daryaganj, Delhi - 110002, India

79 Anson Road, #06-04/06, Singapore 079906

Cambridge University Press is part of the University of Cambridge.

It furthers the University's mission by disseminating knowledge in the pursuit of education, learning and research at the highest international levels of excellence.

www.cambridge.org
Information on this title: www.cambridge.org/9781107677265

© Clifford J. Carrubba and Matthew J. Gabel 2015

This publication is in copyright. Subject to statutory exception and to the provisions of relevant collective licensing agreements, no reproduction of any part may take place without the written permission of Cambridge University Press.

First published 2015
First paperback edition 2017

A catalogue record for this publication is available from the British Library

ISBN 978-1-107-06572-7 Hardback
ISBN 978-1-107-67726-5 Paperback

Cambridge University Press has no responsibility for the persistence or accuracy of URLs for external or third-party internet websites referred to in this publication, and does not guarantee that any content on such websites is, or will remain, accurate or appropriate.

Contents

Acknowledgments		*page* vii
1	International courts and compliance	1
2	A theory of courts and compliance in international law	21
3	Putting the theory to the test: evaluating the hypotheses in the European Union	57
4	Preliminary considerations: designing a control for the legal merits	86
5	The Political Sensitivity Hypothesis: third-party briefs and European Court of Justice rulings	125
6	The Conditional Effectiveness Hypothesis: the European Court of Justice and economic integration	156
7	Conclusion	191
References		220
Index		233

Acknowledgments

Our collaboration on this book began as a conversation about the European Court of Justice (ECJ) and its role in the process of European integration. Over the last fifteen years, that conversation prompted us to engage broader theoretical questions about the impact and limits of international courts. It also incited our effort to collect and examine evidence that would allow us to distinguish how and under what conditions international courts (and the ECJ in particular) shape the behavior of their member states. This book represents the current state of that (now very long) conversation.

In executing this project, we have been very fortunate to receive the generous financial support of several organizations. The National Science Foundation (SES-079084) provided funding for the collection of data regarding rulings by the ECJ and the development of our theoretical account. The University of Kentucky and the Halle Institute at Emory University also contributed financially to the data collection. The John Simon Guggenheim Foundation provided Dr. Gabel with a fellowship to write a large portion of this manuscript. Caitlin Ainsley, Don Beaudette, Bethany Blacktsone, Marc Hutchison, Michael Malecki, Toby Rider, and Joe Sonka provided valuable research assistance.

We have had the opportunity to present various parts of the book at a number of conferences and seminars. We are particularly grateful for the hospitality and comments from the seminar participants at the European Union Centers at the University of Colorado and Syracuse University; the schools of law at the University of California–Berkeley, Georgetown University, University of Texas, Hebrew University of Jerusalem, and Tel Aviv University; the Europe Center at Stanford University and Duke University; the departments of political science at the University of Colorado, Duke University, the University of Georgia, the University of South Carolina, the University of Wisconsin, the University of Rochester, and SUNY-Buffalo.

Along the way, we benefited from comments, criticism, and advice from numerous people, including David Anderson, Pablo Beramendi, Bill Bernhard, Abby Blass, Carles Boix, Dan Brinks, Damian Chalmers, Terry Chapman, Tom Clark, Jens Dammann, Marie Demetriou, George Downs, Zach Elkins, John Ferejohn, Geoffrey Garrett, Jeff Gill, Mark Hallerberg, Gretchen Helmke, Imelda Higgins, Simon Hix, John Huber, Nate Jensen, Leslie Johns, Joe Jupille, Luke Keele, Jay Krehbiel, David Leblang, Gail McElroy, Christine Mahoney, William Minnozi, Jamie Monogan, Harvey Palmer, Kirk Randazzo, Nils Ringe, James Rogers, Kenneth Scheve, Charles Shipan, Jim Spriggs, Jeff Staton, Georg Vanberg, Erik Wibbels, David Wildasin, and Chris Zorn.

We would also like to thank the managing and series editors for the comparative constitutional law and policy series, Zach Elkins, Tom Ginsburg, Ran Hirscl, and John Berger. Christina Yeager provided superb copyediting.

Finally, we are particularly indebted to our families and loved ones. Cliff would like to thank his wife, Dana, and three cats, Clea, Csavo, and Daisy, for their unending patience and support. Matt is very grateful to his wife, Angela. Her encouragement, support, and patience were critical to the completion of the project, particularly since the book's development coincided almost exactly with their ongoing adventure in parenthood.

Some of the material in the book has appeared in our previously published articles. Much of the material in Chapter 2 appeared in "Courts and Compliance in International Law" (*Theoretical Inquiries in Law* 14 (2): 505–41, 2013, © 2013 Theoretical Inquiries in Law, reprinted with permission). Parts of Chapters 3 and 5 appeared in "Understanding the Role of the European Court of Justice in European Integration" (*American Political Science Review* 106 (1): 214–23, 2012, © 2012 American Political Science Association, reprinted with permission) and "Judicial Behavior under Political Constraints: Evidence from the European Court of Justice" (*American Political Science Review* 102 (4): 435–52, 2008, © 2008 American Political Science Association, reprinted with permission). Parts of Chapter 6 appeared in "Of Courts and Commerce" (*Journal of Politics* 74 (4): 1125–37, 2012, © 2012 Southern Political Science Association, reprinted with permission).

1

International courts and compliance

The number of international agreements has exploded since World War II. As of today, some 3,000 multilateral and 27,000 bilateral treaties are in force.[1] These agreements cover an enormous array of activity. As a result, international laws are now in place to regulate trade relations, human rights, environmental policy, social policy, immigration rights, and competition (antitrust) policy, among other areas. In joining these international agreements, signatories make written commitments to bring national policies and practices in line with the rules of the common regulatory regime. These agreements are typically necessary because signatories would not adopt the prescribed behavior voluntarily as a result of domestic political, economic, or social pressures.

Of course, adoption of the agreement does not, by itself, change those domestic pressures. Consequently, once the agreement is signed, governments still may not follow through on their commitments. To help ensure government compliance with these agreements, countries often create international institutions, and legal institutions – permanent and ostensibly neutral third-party institutions to review potential violations of these agreements – in particular (Smith 2000). Table 1.1 lists 54 recent and current multilateral international regulatory regimes and describes characteristics of their dispute settlement mechanisms (DSMs).[2] Although not exhaustive, this list gives a general sense of the prevalence of various legal institutions prescribed in international agreements. Two-thirds (42) of these regimes feature a means of third-party review by a panel to which member states (and others, depending

---

[1] Numbers reported in Simmons (2010).
[2] The information in the table was derived from the treaty and, where available, the rules of procedure of the dispute resolution mechanism. The table identifies whether certain features are stipulated in the treaty or rules of procedure, not whether these features are currently operational. Our list does not include subsidiary agreements because they often share the DSM of the overarching organization.

TABLE 1.1 *Multilateral international regulatory regimes*[a]

Organization	Third-party review	Standing tribunal	Amicus briefs
African Economic Community	Yes	Yes	
African Union	Yes	Yes	Yes
Agadir Agreement	Yes	No	
Andean Community	Yes	Yes	Yes
Arab Maghreb Union	Yes	Yes	
ASEAN Free Trade Agreement	Yes	No	
Asia-Pacific Economic Cooperation	No	No	
Asia-Pacific Trade Agreement	Yes	No	No
Association of Caribbean States	Yes		
Association of Southeast Asian Nations	Yes	No	Yes
Benelux Economic Union	Yes	Yes	Yes
Caribbean Community	Yes	Yes	Yes
Central American Common Market	Yes	Yes	No
Central American Integration System	Yes	Yes	No
Central European Free Trade Agreement	Yes	No	Yes
Common Market for Eastern and Southern Africa	Yes	Yes	Yes
Common Market of the South	Yes	Yes	No
Commonwealth of Independent States	Yes	Yes	Yes
Community of Latin American and Caribbean States	No	No	No
Community of Sahel-Saharan States	No	No	No
Council of Arab Economic Unity	Yes	Yes	
Dominican Republic-Central America-US FTA	Yes	No	Yes
East African Community	Yes	Yes	Yes
Economic and Monetary Community of Central Africa	Yes	Yes	
Economic Community of Central African States	Yes	Yes	
Economic Community of the Great Lakes Countries	Yes	Yes	
Economic Community of West African States	Yes	Yes	Yes
Eurasian Economic Community	Yes	Yes	
European Economic Area	Yes	Yes	Yes
European Free Trade Association	No	No	No
European Union	Yes	Yes	Yes
Georgia, Ukraine, Azerbaijan, Moldova Free Trade Agreement	No	No	No
Greater Arab Free Trade Area	Yes	No	
Gulf Cooperation Council	Yes	No	No

TABLE 1.1 (cont.)

Organization	Third-party review	Standing tribunal	Amicus briefs
Intergovernmental Authority on Development	No	No	No
Latin American Integration Agreement	Yes	No	No
Mano River Union	No	No	No
Melanesian Spearhead Group	No	No	No
North American Free Trade Agreement	Yes	No	Yes
Organization for the Harmonization of Corporate Law in Africa	Yes	Yes	Yes
Organization of East Caribbean States	Yes	Yes	No
Organization of Islamic Cooperation	Yes	Yes	Yes
Pacific Island Countries Trade Agreement	Yes	No	Yes
Pacific Islands Forum	No	No	No
South African Customs Union	No	No	No
South African Development Community	Yes	Yes	Yes
South Asia Co-operative Environment Program	No	No	No
South Asian Association for Regional Cooperation	Yes	No	No
South Pacific Regional Trade and Economic Cooperation	No	No	No
Trans-Pacific Strategic Economic Partnership	Yes	No	Yes
United Nations Convention on the Law of the Sea	Yes	Yes	
West African Economic and Monetary Union	Yes	Yes	
World Intellectual Property Organization	Yes	Yes	No
World Trade Organization	Yes	Yes	Yes

[a] When we could not find relevant information, we left the cell blank.

Source: The classifications are based on the treaties governing the organization and official rules governing the dispute settlement procedure.

on the regime) can challenge a member-state government for alleged violations of treaty obligations. This third-party review is commonly executed by an independent standing body with a permanent staff. We refer to these panels as international "courts." Also note that, as will become important later, these courts often formally allow nonlitigant governments to intervene in a case through amicus briefs.

Are these international courts effective? There is fairly wide variation in activity, with some institutions lying dormant or wilting on the vine while others thrive and appear to provide substantial benefits to their membership.[3] The most successful and deepest international agreements, such as the World Trade Organization (WTO)/General Agreement on Tariffs and Trade (GATT) and the European Union (EU), have vibrant courts that routinely review substantively important aspects of their agreements.[4] This suggests that international courts, where used regularly, support international cooperation in the face of the, sometimes severe, incentives for members to defect from the agreement.

Yet international courts are generally considered weak institutions. They lack the means (physical, financial, or political) to compel states to comply with their international obligations. Thus, it is far from obvious why international courts are both active in reviewing alleged violations of international agreements and apparently influential on the level of compliance with these agreements. The resulting puzzle – whether and how international courts can promote compliance with international agreements – is the central focus of this book.

This puzzle is substantively and normatively important. If international courts can constrain sovereign government actions through their rulings, these institutions can help solve many of the world's most pressing international policy challenges. For example, they can advance global economic prosperity by supporting increasingly liberalized trade through agreements such as the WTO, they can help resolve long-term environmental challenges (such as fisheries resources, pollution, global warming, and more), and they can improve the protection of human rights through such treaties as the European Convention on Human Rights. If not, the proliferation of these institutions is, at best, a distraction and waste of resources. At worst, these institutions are tools governments can use to deceive the global public into believing they are serious about solving major global challenges. Thus, solving this puzzle is important not just for knowing whether these courts facilitate global policy change but also for evaluating the goals and character of the governments that created these institutions.

In this chapter, we first review the classic arguments regarding the difficulty of international cooperation and the potential contribution of international

---

[3] For example, Gray (2012) provides a comprehensive overview of regional trade agreements and the state of their institutions. Gray finds that a large share of these are either dead or in a "zombie" state, where the organization exists in name only.
[4] On the coincidence of "deep" agreements and legalized DSMs, see Helfer and Slaughter (2005: 938). On the performance of legalized DSMs, see Gray and Slapin (2012), Helfer and Slaughter (2005), and Kono (2007), but see Posner and Yoo (2005).

institutions to overcoming these problems with government noncompliance. We then turn to international courts. Specifically, we engage arguments about how courts can facilitate cooperation in the absence of coercion. In the last part of this chapter, we sketch out our argument and describe our strategy for bringing evidence to bear on two of its implications. Our empirical focus is on one particularly important and successful international organization, the European Union (EU). We conclude the chapter by discussing our methodological approach and the organization of the book.

I. THE DEBATE ON INTERNATIONAL INSTITUTIONS

Historically, international relations scholars have been fairly skeptical of the value of international agreements and the institutions created to implement them. In particular, realists believe the international environment is fundamentally anarchic and therefore hostile to international cooperation. As Hoffman (1956: 364) described it, a state is "a legally sovereign unit in a tenuous net of breakable obligations." International agreements and institutions therefore can do little to shape or constrain state behavior (Bork 1989–90; Boyle 1980). These scholars are particularly dubious of the ability of international legal processes to influence state behavior (Bulterman and Kuijer 1996; Diehl 1996; Fischer 1981, 1982). Rather, power relations among states determine when and how governments obey international law (Morgenthau 1985). This does not preclude all compliance with international agreements. But any such cooperation should reflect a convergence of interests among states and the fact that these agreements reflect the international balance of power (Morgenthau 1985). Similarly, Aron (1981: 820) concludes, "International law can merely ratify the fate of arms and the arbitration of force."[5] International institutions are therefore epiphenomenal and have no influence on the behavior of sovereign states.

The first principles of the realist position seem compelling. It is certainly true that states are powerful, sovereign entities in the international environment. It also is true that these agreements cannot literally compel states. And finally, it is hard to imagine that the agreements do not reflect power politics among these states. However, many scholars ultimately reject the realists' conclusions. We observe states creating and maintaining international agreements, some of which involve the creation of enduring independent institutions. What is more, governments frequently appear to comply with agreements and

---

[5] See Simmons (1998: 79–80) for a more extended summary of the realist position.

participate in their institutions. Traditional realists are at a loss to explain why (Keohane and Martin 1995).

What might the realists be missing? One set of responses, based in constructivist and normative arguments, revolves around the notion that legally formalizing an international agreement ultimately constrains state behavior. For example, the managerial model argues that treaties are consent-based arrangements designed to serve the interests of the participating states. As such, incentives to deviate should be weak by definition. Further, when such occasions do arise, the norm of compliance with legal obligations should constrain potentially deviant behavior (Chayes and Chayes 1995: 8). Others argue that the notion of consent itself drives compliance. Because treaties are voluntary agreements consented to by the signing states, once a treaty is signed it creates a general legal obligation that necessitates compliance (Byers 1999: 7; Setear 1997: 156; Smith 1991: 1565–6).

The domestic political context could also be important. For example, democracies are accustomed to using negotiation rather than violence as a resolution to conflict, which may reinforce a norm among democracies of resolving international disputes through international institutions (Dixon 1993). Alternatively, the domestic interaction of state and nonstate actors under a new international agreement could promote compliance with the agreement (Koh 1996: 204).[6]

In one sense, these arguments answer the realists' concerns about the effectiveness of international agreements. However, they do so, in part, by assuming away the realists' challenge. They claim that exogenous factors ultimately constrain governments so as to reduce, if not eliminate, the temptation to renege on agreements. Consequently, there is no compliance problem for which international institutions or courts could offer a solution.[7]

For a different set of scholars, this line of argument does not provide compelling answers for why states comply and why international institutions influence the level of compliance with agreements. These scholars, coming from

---

[6] Scholars have criticized these types of arguments along a number of lines (e.g., see Guzman 2002a). For our purposes here, these theories do not provide the theoretical foundations for when and why noncompliance should occur. For example, Dixon (1993) argues that democracies are more likely to engage in dispute resolution at the international level when engaged in conflicts with each other. But why do we sometimes see democracies following rulings issued by third-party DSMs and sometimes not? Similarly, an argument that the act of consenting to these agreements gives them a self-sustaining normative force cannot explain the conditions under which we should observe noncompliance.

[7] We discuss how our theoretical approach does and does not complement these arguments in the conclusion.

a liberal institutional (or functional rationalist) perspective, propose answers more closely rooted to the first principles of the realist position.

a. *International agreements from a liberal institutional perspective*

As with the realists, liberal institutionalists start with the assumption that governments must voluntarily choose to comply with international agreements. However, they elaborate on this challenge by more fully characterizing what governments hope to gain from signing an international agreement. Specifically, they argue that governments sign international agreements to help resolve common problems that require some collective action, or coordination, among the signatories (Bilder 1989; Keohane 1984). Generally, the collective action challenges are described as a prisoners' dilemma. Two or more governments identify policies that, if adopted by each government, leave the participant states jointly better off. However, each government individually has an incentive to defect and retain its original policies. The challenge is to find a mechanism that helps governments realize the benefits of mutual cooperation despite the incentive to defect. International trade is a typical example of this kind of policy area: two governments might benefit from each lowering trade barriers on goods the other state wants to export, but each government individually has an incentive to cheat and to try to keep its trade barriers high in order to protect its import-competing firms.

According to liberal institutionalists, international agreements can help governments realize the benefits of international cooperation by overcoming the collective action problem. International agreements lay down a codified set of rules that establish expectations for behavior among the agreements' participants. These clearly coordinated expectations of what is and is not permissible behavior allow states to build and cue off of reputations. Specifically, if a state develops a bad reputation for not following the rules, the other participants can point to the violations and punish the state for its bad behavior (e.g., by retaliating in turn). Assuming the threatened punishment is sufficiently severe, the potential transgressor will prefer to obey the agreement (despite the incentive to defect), and otherwise unsustainable international cooperation can be supported (e.g., see Keohane 1984; Schachter 1991). Thus, these scholars argue that governments, motivated by the same first principles identified by realists, have a rational incentive to make and comply with international agreements.[8]

---

[8] These scholars also argue that the international institutions that often accompany these agreements can help states overcome informational problems that might otherwise undermine

Although a compelling argument, the liberal institutional perspective suffers from two limitations. First, Downs, Rocke, and Barsoom (1996) demonstrate that this liberal institutional logic can explain only *shallow* (as opposed to *deep*) agreements. They show that governments will agree to policy change under an international agreement only that they would agree to without the formal agreement (because reputation building is possible without a formal, written agreement). Yet, as stated earlier, agreements seemingly deeper than those described by Downs, Rocke, and Barsoom (1996) exist. For example, both the WTO and the EU appear to be much more than simple, shallow agreements. That we observe governments frequently obeying the rules and regulations of these regimes is something for which the standard liberal international argument cannot account.

Second, the liberal institutional argument is predicated on the traditional prisoners' dilemma. In this model the costs and benefits of cooperation do not change over time. However, we know this is not the case. And, critically, not only can the costs of complying with the regime's rules vary but sometimes those costs can be large enough relative to the benefits that the governments are no longer playing a prisoners' dilemma (e.g., Carrubba 2005). In this extreme case the governments would be better off with mutual defection than with mutual cooperation. This raises challenges for the traditional liberal institutionalist arguments about the value of international institutions for sustaining cooperation.

In sum, the standard liberal institutionalist argument cannot explain why we see deep agreements, and it cannot explain how states can maintain cooperation in the face of potentially severe variability in the costs of compliance. These two concerns reinforce each other because it is exactly the deeper agreements that are likely to have the more problematic, higher-variability costs. We are therefore left with the questions of how governments sustain cooperation in deeper agreements and what role, if any, international institutions play. Scholarship in what has become known as the rational design literature addresses these issues.

---

cooperation (Keohane 1984). For example, mutually beneficial agreements can be undermined if there is asymmetric information among the contracting parties (Keohane 1984: 92–5). Suppose one state knows more about the likely consequences of a potential international agreement than its contracting party does. Even if the agreement would be mutually beneficial in reality, the less informed party might be sufficiently concerned with the possibility of deception that it will not sign the agreement. International institutions can help resolve this dilemma if they can act as neutral third parties that facilitate information transmission (Keohane 1984: 94). Our argument explicitly incorporates informational challenges in international agreements, but in a very different way.

b. *International institutions from a rational design perspective*

Building off of liberal institutionalism, rational design scholars start from the premise that "states use international institutions to further their own goals, and they design institutions accordingly" (Koremenos, Lipson, and Snidal 2001: 762). However, unlike the previous work, the rational design literature focuses on the specific design features of international agreements. Koremenos et al. (2001: 764) argue that these design features are of interest because they can help make international cooperation "more feasible and durable." Stated slightly differently, the rational design literature argues that international institutions can help governments achieve otherwise unsustainable – in Downs, Rocke, and Barsoom's (1996) terms, deeper – international cooperation, in part because they can help sustain cooperation in the face of sometimes highly costly shocks to the incentive to cooperate.

To see how, consider the flexibility of an international agreement. These scholars believe that the flexibility of an international agreement allows otherwise unsustainable cooperation (Koremenos, Lipson, and Snidal 2001: 773). As the incentives to comply with the regime's rules change, introducing flexibility into the agreement can help keep states from either violating or leaving the agreement. For example, Rosendorff and Milner (2001) demonstrate how escape clauses in the WTO agreement can help governments sustain otherwise unsustainable international cooperation in trade. These authors do so by explicitly modeling the costs of cooperation as changing over time. Escape clauses allow governments to opt out of complying when the costs are sufficiently high such that the government would defect from the regime if not allowed to use the escape clause. As a result, the international agreement survives. Another institutional feature that can facilitate cooperation is a formalized adjudication process. We now turn to that institutional feature in detail.

c. *Courts as rational design*

From one perspective, courts are a straightforward solution to the challenge of maintaining government compliance with international agreements. By construction, courts are designed to be the institution that parties turn to when they feel their legal rights have been violated. Upon an appeal, courts are responsible for interpreting and applying existing law, and their decisions, once made, are supposed to be binding. Further, some argue that highly legalized international courts are in a particularly strong position to enjoy compliance by the agreement's member states (Keohane, Moravscik, and

Slaughter 2000a; Kono 2007: 749; Smith 2000). A highly legalized international court issues binding rulings that are integrated into the domestic legal systems of the member states through *direct effect*, which means the international agreement and its rulings can be invoked and enforced in domestic courts. Thus, to the extent national governments change policy when confronted by an adverse ruling in a national court, highly legalized international courts can overcome the compliance problem. Yet, although legalized international courts are commonly associated with enduring and successful international agreements, existing evidence does not support the argument that legalization *causes* success (Kono 2007).[9]

This empirical finding is hardly surprising given the long tradition of research on judicial impact that shows the limited effect of national court rulings on government policy. The primary actor in the domestic setting that enforces court decisions is the government. Thus, the policy impact of a national court depends critically on the willingness of the national government to change policy as prescribed by the court's rulings. Governments often do so only grudgingly. This is the general point made by Epp (1998) in his seminal work on the "rights revolutions" in the United States, Canada, India, and the United Kingdom. Furthermore, a vast body of research on the United States and, increasingly, other countries indicates that the executive and legislative branches do not routinely acquiesce to adverse court rulings (e.g., Canon 1991; Staton and Moore 2011; Vanberg 2005; Wood and Waterman 1991, 1993).[10]

This is not to say that domestic courts are completely impotent to change government policy – they could provide some leverage over governments for international courts. But the judicial impact literature does highlight that such judicial power should not be assumed; rather, we need an argument for how and under what conditions a domestic court ruling can influence government behavior. A relatively recent and growing set of studies does just that (e.g., Carrubba and Zorn 2010; Conant 2002; Staton 2010; Vanberg 2005). In sum, existing work on domestic courts suggests that domestic court influence on government behavior is no more than conditional and therefore casts doubt on the argument that highly legalized international courts, by borrowing on the authority of national courts, automatically gain compliance with their rulings.

---

[9] Kono (2007) investigated whether more legalized dispute settlement mechanisms (DSMs) promoted greater trade liberalization in preferential trade agreements than less legalized DSMs did. He found that the existence of a standing third-party review body was associated with greater trade liberalization. But there was no difference in trade liberalization that resulted from more legalized attributes of the DSM, including whether the rulings could be enforced through domestic courts.

[10] We provide a detailed discussion of this subject in Chapter 6.

The rational design literature suggests an alternative mechanism for court influence. As described previously, this literature assumes governments are playing a version of a prisoners' dilemma in which the costs of compliance are highly variable. This fact can make unconditional compliance with the regime's rules unsustainable. Consequently, the success of the agreement can depend on an ability to selectively enforce cooperation. A court can help governments implement such a strategy.

Rosendorff (2005) and Carrubba (2005) have developed formal theoretical arguments of international court influence along these lines. Consistent with the rational design perspective, they assume that the member governments to an agreement design the court so that it enhances net beneficial compliance (and only net beneficial compliance). Both models assume an underlying collective action problem that governments intend the international agreement to overcome. Further, the costs and benefits of compliance can change over time. Rosendorff (2005) demonstrates how the WTO Dispute Settlement Body (DSB) allows cooperation to be sustainable under a wider range of conditions than would be sustainable without the DSB. Carrubba (2005) demonstrates how a generic international court can help governments sustain a selective compliance regime in which governments comply with the regulatory regime's rules if and only if cooperation is net beneficial (i.e., governments comply only when reciprocal compliance over a particular level of cost leaves both governments better off). Further, Carrubba (2005) demonstrates when governments prefer an agreement with a court versus one without a court. This literature continues to evolve with additional work by Johns (2011, 2012) and others (e.g., Gilligan, Johns, and Rosendorff 2010; Rosendorff and Milner 2001).

This growing area of research suggests that international courts, even without enforcement powers, can contribute to the performance of an international regulatory agreement. And, by assuming courts cannot enforce compliance directly, these models put the compliance problem at the center of their arguments.

II. OBJECTIVE OF THE BOOK

In this book we build off of the rational design literature. Specifically, we ask how a weak international court – one with no direct enforcement mechanism and no assumed informational advantage (i.e., the court does not know things that governments or litigants do not know) – can effect national government compliance with international law. To what degree can these courts obtain government compliance with international law and their rulings on international law? What are the limits to what these courts can do? What do answers to these questions suggest about the international rule of law? Are nation-states losing a degree of sovereignty? Or, in the opposite extreme, are these institutions ultimately impotent in the face of these challenges? If the answer is somewhere in between, how can we understand exactly what these courts are able to accomplish?

To answer these questions, we propose and test a formal theory of international court influence. The theory is an extension of the formal model presented in Carrubba (2005) and has five key features. First, it captures the key challenge we are interested in studying: a court is tasked with ruling on cases in which governments have allegedly failed to obey international law, but governments can freely evade adverse court decisions. Second, the model is designed to be as general as possible. We believe this core strategic challenge regarding compliance is a common one among international courts. As such, we want a model that clearly analyzes this challenge and applies generally. The more institution-specific detail we build into our model, the harder it is to see how the model applies to settings without those specifics. For example, if we explicitly model the infringement procedure of the European Court of Justice (ECJ) in its entirety, we massively restrict the generality of the model because no other courts have that exact mechanism for litigation. To the degree that adding in this institutional detail clouds our ability to see how the theory applies outside of the ECJ, and to the degree that the fundamental challenge we are interested in studying holds independent of the specifics of the legal process, adding that detail is ultimately counterproductive to our theoretical exercise. Thus, although interesting in its own right, we are not attempting to explain how the particular institutional nuances of any given court shape that court's influence.[11]

Third, the theory is designed to apply to a wide range of substantive regulatory regimes. As long as the policy area is one in which governments perceive a benefit from mutual cooperation but simultaneously face at least intermittent incentives to defect from the regime's rules, our model will apply. At a minimum, then, the theory applies to international trade, environmental policy, and a variety of social policies. That said, the theory is not universalistic. For example, it is not clear that our theory applies to international human rights law. This depends on whether the international human rights regime addresses a collective action problem and whether enforcement of the regime's rules is potentially problematic.

---

[11] For example, Rosendorff (2005) offers some very compelling insights about how specific features of the WTO's dispute settlement procedure influences the extent to which that body can sustain cooperation with the WTO legal regime. Our contribution is consistent with, and complementary to, this more nuanced approach. Also see Rosendorff and Milner (2001) for examples of work studying these more institution-specific questions.

Fourth, our theory also is complete in a very specific sense. Many models of judicial politics start from an intermediate stage. For example, they assume some laws exist, wherever they have come from, and a case contesting the validity of some defendant's action has reached a particular court, for whatever reasons. Given that starting point, how should we expect the case to resolve? Although a useful and appropriate starting point for many questions, this is not a good strategy for the issues this book seeks to address. To understand an international court's ability to facilitate international rule of law, we must know not only how a case will resolve when it reaches the court but also what sorts of cases will reach the court and, even before that, the conditions under which a government will choose to violate the regime's rules in the first place. Further, it also is critical to define the microfoundations for why the governments created the particular regulatory regime and chose to provide for a court.[12] Only with all of these factors taken into account can we draw well-reasoned inferences about judicial influence in the courts we are studying. We address all of these factors in our model.

Finally, the model proposed here is a generalization of Carrubba (2005) in two important ways. First, in Carrubba (2005) only two nations are involved in the international agreement. Here we model a multinational agreement. This generalization is important because it allows us to characterize the role of governments not directly involved in the judicial dispute. These third-party nations may have preferences about the outcome of the dispute and they may choose to make their preferences known. In the model we formally allow them to file briefs on behalf of one disputant or the other. However, formal participation in the case is not necessary for the model's applicability. The key elements are that third-party governments may choose to weigh in, however informally, on how a case should be resolved and that the court is aware these governments are taking sides. Second, in Carrubba (2005) the court is assumed to provide a venue in which all information becomes common knowledge. This assumption is important because it allows governments to learn the defendant government's cost of compliance, which in turn allows the aggrieved nation to determine whether it wants to punish noncooperation. However, defendant governments have an incentive to strategically misrepresent their actual costs of compliance. Thus, here we explicitly model the information transmission process.

To evaluate whether the theoretical model captures how real-world international courts contribute to the performance of international regulatory regimes,

---

[12] As Hirschl (2008: 113) concludes, we should assume that the transfer to a court of the responsibility to review politically sensitive policies should be in the interests of the political stakeholders.

we test two of the key predictions of our theory with an original data set covering rulings by the European Court of Justice (ECJ) from 1960 to 1999.[13] During this period, the ECJ served as the court of the European Union (EU), an exceptionally deep international agreement, covering a broad range of policies related to the free movement of goods, services, capital, and labor. This includes social, environmental, and consumer protection policies. The EU also governs a complex system of agricultural policies. The commitments of membership entail substantial domestic costs on the member-state governments, leading to a standard collective action problem. Furthermore, given the high saliency of these policies to domestic constituencies, these costs can vary substantially and reach prohibitively high levels on occasion. Thus, the EU member states have signed on to an agreement with the critical attributes of our theoretical model.

The ECJ is a standing tribunal that annually hears hundreds of cases regarding the full gamut of EU policy areas. These cases include questions of member-state compliance with their obligations under the treaties and secondary legislation. The ECJ is a typical international court in that it cannot directly enforce its own rulings against member-state governments. And, as we describe in Chapter 3, the ECJ frequently faces compliance problems with its rulings. Thus, the ECJ and its role in the EU are reasonable empirical matches to the contours of our theoretical model.

It is important to note that the ECJ is also interesting because it is perhaps the most influential and most studied international court in history. This has two implications for our study. First, it means the findings of our study should be substantively interesting, independent of the theoretical concerns we seek to address. Second, the ECJ context presents perhaps a more difficult test of our predictions than we might encounter with other international courts. Recall that pervasive compliance problems are central to our theoretical model, and thus we are likely to find the greatest empirical support for our predictions from international courts where the compliance problem is most severe. The ECJ is not commonly depicted as a most severe case. It regularly faces threats of noncompliance, but it is considered unusually influential for an international court because these threats are perceived to be less severe than those encountered at other international courts. Assuming this perception is accurate, any empirical evidence we find for our theory in the ECJ context suggests it should be only more likely that our theory applies to other international courts.

---

[13] The ECJ is the appropriate acronym for this particular time period. The court's name has changed recently to the Court of Justice of the European Union.

Finally, we should note that we have considered testing our theory on other prominent international courts such as the WTO dispute resolution body (the DSB) and the International Court of Justice (ICJ). The model is potentially applicable to the WTO DSB because of that body's focus on trade issues. Trade falls squarely in the realm of intergovernmental collective action problems. Further, the DSB, although very different from the ECJ on particular institutional details (e.g., it can formally sanction retaliation, as modeled by Rosendorff 2005), faces the same broad challenges as the ECJ does. It must adjudicate disputes among participant states with no direct means of enforcement. Rather, it must rely on the threat of retaliation by the affected state or states to enforce its rulings. Further, third-party governments can and do make their preferences for the resolution of a dispute known during the litigation process. We chose not to study the WTO DSB in part because the WTO DSB does not allow us to test as carefully for the impact of political preferences on dispute resolution. As we address in great detail later, we need to account for the legal merits of each dispute's case. The ECJ provides us with an excellent way of controlling for the legal merits; an equivalent method is not as apparent for the WTO DSB. That said, work by Busch and Reinhardt (2006) provides some meaningful evidence that the WTO DSB is sensitive to political preferences in a similar way to that of the ECJ, and thus that our argument is applicable in this setting as well.

The ICJ is not as clear a case. To the degree that disputes the ICJ hears entail collective action dilemmas among the participant states, the argument can apply. However, we believe that for many cases the ICJ hears, an underlying collective action dilemma is not obvious.

a. *Our theoretical approach*

The theoretical core of the book is a formal model. We employ formal modeling because of the complex strategic environment we wish to study. First, many actors' interests must be taken into account. An arbitrarily large number of governments may participate in these regulatory regimes, an arbitrarily large number of litigants can bring cases, and a court must decide how to rule once confronted with a dispute. Second, all of these actors have potentially cross-cutting interests. The court will want to rule as it sees fit, but it does not want to issue rulings that will be circumvented. Potential litigants would like the court to protect their rights when those rights have been denied, but bringing cases is a risky gamble because there is no guarantee the litigants will win. And governments have agreed to form a common regulatory regime presumably because they perceive value in having that regime's rules obeyed, but that does not mean that a government does not have an incentive to shirk those rules at least some of the time. Finally, these actors have a strong incentive to consider how the other actors are likely to behave before choosing a course of action; that is, the actors have a strong incentive to behave *strategically*. How the court wants to rule depends on how governments are likely to react to the issuance of that ruling, whether a potential litigant wants to bring a case depends on the odds that litigant will win the case, and whether a government wants to violate the regime's rules depends on the probability of the government being brought to court and losing a case.

Formal modeling, or game theory, is a very useful tool for theorizing when confronted with these challenges – a multiplicity of actors, crosscutting interests, and powerful strategic incentives. Formal models require scholars to transparently and rigorously define and characterize exactly the actors, their goals (preferences), and the available choices for achieving their goals. Then, having explicitly laid out these first principles (i.e., assumptions), the model allows scholars to logically derive the choices those actors will make *given each actor is anticipating how the other actors are likely to respond to its choices*. Thus, the formal model in this book is designed to help ensure that the actions our theory predicts, and that motivate our tests in the subsequent chapters, are actually the actions a strategic theory based on the first principles laid out in Chapter 2 would predict. The approach is powerful because it allows us to be rigorously deductive in our reasoning even in the face of complex strategic environments like this one.

b. *A note about assumptions*

Our purpose is to derive a deductive theory of international court influence. Any deductive argument must start with a well-defined set of assumptions from which all findings logically follow. This fact holds whether we want to employ mathematical or nonmathematical theories. In other words, whether or not one uses game theory, if one wishes to make a deductive argument, one must specify the foundational assumptions for the argument.

But what are good or reasonable assumptions? One measure of the likely utility of a theory is the plausibility of the assumptions being employed. For example, is it plausible that politicians value reelection? If so, that is a reasonable building block on which to construct an argument. More generally, plausibility should be thought about within the context of the question the theory is trying to answer. This point is critical when we consider not just what is defined into the theory through assumption (i.e., assuming politicians value reelection) but especially what is defined as out of scope (i.e., we are not assuming politicians are social welfare maximizers). Because everything we do not explicitly assume into the model is implicitly assumed away, we want to avoid assuming away something that would interfere with the inferences we are trying to draw over the specific question at hand.

Consider the question being asked in this book: How can an international court influence national government behavior in the face of severe enforcement challenges? It is important that we start with plausible assumptions defining what is in scope for our model. For example, we assume the governments face a collective action problem over compliance with some set of international laws. They perceive benefits from having others comply with the laws, but at least some of the time they have strong incentives to defect from those rules themselves. This foundational assumption is substantively plausible for an array of policy areas (e.g., free trade regimes).

Equally importantly, we also must define what is out of scope for our model. For example, our model does not include an international bureaucracy (e.g., the European Commission) as an independent actor capable of exerting any special influence on the outcome of government–court interactions. We do not omit this actor because we believe it cannot be an important influence on the international stage, but rather because we do not believe its role changes the fundamental dynamic we wish to study. That is not to say that such an actor does not potentially influence court decisions. In fact, there is long-standing evidence of exactly such influence with the European Commission. However, the purpose of our model is not to capture every factor that might influence court decision making, but rather to capture how the threat of noncompliance by governments might influence the ability of an international court to regulate government behavior. We do consider the other factors at the point of testing the implications of our model because they may confound the relationships we seek to estimate. Thus, we control for those out-of-model factors that we think are important and that might otherwise undermine our empirical, if not our theoretical, inferences.

In sum, a strong foundation for a theory is a set of assumptions that are well tailored for the question being asked. We would like the assumptions of the model – both in terms of what is defined as in scope and out of scope – to be sensible given the question being asked. We have strived to achieve that goal in our theoretical development. As such, we conceptually motivate the key assumptions of our argument in the theory chapter and intersperse substantive examples to motivate and illustrate the key features of the model (e.g., see Table 1.1 and the discussion of the *Schmidberger*[14] case in the concluding chapter).

---

[14] *Schmidberger* v. *Republic of Austria* (Case 112/00 ECJ).

That said, assessing plausibility can be somewhat subjective. How many and what types of evidence and examples are sufficient to establish the possibility of a systematic threat of government noncompliance with a court decision? How do we establish which factors judges consider when deciding a case? For example, one rarely finds even the hint of political considerations in the written judgment of a court. However, some of the judges on that court might, in a published memoir or interview, indicate that the political considerations were important to the decision. Other judges might write the opposite. How do we evaluate who is telling the truth and who is not? Ultimately, we believe the answer to these questions, and more generally the veracity of a deductive argument, is best evaluated by testing a theory's predictions with data. Because we are relying on game theory to ensure that our predictions logically derive from our foundational assumptions, if the assumptions are not capturing an important part of reality, and we have appropriately controlled for alternative explanations, then we should not observe evidence systematically consistent with the model's predictions. Thus, it is important to evaluate the plausibility of a theory's assumptions if for no other reason than to help ensure the likely relevance of the argument. But we do not believe this evaluation should be a litmus test, both because the assessment of plausibility can be difficult and somewhat subjective and because we can rigorously evaluate the veracity of the assumptions by testing the model's predictions in any case.

c. *Our empirical approach*

The core of our empirical work is large-N quantitative analysis. The theoretical questions we are interested in focus not on single "big cases" or transitional events but rather on the day-to-day operations of international courts. In which instances are governments likely to try to shirk the law, and when will they be taken to court? When confronted with a case in which a government has a direct interest in the outcome, how are those courts likely to behave? When is the court likely to rule against that government's interests? When is that decision likely to actually change government behavior? In translating the abstract model to a specific empirical context, we derive empirical implications about general patterns of behavior, not deterministic predictions. That is, our empirical expectations are of the following sort: "on average, the likelihood of a ruling for the government defendant should increase with..." We cannot evaluate that sort of expectation with a single ruling or a small set of rulings. Our empirical expectations apply to the aggregate and thus show up only in the aggregate.

Further, we need to tease out our causal inferences from among a number of highly correlated alternative explanations.[15] For example, we are interested in whether court decisions are responsive to threats of noncompliance. We use the positions of third-party governments as indicators of how likely a ruling against a litigating government would result in noncompliance. However, to isolate that effect, we must control for other factors that might cause both third-party briefs and the ECJ ruling to favor one litigant over the other. For example, one might consider the balance of the legal merits of the case as one such factor. As we show in Chapters 4 and 5, that factor and other potential confounding factors are fairly highly correlated with both the positions of third-party governments and the court's ultimate decision. Thus, a careful reading of a few cases, or a more cursory review of a number of cases, would leave us unable to draw a clear conclusion about the relationship of interest. Large-N statistical analysis helps us with this challenge. We employ a variety of statistical techniques designed to reduce (if not eliminate) potential errors in inference arising from these concerns. This approach helps ensure that any conclusions that support our predictions are well grounded in systematic patterns in the rulings and related data.

III. OUTLINE OF THE BOOK

Chapter 2 presents our general theory of international court influence on nation-state behavior in an international regulatory regime. We derive a nuanced understanding of the role of an international court. The court can facilitate cooperation, but only within certain political constraints. Two central empirical implications follow from our argument. First, if the ECJ is playing this nuanced role, ECJ decisions should be sensitive to the positions of the third-party governments as expressed through their filing of amicus briefs. We label this implication the Political Sensitivity Hypothesis. Second, again, if the ECJ is playing this nuanced role, the impact of ECJ decisions should depend on whether third-party governments are willing to punish noncompliance with adverse court rulings. We label this implication the Conditional Effectiveness Hypothesis. These two implications are the basis for our empirical work in the rest of the book.

Chapters 3 through 6 test the predictions generated in Chapter 2 with data on rulings by the European Court of Justice. Chapter 3 provides an

---

[15] See Pollack (2003: 196) on the disadvantages of considering only a small number of ECJ cases in resolving the sorts of issues we face in our study.

overview of the correspondence between the model and the European Union. It includes a detailed description of the operation of the ECJ and data we have collected about its rulings. This background provides a foundation for tests of two empirical implications of the model. Chapters 4 and 5 focus on the Political Sensitivity Hypothesis. One key difficulty with testing this hypothesis is developing a strategy for isolating the hypothesized relationship from a plausible alternative explanation: that the relationship between third-party government briefs and the court's decision reflects the fact that both positions are positively correlated with the merits of the case. Chapter 4 proposes and validates a control for the merits of the legal arguments. Chapter 5 then tests the hypothesized relationship and evaluates its robustness in the face of a variety of potential confounds, including the legal merits. We find strong support for the hypothesis.

Chapter 6 turns to the second empirical implication derived from the theory in Chapter 2, the Conditional Effectiveness Hypothesis. We test this hypothesis by evaluating whether intra-EU imports into an EU member state increase as a function of the (lagged) number of pro-liberalizing trade decisions made by the court. Consistent with our theory, we find that intra-EU imports increase in response to pro-liberalizing trade rulings if those rulings have the support of third-party governments, but not otherwise. Further, we find that decisions with third-party government support have a long-term impact on trade.

In the concluding chapter, we discuss a variety of implications from our analysis. We describe what our findings imply about the theory of international court influence proposed in this book, what our findings imply for alternative theories of international court influence, what our findings imply for the design of international courts, and what our findings imply for judicial politics writ large. In this last point, we connect to both the international and domestic courts literatures.

2

A theory of courts and compliance in international law

As discussed in Chapter 1, the number of international agreements has exploded since World War II. These agreements regulate everything from trade to the environment to human rights and much, much more. In these agreements, particularly the deeper ones, the signatories consent to bring national practices and policies in line with the rules of a common regulatory regime.

As Table 1.1 in Chapter 1 demonstrates, many of these international agreements feature highly legalized courts. Two-thirds of the regimes include third-party review by a court or arbitration panel before which member-state violations of treaty obligations can be challenged. Frequently, these bodies are standing tribunals with permanent staff. Furthermore, the tribunals frequently allow nonlitigants (primarily governments) to intervene in a case through amicus briefs.

Also as described in the last chapter, the deeper international agreements often have the most developed courts. For example, the most inclusive trade regime in the world, the World Trade Organization (WTO), features a standing tribunal with a well-defined adjudication procedure. Similarly, the most significant international economic agreement in the world, the European Union (EU), has a highly integrated supranational legal system with the European Court of Justice (ECJ) at its head.

These highly legalized courts have become more than simple legal veneers to the agreements. Governments are frequently brought to court and ruled against for violations of international law.[1] Continuing with our examples, the WTO Dispute Settlement Body regularly hears complaints on possible violations of the General Agreement on Tariffs and Trade (GATT) rules. Between 1990 and 1993, under the GATT system, an average of 15.8 complaints

---

[1] See Chayes and Chayes (1993); this point is also discussed in Downs, Rocke, and Barsoom (1996).

was brought each year before the panel. Since the inauguration of the WTO, the average rose to 33.8 for 1995–2000 (Drache, Arnott, and Guan 2000). All of these cases are against governments, and of those cases, the adjudicating body has ruled against the defendant in approximately 90 percent of the cases (Wilson 2007). Similarly, the European Court of Justice went from hearing tens of cases a year in the early 1960s to hundreds a year. In total, between 1959 and 2000 the European Court of Justice heard nearly one thousand cases in which member-state governments were defendants, and of those cases the Court ruled against the governments in approximately 80 percent of the cases.[2]

The question of what happens once the courts rule is another matter. Simply put, compliance with a court ruling cannot be taken for granted. If the WTO Dispute Settlement Body (DSB) declares that a US subsidy to domestic steel producers is illegal under WTO/GATT law, the US government must choose whether to drop the subsidy. The DSB ruling can authorize retaliatory sanctions, but no more (e.g., see Rosendorff 2005). If the ECJ declares invalid a German restriction on the sale of Cassis de Dijon in German liquor stores, ultimately the German government must allow Cassis de Dijon to be sold for the ruling to have effect. Under some conditions the ECJ may be able to demand that Germany pay a fine if Germany refuses to comply,[3] but even then the German government must voluntarily choose to pay that fine. And, more generally, even if the government respects the decision of the court in some particular case, it does not mean the decision has a broader policy impact; the government could continue with its preexisting practices outside of that particular application of the law.

Does lack of enforcement powers actually undermine a court's influence? There is no straightforward answer to this question. Some scholars believe that in practice it does not. They argue that we observe high levels of compliance with international courts, and where we see noncompliance, it is frequently a result of misunderstandings and errors in implementation, not bad faith.[4] These skeptics generally use reported figures on rates of compliance with Court decisions to substantiate their claim. Although an obvious metric to turn to, compliance with Court decisions alone cannot resolve the question. For example, these reported figures do not account for situations in which

---

[2] C. J. Carrubba and M. Gabel, European Court of Justice Data, http://polisci.emory.edu/home/people/carrubba_ecjd/index.html.

[3] After 1993, the Commission could bring a challenge under Article 171 of the Treaty on European Union for a failure to comply with a previous infringement decision. If the Court found against the government, it could then issue a ruling declaring that the government owed a fine for its failure to comply.

[4] See, e.g., Chayes and Chayes (1996).

governments would not have complied and, anticipating that fact, are not brought to court in the first place. Or similarly, courts with discretionary dockets might choose not to hear the case.

To illustrate this point, consider the following example. In September 2003, France decided to bail out Alstom, a large French company that at the time employed approximately 30,000 French citizens. France made this decision without consulting the European Commission, despite the fact that EU law requires it to do so.[5] Although the Commission quickly responded by declaring that the French plan would constitute illegal state aid under EU competition law,[6] ultimately the Commission did approve a version of the bailout on May 25, 2004. This agreement came after the first tranche of support from the French state – support based on the plan deemed illegal by the Commission – was coming to a close.[7]

Although France and the Commission might argue that the final version of the bailout was not illegal, clearly France had pursued and executed state aid that the Commission could have prosecuted before the Court. Yet this did not happen. One plausible explanation is the Commission avoided court on purpose. Specifically, the Commission may have anticipated that a French government willing to blatantly ignore its EU obligations at the outset might be equally willing to ignore an adverse ruling from the Court. As a result, no court case was brought and therefore no opportunity for noncompliance with the ruling could appear in the record.

How can a court be effective in the face of these compliance and enforcement challenges? And what influence does a court facing such challenges actually wield?

In this chapter we propose a formal model designed to answer these questions. We find a number of interesting results that add nuance to previous understandings of court influence. Most importantly, we find that these courts can facilitate levels of international cooperation that *would not exist without them*. But, at the same time, there are real limits to what the courts can accomplish. Specifically, these courts can help promote levels of cooperation that governments, *ex ante*, want the international regime to sustain, but they cannot force governments to comply with international law beyond that level.[8] This

---

[5] "All for One and One for Alstom," *The Economist*, August 8, 2003, www.economist.com/node/1973533?story_id=1973533.
[6] "France Warned on 'Illegal' Alstom Aid," BBC News, August 5, 2003, http://news.bbc.co.uk/2/hi/business/3126357.stm.
[7] "France, EU Agree on the Fate of Alstom," *Taipei Times*, May 27, 2004, www.taipeitimes.com/News/worldbiz/archives/2004/05/27/2003157180.
[8] At the end of the chapter we discuss how this result does not imply that cooperation cannot evolve over time.

finding is a version of the efficient breach argument of international agreements. Courts help ensure that certain levels of cooperation are sustained, but they allow breaches of the agreement when trying to sustain cooperation would be at best ineffectual and at worst counterproductive.

In a very specific sense, defined in detail later, the court serves this purpose by acting as a *fire alarm* and *information clearinghouse*. Briefly, the court acts as a fire alarm by being a venue in which aggrieved parties can bring claims of violations of international law, and the court acts as an information clearinghouse by being a venue in which litigants can make their arguments and third parties (particularly other governments) can weigh in on the case.

Beyond this core finding, we also demonstrate two important, testable empirical implications. If our argument is correct, the court should cue heavily off of revealed government preferences on how a case should be resolved. The more governments opposed to the defendant government's actions, and the fewer in support, both the more likely the court will rule against the defendant government and the more likely the defendant government will obey the adverse decision.[9]

In the next section, we discuss the motivation behind our modeling approach. Then, we get into specifics. We consider why governments would join an international regulatory regime, why they would create a court to oversee compliance with that regime's rules, and what sorts of behavior we should see in equilibrium as a result. We finish the chapter by discussing implications of this equilibrium for international court influence, derive testable predictions of the model, and conclude.

I. FEATURES OF A COMPLETE THEORY

A theory designed to answer how an international court can influence government behavior ideally should be able to address the following points. Most obviously, the theory must provide some motivation for voluntary compliance. If a government has no incentive to comply with an adverse decision, why would a government ever obey the ruling?

Second, the theory should explain activation of the legal system. This requirement actually consists of two components. For one, potential complainants must have a reason for bringing a case. Challenging a government

---

[9] Smith (2003) and Busch and Reinhardt (2006) advance a similar argument to explain adjudication by the WTO. They contend that WTO adjudication is influenced by the positions taken by third-party governments involved in the case. Our model provides a specific theoretical justification for that argument.

in court requires use of scarce time and resources, whether or not the challenger is a government, a firm, or an individual. Because of this fact, the potential challenger must believe that he/she has a legitimate chance of not only winning the case but also having the defendant comply once the verdict is in.[10] But activation of the system, then, is not just about the decision of a potential complainant to bring a case; it is also about the decision of the potential defendant to engage in a potentially punishable activity in the first place. Thus, the theory must account for the decision of a government to comply (or not) with the regulatory regime's rules before a case even arises as well as the complainant's decision to bring a challenge.[11]

Third, the theory should motivate why governments would create a court in the first place. As previously discussed, the legalization of dispute resolution varies considerably across international agreements.[12] This fact suggests that more legalistic adjudication mechanisms are designed for a purpose. Motivating the decision to create a legalistic system for adjudication is useful because it may provide both a rationale for court influence and a rationale for the limits of what a court can do.

Finally, a complete theory should motivate why the participating governments wanted to create a common regulatory regime in the first place. It takes time and resources to create a common regulatory regime. Unless governments are irrational, that means they must have some vested interest in it. And, unless that interest is purely symbolic, this means the governments expect at least some compliance with the regulatory regime's rules.[13] Consequently, if we do not account for what governments hope to get out of joining the regulatory regime, we cannot say much about what courts can do above and beyond the goals these governments have set for themselves.

In sum, a complete theory of court influence in an international regulatory regime should start by specifying what the regulatory regime is intended to

---

[10] We set aside litigation strategies that are certain of defeat yet are pursued for some public relations or other benefit just from having engaged in the battle.
[11] Note also that a sensible explanation for activation of the legal system should imply realistic legal activity. Just as sensible microfoundations must motivate activation of the legal system, they also should not lead to governments always defecting from the regulatory regime's rules and always being taken to court, and therefore for the court to have an effectively infinite, and unmanageable, docket.
[12] In some systems, such as the European Union, all of this legalization was not designed into the treaties initially. See, e.g., Alter (1998, 2001).
[13] For example, a government might sign a human rights treaty to appease a domestic constituency, nongovernmental organization, or foreign government, say, with no real intention of ever complying with the treaty's terms or with no expectation that other parties will comply. However, with other agreements, such as the WTO/GATT and the EU, it is hard to imagine that participants did not have real policy goals.

accomplish and finish by deriving what happens once a decision is rendered. In the next section we present a model that addresses these points. The model is based on first principles that explain why governments would join a common regulatory regime with a court, and then it endogenously derives when governments will violate the agreement, when they will be taken to court, when they will be ruled against, and when they will comply.

II. A THEORY OF INTERNATIONAL AGREEMENTS AND THEIR SYSTEMS OF ADJUDICATION

In this section we present a model that extends previous work (Carrubba 2005). This model is but one of an excellent and growing formal (game-theoretic) literature that studies how international adjudicating bodies can affect government behavior under international agreements. This literature is characterized by game-theoretic models that vary in two important ways. First, some are general models of international organizations with courts,[14] while others examine institutional details associated with specific agreements (e.g., models designed to demonstrate how the escape clauses and authorized retaliatory sanctions associated with the WTO DSB support international cooperation).[15] Second, these models vary the degree to which they endogenize each step of the dispute resolution process. For example, some assume disputes are exogenously generated (Johns 2011); that is, the models assume a government deviated from the regime's rules and a plaintiff brought that government to court. Others assume the court's decision to hear a case and its judgment are determined probabilistically, in contrast to allowing the court to be a strategic actor that chooses how to rule on the dispute (Gilligan, Johns, and Rosendorff 2010; Johns 2012). Here we want a model that is general (not tailored to a specific regime) and that explicitly endogenizes each step of the adjudication process. Extending on Carrubba (2005) allows us to have such a model.

a. Why create a common regulatory regime?

Substantively, we observe common regulatory regimes designed to address a variety of policy goals. Sometimes governments try to liberalize interstate trade (e.g., WTO/GATT and North American Free Trade Agreement [NAFTA]). Sometimes governments want to regulate environmental standards (e.g., Kyoto). Sometimes governments try to promote human rights (e.g., the

---

[14] See, for example, Gilligan, Johns, and Rosendorff (2010), Johns (2011, 2012), and Maggi (1999).
[15] See, for example, Rosendorff and Milner (2001) and Rosendorff (2005).

European Court of Human Rights). And sometimes governments are doing all that and more (e.g., the EU).

But the policy goals do not, in themselves, explain why governments choose to create a common regulatory regime to realize those goals. If governments independently have a straightforward preference for these policies, then investing the time and effort to create a common regime is a waste. They should all just unilaterally lower barriers to trade, improve the environment, increase human rights protections, and so on. Thus, there must be something more driving their desire to create and join these regimes. Here we focus on one powerful and widely applicable motivation: the need for *collective action* over some set of policies among a set of states.

Policy challenges that require collective action can be relatively straightforward. For example, governments specify traffic rules. Everyone drives on the right side of the road and red means stop at an intersection. As long as everyone follows a common convention, all is well. These types of challenges generally are referred to as coordination problems. However, international regulatory regimes frequently present collective action challenges that go well beyond simple coordination. To see how, consider the examples of trade, environmental policy, and social provisions, three of the most common international policy domains.

According to traditional trade theory, economies benefit from unilaterally lowering domestic barriers to imports. However, despite this fact, the historical record is replete with examples of national barriers to trade. The reason is generally thought to be political. When governments lower barriers to trade two consequences follow. The previously protected domestic industry must adjust to the new levels of competition, and consumers pay less for the newly liberalized commodity. Stated in standard terminology, lowering trade barriers delivers concentrated costs to the import-competing firm and diffuse benefits to consumers. Thus, although consumers have a modest incentive to reward politicians for the lower prices, import-competing firms have a very strong incentive to punish those same politicians. And, as a result, governments rarely unilaterally lower trade barriers.

Whereas lowering one's own trade barriers is generally politically costly, a trading partner lowering its barriers to trade is an unalloyed good. By lowering its trading barriers, the partner country makes exporting into its market easier. As a result, domestic exporters increase sales and the economy grows, all with no discernible political costs.

The desire to have trading partners lower their trade barriers, in conjunction with the reluctance to lower one's own barriers, creates fertile ground for a political bargain between the potential partners to liberalize trade. Properly

		State 2	
		Lower Trade Barrier	Not Lower Barrier
State 1	Lower Trade Barrier	$b-c, b-c$	$-c, b$
	Not Lower Barrier	$b, -c$	$0, 0$

FIGURE 2.1 The trade game

sculpted, a set of governments can realize mutual benefits from liberalizing trade as long as the benefits each government derives from partners lowering barriers to trade exceed the domestic costs of lowering trade barriers. But realizing these benefits is not simple because each individual government faces a temptation to maintain or reconstruct trade barriers. Thus, governments face a form of a prisoners' dilemma. Every state wants a mutually beneficial lowering of barriers to trade; however, each state is better off if the others all lower their barriers while it maintains its own barriers.

This tension is modeled in Figure 2.1. If both states lower their trade barriers, they each gain the benefit ($b > 0$) of the other state lowering its trade barriers while they pay the cost ($c > 0$) of lowering their own. If only one state lowers its trade barriers, that state pays a cost and the other state gains the benefit. And if neither lowers its barriers, neither state gains a benefit or pays a cost.[16]

Raising environmental standards frequently has the same political dynamic as trying to lower trade barriers. Consider two of the biggest environmental concerns, air and water quality. Imposing more stringent domestic requirements unilaterally is problematic for at least two reasons. First, the targeted industry is going to lose profitability, and thereby domestic and international competitiveness. This is true whether governments raise standards by imposing more stringent production requirements on domestic firms, require the goods firms produce meet higher environmental standards, impose targeted taxes (e.g., a fuel tax to increase the cost of driving and thereby decrease car use), or employ any other equivalent policy instrument. Thus, while the population enjoys diffuse benefits from higher environmental quality, affected industries once again experience concentrated costs.

The second problem is that other states can free ride. For example, suppose France imposes laws requiring cleaner energy in order to reduce air pollution. This change will likely affect air quality in neighboring European states as well. Thus, any one country raising environmental standards can face opposition in

---

[16] For an explicit derivation of the prisoners' dilemma tension from a simple model of a state economy, see Rosendorff and Milner (2001) and Rosendorff (2005).

its domestic arena because doing so unilaterally can decrease domestic firms' competitiveness in the international market and because pollution policies in one state affect pollution in neighboring states. A set of states may benefit from a mutual increase in environmental standards, but each has an individual incentive to defect and free ride off of the others. Simply relabel the moves in Figure 2.1 as "increase environmental standards" or "not" and the payoffs apply.

Finally, a variety of social policies also fit this characterization. For example, in the EU, member states grant workers from other member states a selection of rights and access to social provisions as if they were domestic workers. This policy decreases transaction costs for cross-border workers, which in turn leads to a more efficient mapping of potential employees to jobs within the EU. As a result, all states benefit from the stronger economy. This is the equivalent of free trade benefits, just in labor. However, as with trade, the benefits of participating in this regime are diffuse while the costs are concentrated; everyone benefits somewhat from a faster growing economy, but providers of the social provisions have to cover the costs (be they governments or firms), and domestic workers and unions do not like competing with foreign labor. Thus, governments might like to agree to a mutual provision of these social policies, but they have little incentive to do so unilaterally. Further, each state benefits the most if all other states provide social provisions to out-of-state workers while it limits its own provision. As a result, these policies also follow the logic of a prisoners' dilemma outlined in Figure 2.1.

So, why create a common regulatory regime in these sorts of policy areas? The short answer is to help resolve the underlying strategic dilemma presented in Figure 2.1. All of the participant states perceive a benefit from mutual adherence with the proposed regulatory regime's rules. However, they have no incentive to unilaterally follow the rules. They would rather everyone else follow the rules while they go their own way. Forming a common regulatory regime is one way to try to overcome this challenge. Each state ties its commitment to the regime's rules to the other participating states' commitments. Making explicit commitments to each other helps states to build and cue off of reputations. Specifically, if a government has a history of complying with the regime's rules (i.e., a good reputation), the other governments can trust the state and reward it by continuing to comply as well. If a government has a history of flouting the rules (i.e., a bad reputation), the other governments can retaliate by not complying themselves. The ability to tie the threat of future retaliation, or *punishment*, to bad behavior today is what allows these regimes to help sustain cooperation. The long-run cost of being punished tomorrow can dissuade governments from pursuing the short-run benefit of defecting today. The idea that, in an infinitely (indefinitely) repeated setting, these strategies can sustain cooperation is well established in the literature.[17]

b. Why create a court?

The difficulty of monitoring compliance in these regulatory regimes can vary greatly. For some regimes, the task is comparatively simple. The regime has relatively few rules and compliance with those rules is easy to observe. For example, suppose Germany agreed to place no higher than a 10 percent tariff on wine imports, and France agreed to do the same with regard to beer. Each government has a relatively simple task. The German government has only to watch that France does not overtax beer imports, and the French government has only to watch that Germany does not overtax wine imports.

However, regimes often have more general and more complicated policy goals. For example, suppose the goal of Germany and France in the preceding example is not to constrain each other's tariff rates, per se. Rather, it is to ensure access for French wine in the German market and German beer in the French market. Monitoring compliance with this sort of goal is far from simple. For example, Germany could meet the 10 percent tariff rule but introduce a health standard, or other nontariff barrier on wine imports, that has an effect equivalent to a higher tariff.

Similarly, expanding membership and policy jurisdiction complicates monitoring compliance. Returning to the example, suppose Germany and France are part of a fifteen-member organization in which the agreement is to regulate any barriers to trade (nontariff as well as tariff) across the entire economy. This scenario presents the participating governments with an extremely challenging task. The agreement includes many more goods, violations are harder to monitor, and retaliatory sanctions for violations have to be coordinated among a variety of governments.

Monitoring is not the only challenge for these agreements. Once an agreement is signed, changes in domestic political, social, and economic contexts faced by a government cause the incentive to defect from the regime's rules to vary over time. Foreign supply could suddenly spike, thereby flooding the domestic market, driving down the price of the good, and increasing pressure from import competitors to raise trade barriers. The political leadership could

---

[17] For a few examples of using this approach to model international agreements, see Maggi (1999), Carrubba (2005, 2009), Rosendorff (2005), Rosendorff and Milner (2001), and Johns (2011). But see Downs, Rocke, and Barsoom (1996).

change, providing the previously protected industry with greater clout than it had under the leadership that signed the agreement. Or a government could be nearing a hotly contested election in which voters in a vulnerable industry are pivotal, thereby increasing the government's incentive to deviate from the rules and protect the industry.

The deeper the agreement, the more likely these costs could undermine the regulatory regime. First, recall that cooperation is sustainable as long as the long-run benefits from cooperation exceed the short-run costs of complying. However, deeper agreements lead to more variable costs, and the more variable the costs, the more likely a government will face a situation when the short-run cost of compliance is simply too severe, and the government will defect, even knowing that doing so will lead to punishment at a minimum and the end of cooperation entirely in the worst-case scenario.[18] Standard punishment strategies involving future interactions are not sufficient to deter such defections. As a result, governments may prefer rules that allow exceptions for defections because of temporary domestic crises.[19]

Second, whether a government faces a domestic crisis that warrants such a defection is not common knowledge. Only the government itself knows the true costs it faces. Put differently, its payoff from defection is private information. This asymmetry of information is important because it complicates efforts to allow the flexibility necessary to accommodate the highly variable costs deeper agreements induce. If governments assume any defection is a result of difficult domestic conditions, the threat of punishment would be nullified and cooperation would soon break down. If governments punish any defection, eventually highly costly situations would arise and cooperation would break down as well.

A court is an institution that can help manage these two challenges by acting as a *fire alarm* mechanism and an *information clearinghouse*. To understand these roles, start by considering a very simple agreement. Two states have signed a treaty, and they have agreed that only national governments have the right to challenge each other over possible violations of the regime's rules. In this case, a court would serve little purpose. Anything the governments could

---

[18] In fact, when costs are large enough and cooperation is mutually costly, the game is no longer a prisoners' dilemma.

[19] As mentioned in Chapter 1, some work in the rational design literature explicitly models a stochastic cost of complying with international agreements (Rosendorff and Milner 2001; Rosendorff 2005). Rosendorff (2005) explicitly models how an international court can help governments overcome variable costs. In his model, the court helps sustain cooperation by allowing for utility transfers between states when one state wants to derogate from an agreement. Here the court serves a different function.

do in front of a court, they could do just as efficiently through state-to-state meetings.

Now consider the same regime, but with multiple members. In this scenario, enforcement of the regime's rules relies on the actions and reactions of not only the states directly involved in the conflict but also the other regime participants. Each time there is a conflict, these states have to decide whom to back, if anyone. A court acts as a *fire alarm* by being an institutionalized venue in which a state brings a challenge, making both the challenged state and the third-party states aware of the conflict. A court acts as an *information clearinghouse* by being a venue in which these states then argue over the challenge. The challenger makes its case, the defendant responds, and the third-party states support (e.g., file amicus briefs in favor of) whichever positions they wish. Further, the states are free to engage in focused, back-channel negotiations in which information perhaps not material to the trial but material to the participating states is conveyed. Engaging in this behavior, the making and weighing in on arguments, creates an opportunity for the participant states to credibly exchange information over the consequences of the defendant state complying with the agreement. Third-party states can signal any consequences they would experience, and the defendant state can attempt to communicate to the other states exactly how costly compliance would be.[20] Although in theory all of this could be done without a court, the denser the regulatory regime and the higher the number of states participating in the regime, the more having an institutionalized venue for dealing with conflicts over application of the regulatory regime's rules makes sense.

Finally, modify this regime by allowing other actors – perhaps private individuals, firms, special interests, or subnational governments – to have standing in front of the court. Now the court provides a service as a fire alarm mechanism well beyond simply being an institutionalized venue for interstate disputes. Governments no longer have to invest time and resources identifying possible violations and bringing challenges. Rather, they can rely on affected parties to bring their own challenges.

In sum, we start with the first principles that a set of governments joins a common regulatory regime to overcome a collective action problem. The governments would like to sustain mutual cooperation with the regime's rules, but every government has an individual incentive to defect. What is more, the incentive to defect from the regime varies over time. Sometimes it is small enough that cooperation is sustainable, sometimes it is large enough that a government would rather avoid the short-run cost, even at the expense

---

[20] How this information can be credibly exchanged is derived in the formal model.

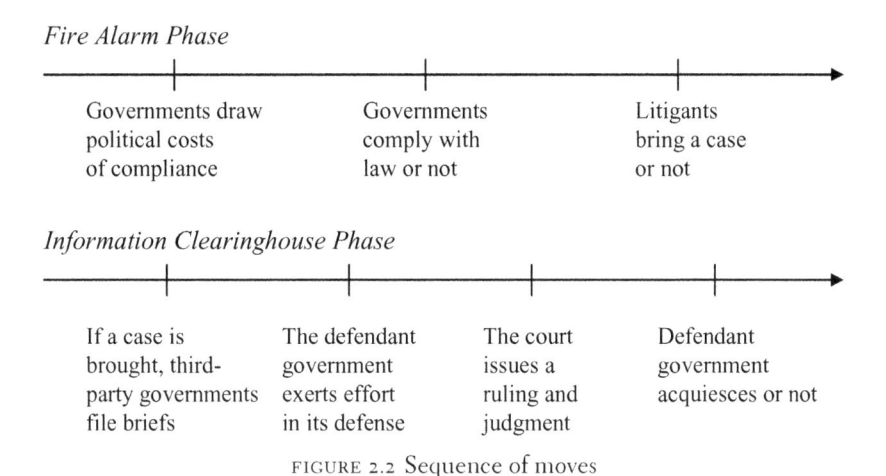

Fire Alarm Phase

| Governments draw political costs of compliance | Governments comply with law or not | Litigants bring a case or not |

Information Clearinghouse Phase

| If a case is brought, third-party governments file briefs | The defendant government exerts effort in its defense | The court issues a ruling and judgment | Defendant government acquiesces or not |

FIGURE 2.2 Sequence of moves

of undermining future cooperation. The governments create a court that can help them overcome these challenges by acting as a fire alarm and information clearinghouse; the court provides a venue both for aggrieved parties to raise challenges over possible instances of noncompliance and for interested parties to learn more about the possible violation. Next we present a model based on these first principles and derive what they would imply about international judicial influence in this context.

c. *The model*

The following model of a dispute generation and resolution process captures all of the necessary dynamics for this study. (See Figure 2.2.) Assume $N \geq 2$ governments are participating in a common regulatory regime. By joining the common regulatory regime, the governments have agreed to abide by a set of policies for the foreseeable future. As such, the agreement is modeled as an infinite (indefinite) horizon game consisting of an infinite (indefinite) number of rounds, or periods, of play. Each period starts with each government drawing its own cost of compliance c_i from some continuous distribution of costs bounded between zero and some maximum $\bar{c}$.[21] (Assume $0 < b < \bar{c}$.) A government's cost is not common knowledge; that is, only the government drawing the cost knows for sure the political and economic costs of compliance

---

[21] We suppress the period and government-specific notation and instead simply represent it as a random cost drawn from a distribution c_i to avoid notational clutter. All proofs in the appendix require indexing only by the specific cost drawn. The same is done with all subsequent notation except where necessary.

		State 2	
		Lower Trade Barrier	Not Lower Barrier
State 1	Lower Trade Barrier	$b - c_i, b - c_i$	$-c_i, b$
	Not Lower Barrier	$b, -c_i$	$0, 0$

FIGURE 2.3 The trade game with variable cost

it faces. Again, this informational asymmetry captures the fact that political pressures are better understood by those experiencing them than by those trying to draw inferences from afar.

The dispute generation process

Once costs are drawn, each government decides whether to comply, formally notated as a decision X, in which X = {comply, defect}. Complying ensures that at least one other government receives a benefit b and the complying government pays its cost c_i.[22] Each of the other $N - 2$ states may also be affected by the government's decision to comply or not. Compliance can yield a benefit (b), a cost ($-c < 0$), or have no effect at all (0). Formally, a third-party government's payoff is noted as β_j, where $\beta_j = \{b, -c, 0\}$, with probability $Pr[\beta = b]$, $Pr[\beta = -c]$, or $Pr[\beta = 0]$, for government j. If a government does not comply, all other governments get a payoff of zero.

These payoffs allow for the possibility that compliance at times may be undesirably costly to the participant states. We establish and label the conditions under which cooperation would be undesirably costly in three steps. First, consider a simple two-state version of the model in which each government receives a certain benefit if the other government complies, and each government pays a variable cost if it complies. Figure 2.3, a reproduction of the trade game in Figure 2.1 but with variable costs, captures this scenario. If both governments have low costs (i.e., $c_i \in [0, b)$), the game in Figure 2.3 is the standard prisoners' dilemma. Compliance with the regime's rules is mutually beneficial; the benefit a government receives from the other government complying outweighs the costs it pays from complying itself. Thus, each side is better off with both sides complying than with neither complying when costs are sufficiently low (i.e., $b - c_i > 0$). However, if both governments

---

[22] This assumption is made solely to ensure that at least one member of the regime benefits from compliance.

have high costs (i.e., $c_i \in [b, \bar{c}]$), the game in Figure 2.3 is no longer a prisoners' dilemma. Now compliance is mutually costly; the benefit a government receives from the other government complying *is outweighed* by the cost it pays from complying itself. Thus, each side is worse off with both sides complying than with neither side complying when costs are too high ($b - c_i < 0$). Thus, in this game governments would like to ensure compliance with the regulatory regime's rules when the costs of compliance are sufficiently low, but not when they are too high. While maintaining compliance even over high costs may be possible, it is undesirable from the perspective of the governments. This cost structure captures the variability of costs supposed in deep agreements and highlighted in the rational design literature on international organizations (e.g., Koremenos, Lipson, and Snidal 2001).

Next, allow the costs of compliance to vary independently for the two governments. If a government with low costs complies (i.e., $c_i \in [0, b]$), we can think about compliance as being *net beneficial* because the benefit the other government receives *is larger* than the cost the complying government pays. Conversely, if a government with high costs complies (i.e., $c_i \in [b, \bar{c}]$), we can think about compliance as being *net costly* because the benefit the other government receives is *less than* the cost the complying government pays. As long as each participant has a sufficient chance of being the beneficiary of a net beneficial instance of compliance,[23] all states are better off in the long run if they comply whenever compliance is net beneficial. And, as long as each participant has a sufficient chance of being the "victim" of a net costly instance of compliance, all states are worse off in the long run if they comply whenever compliance is net costly. Although in any given round of play a government might comply because it drew a sufficiently low cost, but not be complied with because the other state drew too high a cost, over time the situation would even out; the state getting nothing in the immediate round would be the beneficiary of the same circumstance some time in the future.

Finally, generalize the game to the N government version. The only change is that compliance is net beneficial if and only if the total cost of compliance for a government is less than the total benefits, or when $\eta b - \mu c - c_i > 0$, where $\eta \geq 1$ governments gain a benefit from compliance and $\mu \geq 0$ other governments pay a cost if the government complies. In other words, when the total costs of compliance for all governments participating in the agreement are less than the total benefits in any particular instance, cooperation is net

---

[23] And assuming they do not discount the future too highly, as with any iterated prisoners' dilemma.

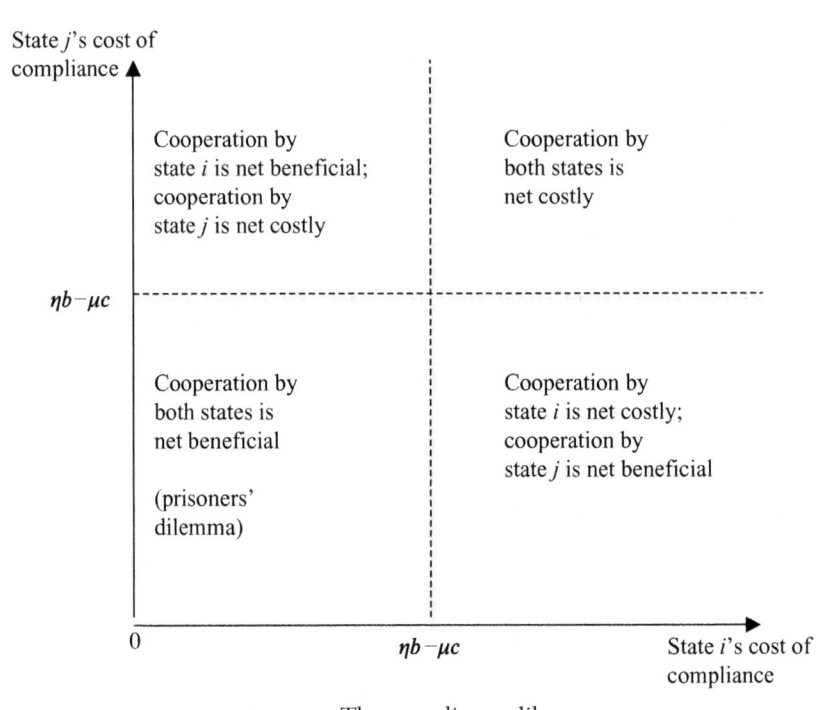

```
State j's cost of
compliance ▲
             │
             │  Cooperation by         │  Cooperation by
             │  state i is net beneficial; │  both states is
             │  cooperation by         │  net costly
             │  state j is net costly  │
             │                         │
   ηb−μc     ┼─────────────────────────┼─────────────────────
             │                         │
             │  Cooperation by         │  Cooperation by
             │  both states is         │  state i is net costly;
             │  net beneficial         │  cooperation by
             │                         │  state j is net beneficial
             │  (prisoners'            │
             │  dilemma)               │
             │                         │
             └─────────────────────────┴─────────────────────▶
             0                    ηb−μc           State i's cost of
                                                  compliance
```

FIGURE 2.4 The compliance dilemma

beneficial. Otherwise, it is net costly.[24] Figure 2.4 illustrates this compliance dilemma.

Returning to the structure of the game, if a government defects from the regime's rules, any party with standing can file a challenge. Standing can be as narrow as with the WTO in which only participant governments are allowed to bring actions or as broad as with the EU in which even private individuals can file challenges. To leave the model as general as possible, we simply assume that for each violation there exists some actor who is hurt by that violation and who can bring a challenge if he/she wishes. Formally, litigants are modeled as one-shot players.[25] The litigant's choice set is to bring a case or not, L = {*litigate*, ¬*litigate*}. Bringing a challenge incurs a cost k_l because doing so involves a nontrivial amount of time and resources, even for a government.

---

[24] Recall one government will always receive a benefit from compliance and the rest of the governments draw costs or benefits probabilistically.

[25] Nothing substantively important would change if we modeled them as repeat players. Because governments, individual bureaucrats, and private litigants (where relevant) change over time, we thought it was more natural to model them as one-shot players.

The litigant receives j_i if the court rules in its favor and the government accepts the ruling. The litigant receives zero otherwise.

The dispute resolution process

If a challenge is filed, the case resolves in three phases. First, third-party governments are free to take positions on the case. For concreteness, we allow governments to file briefs on behalf of the petitioner or defendant. Formally, the decision to file a brief is notated as $O \in \{support, oppose, \neg file\}$.[26] Filing briefs costs some modest amount of effort, $\varepsilon > 0$. All parties to the case, including the justices, observe the filing of these briefs. The total number of briefs filed against the government is indexed as n, and the total number of briefs filed for the government is indexed as m. Second, the defendant government decides how much effort to exert in its defense, $e_{n,m}$, where a defendant government's effort can depend on the number of states that file briefs in support of each of the litigants. Unlike the briefs, the defendant's effort is not common knowledge (i.e., all actors observe the briefs, but all actors do not observe the defendant's effort). Recall, although some of the effort of defending oneself occurs in the courtroom, a nontrivial amount can entail behind-the-scenes negotiations among governments. To capture this asymmetry, the governments, but not the court, observe the amount of effort exerted during the trial.

Next, the court issues a ruling. The ruling consists of a disposition (or ruling) and a judgment (or penalty). The disposition is denoted as $R = \{for\ gov, \neg gov\}$, where $R = for\ gov$ if the court supports the government and $R = \neg gov$ if the court supports the petitioner. If the court rules for the petitioner, the court issues a judgment, $j_i = j + c_i$, where $j \geq 0$. This judgment is the price the court declares the government must pay to come back into compliance. For simplicity, the judgment is treated as a direct transfer of utility from the defendant to the plaintiff. If the court rules for the defendant, there is no judgment.[27]

---

[26] Note that we formally model third-party involvement as the filing of briefs before the court. One could equivalently think about these interventions as more informal involvement in which governments make pronouncements about how they want the case resolved.

[27] Compare Oil Platforms (*Iran* v. *U.S.*), 2003 I.C.J. 161 (Nov. 6) (the ICJ ruled that the US Naval attack on three offshore Iranian oil production complexes on October 19, 1987, and April 18, 1988, did not constitute a breach of the obligations of the USA under Article X, paragraph 1 of the 1955 Treaty of Amity, Economic Relations and Consular Rights between the US and Iran. The court ruled for the defense and therefore the reparations requested by Iran were denied) and Appellate Report, *United States – Standards for Reformulated and Conventional Gasoline*, adopted May 20, 1996, AB-1996–1,WT/DS2/9 (Venezuela and Brazil brought suit against the United States for violation of the "national treatment" principle in response to

We define the court's preferences such that they at least occasionally diverge from those of the member governments. We do this because one of the central questions we want to explore is to what degree the court can produce outcomes that reflect the court's, but not the governments', preferences. This approach is standard to principal–agent models in which the principal or principals (the governments) create or hire an agent (the court) to help the principals achieve some goal. However, the principal cannot ensure that the preferences of the agent perfectly match its preferences. Sometimes the agent wants different outcomes.

The court's goals could differ from the governments' in one of two ways. The court could prefer wider or narrower application of the regulatory regime's rules than the governments want. If the court wants narrower application, the court sometimes does not want compliance when the governments do. If the court wants wider application, the opposite is true. Although it is straightforward to allow for either or both differences in tastes, here we focus on the scenario in which the court wants wider application. This is done for two reasons. First, scholars generally believe these courts have an institutionally based incentive to want wider application of the law.[28] This wider application may help enhance their prestige, legitimacy, and/or, most concretely, jurisdictional domain. Second, all of the interesting dynamics in the game relate to how the court handles cases in which governments do not want the regime's rules followed.[29] Allowing the court to prefer at least occasional underapplication of the law makes the model more complex but provides no useful additional empirical leverage.

To capture this divergence in preferences, we assume the court wants to maximize government compliance with adverse rulings. Specifically, each time the court rules against a defendant government and that government acquiesces, the court gains a payoff of 1. This payoff reflects the court's preference for broad application of the rules. Further, consistent with existing research, we also assume that the court suffers some cost k_c for having a decision ignored by a defendant government. Most commonly this cost is thought

---

unequal chemical requirements for imported gasoline. The WTO dispute panel agreed with Venezuela and Brazil, and the United States amended its regulations in response on August 19, 1997).

[28] Garrett, Kelemen, and Schulz (1998) ("The ECJ has a clear institutional interest in extending the scope of Community law and its authority to interpret it.").

[29] The tension between the governments and the court can equally well be thought of as a tension over whether the regime's rules should be more or less expansively interpreted, independent of whether there is consensus over what the correct application of the laws is. We discuss this point more in the conclusion.

of as a *legitimacy cost* (Carrubba 2009). If a decision is ignored, it undermines the court's credibility with the public in a way that weakens the court's potential future influence.[30] This payoff structure incentivizes the court to rule against a government any time the court is sufficiently confident that the government will acquiesce, not just when governments find cooperation net beneficial. Finally, each time the court rules for a defendant government, the court's payoff is zero.

Returning to the game structure, if the court rules for the defendant, no further action is taken and the next period begins. If the court rules for the plaintiff, the defendant must choose whether or not to comply with the ruling (A = {*acquiesce, defy*}).[31] Once the defendant has made this decision, the next period begins. As is standard in repeated games, we discount future payoffs by $\delta \in (0, 1)$ each period. Discounting ensures, for example, that a government gains more from another government complying with the regime's rules today than it does if the other government complies with the regime's rules tomorrow.

d. Analysis

So, what should we expect to see happen? When should governments defect, when should they be taken to court, when will the court rule against them, and how will they respond? As discussed previously, the answer to these questions critically depends on how governments react to transgressions of the regime's rules (either its laws or its court's rulings). Only if a government anticipates getting sanctioned for noncompliance can cooperation be sustained. Thus, to answer these questions we present the equilibrium in two parts. The first part consists of the enforcement, or punishment path, strategies. Which actions by one government will cause the other governments to retaliate and what form will that retaliation take? The second part consists of the on-equilibrium path strategies, the actual answers to the questions posed earlier.[32]

---

[30] For a formal model that derives such a cost, see Carrubba (2009).

[31] Note that we define a decision by the court against the interests of the defendant government as one that requires action by the government to come into compliance with the regime's rules. We conceptualize a ruling by the court against the defendant government that does not require such behavior as effectively not ruling against the government. Thus, we use a specific notion of what an adverse ruling means that has implications for the relationship between compliance and effectiveness (i.e., substantive impact). See Martin (2013) for more discussion on this point.

[32] As with any infinite horizon game, an infinite set of solutions exists. We are interested in identifying those that characterize a plausible solution to the game. See Kreps (1990). As such, we focus on a set of strategies the governments, which designed the regime in the first place, would choose to play.

Enforcement strategies

A government's enforcement strategy consists of two components, what triggers punishment and how punishment is meted out. First, consider what should trigger punishment. Unlike the standard prisoners' dilemma, compliance in this model is not always net beneficial; it is only net beneficial when the total costs of compliance are less than the total benefits (i.e., when $\eta b - \mu c - c_i > 0$). As a result, governments ideally would like to employ a punishment strategy that ensures compliance whenever it is net beneficial and not when it is mutually costly.[33] However, the governments do not know the net impact of compliance *ex ante*. As a result, when noncompliance is observed, the other governments cannot discern whether the noncompliance is justified. Ideally, they want to punish only if it is not justified. But they lack the necessary information to distinguish between the two settings. This informational constraint leaves the governments with a couple of second-best alternatives.

One option is simply to punish any observed defection from the regime's rules. The advantage of this strategy is its coverage: there is no risk that a government is going to get away with noncompliance when compliance would be net beneficial. The downside is that the governments will also end up either enforcing mutually costly cooperation or engaging in costly punishments.

The second option is to condition punishment on the litigation process. That is, the governments can wait to see whether a challenge is brought by a plaintiff and, if it is, observe the positions third-party governments take on the case and the amount of effort the defendant government spends trying to justify its digression before deciding whether to punish. The advantage of this strategy is that governments can target threats of retaliation more effectively because the governments will know how each other feels about the case (and, in equilibrium, whether compliance would be mutually costly). The disadvantage is if a defecting government is not taken to court, that government can get away with defections when compliance would have been net beneficial.

---

[33] Punishment here involves a government denying the benefit of cooperation to another government. Such a punishment could come in many forms. For example, some treaties explicitly provide for retaliatory sanctions (e.g., trade restrictions) as punishment. But members of a regime could punish one another through any number of policies or practices. In the European Union, for example, this could involve disruptive action in diplomatic or legislative settings. It could also involve targeted deviations for treaty obligations that are not explicitly sanctioned by the treaty. In the EU we occasionally see member-states restrict access to their markets for products from specific countries. For example, restrictions on the importation of British beef during the 1990s by Germany and France went beyond EU-specified limits.

That is, the governments forgo the opportunity to punish independent of an adverse court ruling.

Because each of these strategies has trade-offs, *ex ante*, which one is preferable depends on a variety of factors. Trade-offs are discussed in more detail in Carrubba (2005). Here, the key point is that a government has an incentive to invest in creating a court only if it intends to condition its punishment strategy on activation of the judicial system. Thus, we focus on the second option. In particular, punishment is triggered if and only if another government defects, is brought to court, does not invest enough effort in defending itself to convince the other governments that (conditional on the third-party briefs) compliance is mutually costly, is ruled against, and does not comply with the ruling.[34]

Punishment itself is standard to the typical infinitely repeated prisoners' dilemma. For some number of periods t, other governments do not comply, whereas the government being punished does. If for some reason the government being punished does not comply during this phase, punishment continues until the punishee complies for t periods in a row. Once the punishment is completed, the governments return to cooperative behavior.[35]

In sum, governments are free to behave as they wish unless they are caught defecting when compliance is perceived to be net beneficial. Then they are expected to obey an adverse court ruling. If they do, the transgression is forgiven and the governments continue with their normal behavior. If they do not, the defecting governments must cooperate in their punishment for t periods before returning to cooperation.

Predicting the generation and resolution of disputes before the court
Having addressed the punishment strategies, we can now describe how the governments, litigants, and a court behave in equilibrium. A formal statement of this equilibrium is reserved for this chapter's appendix. The equilibrium is presented in a series of propositions. The propositions are presented in chronological order.

Proposition 1: Governments defect from the regulatory regime's rules if and only if the cost of compliance is sufficiently large $(c_i > c_I^*)$.[36]

---

[34] Note that a punishment strategy conditioned upon activation of the adjudicatory process only works if litigants have an incentive to bring cases. Because litigants want to bring cases only if they are going to win at least some of the time, governments have to lose and pay the judgment at least some of the time. In equilibrium, this behavior arises only if punishment is triggered by refusal to obey an adverse ruling.
[35] Formally, this strategy is a t-period, renegotiation proof punishment.
[36] The threshold c_I^*, above which the government defects, is defined in the proofs provided in the appendix.

In deciding whether to defect, each government makes a strategic calculation. If it complies, it pays its cost of compliance with certainty. If it defects, it takes a gamble that has three possible outcomes. If it is not brought to court, the government successfully shirks its obligations. From that government's perspective, this is the best possible outcome. If the government is brought to court, but it gets sufficient support (or lack of opposition) from the third-party briefs, the government can be better off as well. Although it will have to exert some effort in defending itself, the cost of exerting that effort is never more than the initial cost of compliance. Thus, whereas the government would prefer not to have been brought to court, it is still at least weakly better off than when initially complying. Finally, if the government is brought to court and third-party governments are not supportive enough of the defendant government in their briefs, the government will be ruled against and it will obey the adverse judgment. If ruled against, the defecting government is strictly worse off than if it had simply complied in the first place. Thus, a government defects only if the risk is worth it – that is, the initial cost of compliance is sufficiently large.

Proposition 2: A litigant brings a case if the cost of bringing the case is not too high ($k_l \leq k_l^*$).[37]

Bringing a case is a risky gamble. The litigant wins the case and thereby gains some benefit only if the defendant government does not get enough third-party support. Because bringing a case is costly, the litigant does so only if its cost is not too large.

Proposition 3: A third-party government files a brief against (for) a defendant government if it would benefit from (pay a cost for) the defendant government obeying an adverse court ruling.

Filing a brief is costly, even if only minimally. Thus, third-party governments file briefs only if there is some potential benefit from doing so. A government that files a brief on behalf of one of the litigants strictly increases the chances the court will rule in favor of that litigant. Thus, governments that benefit from (are hurt by) the government obeying an adverse ruling file against (for) the defendant government and governments that do not care who wins do not file.

Proposition 4: A government exerts enough effort ($e_{n,m}^* = Pr[k_c \leq k_c^* | n, m]$ ($j^* + n^*b - m^*c$)) to persuade other governments not to punish it for ignoring

---

[37] The threshold k_l^*, above which a potential litigant does not bring a case, is defined in the proofs provided in the appendix.

A theory of international agreements and their systems of adjudication 43

a court decision if the cost of compliance with the regulatory regime's rules is sufficiently large.[38]

Once briefs are filed, the government knows how much effort it must exert to convince the other governments not to sanction it for ignoring an adverse decision. Specifically, it must convince them that, net of the briefs filed, its cost of compliance is large enough such that compliance is net costly. Exerting this amount of effort is worthwhile only if net of the briefs compliance is net costly. Governments with a lower cost prefer to risk having to comply with an adverse ruling, and governments with higher costs of compliance are strictly better off ensuring that they will not have to comply.

Proposition 5: The court rules against a government if and only if the cost of having its ruling ignored is not too severe ($k_c \leq k_c^*$). The court issues judgments that maximize the probability of the government obeying the ruling [$j^* \in (0, CV - CV_p - Nb)$].[39]

Each time a case arises, the court must decide whether to rule against the government. If the court does not rule against the government, there is no risk of paying a cost for being ignored (k_c), but there is also no chance of bringing the government back into compliance with the regime's rules. In deciding whether to risk paying the cost k_c, the court weighs the likelihood that an adverse ruling will be ignored. The more briefs filed against the defendant government, and the fewer in favor of the defendant government, the more likely the defendant government will obey an adverse ruling. As a result, the more briefs against and the fewer in favor, the larger the cost k_c^* for which the court is willing to rule against the defendant. Thus, the court rules against a government if the probability of being obeyed, conditional on the filed briefs, is large enough relative to the cost of being ignored.

Proposition 6: Governments obey adverse rulings if and only if they have not exerted enough effort to persuade the other governments to permit them to ignore the court ruling and the judgment the court imposes is not too large.

If a defendant government exerts enough effort to convince the other governments not to punish it for ignoring an adverse ruling, there is no incentive to obey that ruling. Thus, a government will obey an adverse ruling only if it

---

[38] The effort a government exerts in its defense if it wishes not to be punished, $e_{n,m}^*$, is derived in the proofs provided in the appendix.

[39] The threshold k_c^*, above which the court does not rule against the defendant government, is defined in the proofs provided in the appendix. The judgment j^* the court imposes if it rules against a defendant government is derived in the proofs provided in the appendix.

has not exerted such effort. As long as the court does not impose a judgment so costly that being punished is actually better for the government, the government will obey that ruling. Thus, a government obeys an adverse ruling only if it anticipates sanctioning for ignoring the decision and the judgment is not costlier than the threatened sanction.

In sum, our model involves the following sequence of moves: governments defect when the cost of compliance is sufficiently large, and litigants bring cases when the cost of doing so is not too large. If a case is brought, third-party governments file briefs for the litigant they support, and the defendant government exerts enough effort in its defense to forestall possible sanctions when compliance is net costly. The court then rules. It rules against the government when the probability that the defendant will comply is sufficiently large and the court's cost of being ignored is not too large. The court is careful to ensure that judgments have a chance of being paid, and governments obey adverse court rulings if they will be sanctioned for ignoring them.

e. Implications

Most obviously, the model demonstrates the limits of judicial influence. By construction, the court would like to enforce the regime's rules.[40] Governments, on the other hand, want to comply only selectively. Unfortunately for the court, its hands are tied. Although it can rule against governments independent of the cost of compliance, a government obeys the ruling only if it anticipates being sanctioned by the other governments for ignoring the ruling. Because sanctioning happens only when compliance is net beneficial, the court can help governments achieve their policy goals, but the court cannot push its own agenda beyond that point.

That said, it is important not to read too much into this result. Even a court constrained in such a fashion has room to be legally innovative. To see how, we must first step back and characterize more clearly what we mean by "the law." As described earlier, governments, litigants, and the court all know exactly what the regulatory regime's rules require. In each instance a government decides whether to intentionally violate those rules. If the government violates, the question becomes whether the regime will come back into compliance. Thus, there is a clear sense of the regime's obligations. Governments obey these obligations (mostly) when the costs of compliance are not too high, and do not obey them otherwise.

---

[40] Or, as mentioned in footnote 29, the court would like an expansive interpretation of the regime's rules.

The model was described this way for clarity of exposition. Most models of international regimes describe the governments' choices in this fashion, and so it was simpler to follow that norm. However, that interpretation is unnecessarily restrictive. Regulatory regime rules are better thought of as incomplete contracts than as bright lines that perfectly delineate acceptable and unacceptable behavior. These incomplete contracts provide instructions that sometimes leave ambiguity as to how to apply the law. For example, suppose a regulatory regime declares all nontariff barriers to trade invalid, but at the same time allows certain exceptions for domestic social and environmental policies. Because these social and environmental policies may affect trade, we are left with room for ambiguity regarding which of these policies should be struck down as undue burdens to trade. Seen in this light, governments must decide whether to follow a more or less inclusive reading of the regulatory regime's rules. If they err on the side of not burdening trade, they are being more inclusive and the other state benefits at some cost to the home state.

In this world, there is no legal or illegal decisions, just decisions about whether to be more inclusive or not. As such, the court helps governments fill in this incomplete contract in net beneficial ways. And, by implication, if the court can identify ways to expand the application of the regime's rules beyond its original boundaries that are also net beneficial for the governments, that court can be doctrinally innovative. But it also still means that the court can be legally expansive, *and gain compliance*, only when its interpretation comports with the governments' goals for the regulatory regime.

Relatedly, this model also demonstrates the limits of what we can learn about international cooperation from observing compliance with court decisions. As discussed previously, scholars have pointed to evidence of governments being brought to court and being ruled against and those governments obeying the ruling as prima facie evidence courts are constraining government behavior *independent of the wishes of those governments* (Downs, Rocke, and Barsoom 1996). Previously, we highlighted the potential for selection bias in using these data. Here, we use the model to point to an additional problem with interpreting these data: observational equivalence. We should observe governments obeying court decisions if court rulings are binding in some sense (i.e., if enforcement of those decisions is not problematic). We should also observe exactly the same behavior when the court has to rely on governments to enforce its decisions. This problem of observational equivalence holds no matter how frequently we observe governments obeying adverse rulings. Thus, we cannot easily distinguish between a court that is independently influential (perhaps as a result of governments' commitment to the rule of law) and one whose influence depends on enforcement by others.

That said, in our model a court that cannot depend on voluntary compliance is actively facilitating cooperation that might not otherwise be sustainable. Without the court (or some equivalent mechanism), governments would not be able to target their sanctions for noncompliance. As such, when the costs of compliance are sufficiently high, governments still would defect and the regime would break down. Whereas the whole agreement might or might not collapse, at a minimum participating governments would enter a costly "trade war" in which governments would punish each other with ongoing noncompliance.[41]

Carrubba (2005) uses a simpler version of this model to demonstrate that under a wide range of conditions this untargeted punishment is inferior to a regime with a court. In particular, a court generally (but not always) facilitates cooperation. A court is most beneficial when cooperation would otherwise be unsustainable, but it is also generally beneficial even when cooperation could be sustained without a court. The only time a court actually reduces the benefit of participating in the regulatory regime occurs when enforcement problems (i.e., the incentive to defect from the regime) are particularly small.

f. Predictions

As discussed previously, if correct, this model has important implications for how and why international courts influence national government behavior. However, much of the behavior predicted by the theory is observationally equivalent to behavior predicted by very different theories of international courts. Furthermore, some of the predicted behavior is effectively impossible to test empirically because of measurement and data problems. Thus, a critical question is how to identify discriminating predictions that enable us to evaluate the veracity of our argument. One of the benefits of this modeling approach is that it also generates discriminating, testable predictions. We describe two that are the basis of our empirical work in this book.

First, our theory predicts that a court is more likely to rule against governments when it has more support from third-party government briefs. Briefs act as a credible signal of government preferences. Thus, the more briefs filed against a defendant government and the fewer filed in support, the less likely compliance is net costly and the more likely the defendant government is to

---

[41] Another way to think about this point is that this model demonstrates how a court can maintain cooperation even though cooperation will not always be a prisoners' dilemma. Long-term cooperation can be sustained in the face of intermittent periods in which cooperation is undesirable (i.e., not net beneficial).

acquiesce to an adverse ruling. The more likely the court will have its ruling obeyed, the more likely the court will be willing to take a chance and rule against the government (i.e., for a larger range of costs of being ignored).

Prediction 1 (the Political Sensitivity Hypothesis): The court is more likely to rule against a defendant government the more briefs filed against the government and the fewer briefs filed in support of it.

Second, our theory predicts that court decisions against governments are more likely to change defendant governments' behavior as the support for the ruling from third-party government briefs increases. Ignoring a court ruling can take many forms. Governments might outright disobey the ruling, they might delay implementation of the ruling long enough for it ultimately to be irrelevant, they might engage in behavior that appears to conform to the ruling but that effectively violates its spirit, or they might conform to the decision in the short run and then pass new laws or engage in other behavior subsequently that undermines the impact of obeying that specific ruling in the first place. Whatever the mechanism, the implication of ignoring a ruling is clear: we would observe little, if any, policy impact from the decision. The more support from third-party government briefs the court has, the more likely the defendant will obey an adverse ruling, and therefore the more likely real policy change will occur if the government is ruled against.

Prediction 2 (the Conditional Effectiveness Hypothesis): Court rulings against defendant governments are more likely to change government behavior the more briefs filed in support of the ruling and the fewer filed against it.

III. CONCLUSION

Most international courts face a daunting challenge. They are tasked with helping ensure that independent-minded sovereign states comply with international law. However, courts have no ability to enforce their rulings. There may be consequences to ignoring or otherwise evading an international court's edict, but ultimately national governments are free to react in whatever way they wish. What a court can do is act as a fire alarm, by providing a venue in which disputes can arise, and an information clearinghouse, by providing a venue in which interested governments can make arguments and try to persuade one another whether the defendant government should be held to task. What can a court faced with such a challenge accomplish?

In this chapter we examined judicial influence when the international regulatory regime is tasked with helping resolve collective action problems among the constituent states. The model is intentionally designed to be "institutionally thin," with the goal of providing some conclusions that are generalizable across a variety of policy areas and international organizations. We derive a number of relatively nuanced inferences about international court influence. Our theory implies that these courts can and do promote higher levels of compliance with international law than would exist without them in two ways. First, they prevent otherwise unavoidable periods of systematic noncompliance with the regulatory regime's rules (e.g., trade wars). Second, they help make the regime more stable overall (i.e., cooperation is more easily sustainable when the adjudication of cases serve as a release valve with which governments are occasionally allowed to avoid compliance).

Both of these observations arise from the fact that if governments do not condition punishment on the costs and benefits of compliance, they must punish all violations for any hope of sustaining cooperation. Because the costs of compliance can be quite large, sometimes governments then would defect even knowing they will be punished. As a result, an unconditional response leads to periods in which that government is punished through systematic noncompliance by the enforcing governments. In our model, such periods are avoided because the judicial process helps governments condition their punishment on the costs of compliance faced by the violating government.[42]

This court influence is derived without privileging the court in any way. We make no assumption that governments are credibly committing to follow international law because, for example, domestic publics mobilize and alter governments' incentives once the agreement is signed (Simmons 2009). Further, we make no assumption that the court has an informational or other strategic advantage over the member states that allows it to wield exogenous influence.[43] In fact, our argument effectively maximally disadvantages the court relative to the governments. The court knows less than the governments do about the background political negotiations around a case. The court has no independent enforcement power. And the governments are allowed to

---

[42] Note that this implication speaks to debates on the "efficient breach." Scholars have argued about whether participants in international regulatory regimes such as the WTO should be allowed to occasionally violate the agreement. Some say yes, it makes the system more efficient (e.g., Schwartz and Sykes 2002a). Others say no, obligations need to be respected (e.g., Jackson 2004a). Our analysis supports those who would argue that allowing breaches of agreements can be in the best interests of the agreement and the participants. Without such flexibility, these agreements are likely to be both more shallow than they would otherwise be and ultimately fragile (Johns forthcoming).

[43] For an argument that does include such an advantage, see, e.g., Alter (2001).

Conclusion

prenegotiate how they will respond to various court rulings before the cases even arise (i.e., the governments coordinate on a commonly agreed upon punishment strategy designed solely to serve their purposes). Yet, we still find that courts in such a setting can be important, effectual players in a regulatory regime. The judicial process allows governments to inform each other about the costs of compliance faced by violators. In our model, this happens both through the efforts of the defendant and through the submissions of third-party governments.

Although our theory suggests that these courts are influential, it is important to recognize that this influence is not unlimited. The courts can facilitate levels of compliance that the governments ultimately want to see sustained over the long run. However, they cannot successfully push interpretations of international law that are inconsistent with underlying government preferences. In the parlance of the model, the court can facilitate compliance only with international law that the governments perceive to be net beneficial. Or, put differently, the court can help facilitate compliance only that the member-state governments are ultimately willing for the court to enforce.

These limits may evolve. In the model, government preferences cannot be affected by the actions the court takes. For example, court rulings that governments comply with ultimately could affect the social, economic, and political make-up of the domestic state. This effect, in turn, can induce governments to come to support different policies than they had previously supported. This new support, then, potentially creates opportunities for the court to develop novel interpretations of international laws. Thus, through the operation of the international court, governmental incentives – and thereby international law – can organically change. Similarly, it is always possible that international actors such as a court can identify new opportunities for net beneficial cooperation that the governments did not anticipate when they created the regime. Considering our theory in light of this dynamic process would imply that, within limits, it is perfectly possible for international courts to innovate and change the functioning of an international organization. Some have argued that the ECJ did exactly this with the development of the concept of mutual recognition (Garrett and Weingast 1993).

In sum, to live in a world that recognizes that international institutions work only at the behest of the governments that constitute them is not to imply that these institutions are powerless, purely symbolic, or otherwise utterly ineffectual. That is, it does not imply that classic realist arguments are correct. Conversely, to recognize that these institutions are really doing something – that they are making rulings and changing government behavior – is not to imply that governments are somehow constrained to obey adverse court rulings and that these institutions are international actors run amok, pushing forward agendas independent of and running roughshod over what governments want from them. Rather, our model implies something more nuanced. International courts can be constrained and international courts can have influence, both at the same time. Our theory suggests the contours of exactly how this balancing act would work for a variety of international regulatory regimes.

In the next chapters, we discuss and examine the empirical relevance of this theoretical model to actual international regulatory regimes. Specifically, we test the two predictions extensively in the context of the European Union.

APPENDIX: THE FORMAL MODEL

A. THE EQUILIBRIUM

On-equilibrium path strategies

The Governments

$$X^* = \begin{cases} comply & if\ c_i \leq c_l^* \\ defect & otherwise \end{cases}$$

$$e_{n,m}^* = \begin{cases} \Pr[k_c \leq k_c^*](j^* + n^*b - m^*c) & if\ c_i > n^*b - m^*c \\ 0 & otherwise \end{cases}$$

$$A^* = \begin{cases} acquiesce & if\ c_i \leq n^*b - m^*c\ and\ j \geq CV - CV_p - c_i \\ defy & otherwise \end{cases}$$

$$O^* = \begin{cases} support & if\ \beta = -c \\ oppose & if\ \beta = b \\ \neg file & otherwise \end{cases}$$

The Litigants

$$L^* = \begin{cases} litigate & if\ k_l \leq k_l^* = E\left[\Pr\left(c_i \leq nb - mc | c_i > c_l^*\right)\right] j^* \\ \neg litigate & otherwise \end{cases}$$

The Court

$$R^* = \begin{cases} for\ gov & if\ k_c \leq k_c^* = \Pr\left[c_l < c_i \leq n^*b - m^*c | c_i > c_l^*\right] \\ \neg gov & otherwise \end{cases}$$

$$j^* \in \left(0, CV - CV_p - (N-1)b\right)$$

Off-equilibrium path strategies

Punishee

$$X^*_{p,\tau+j} = \text{comply} \quad \text{if } A_{p,\tau} = \text{defy}, R_\tau = \neg\text{gov},$$
$$j_\tau \in \left(0, CV - CV_p - (N-1)b\right), \text{ and } e_{p,\tau} \leq e^*_{n,m}$$

Punisher

$$X^*_{\sim p,\tau+j} = \neg\text{comply} \quad \text{if } A_{p,\tau} = \text{defy}, R_\tau = \neg\text{gov},$$
$$j_\tau \in \left(0, CV - CV_p - (N-1)b\right), \text{ and } e_{p,\tau} \leq e^*_{n,m}$$

for $j = 1$ to t.
All other strategies as above.

B. PROOF

Assume c_i is drawn from a distribution between zero and some upper bound $\bar{c}$.[44] Assume k_l and k_c are random draws from unbounded distributions. Define $e \geq 0$. Define the number of states to be N. Define $(n-1)$ to be the number of briefs filed on behalf of the plaintiff and m to be the number of briefs filed on behalf of the defendant.

The proof is by construction. We define the continuation values assuming equilibrium play and then derive play in the stage game, demonstrating that best replies in the stage game match the assumed equilibrium play in the continuation values.

The continuation value from on-path play is:

$$CV = \frac{\delta}{1-\delta}\left\{Pr[c_i \leq c_l^*](b - E[c_i|c_i \leq c_l^*]) + Pr[k_l \leq k_l^*](E[Pr[k_c \leq k_c^*|n,m]\right.$$
$$Pr[c_l^* < c_i \leq nb - mc]E[b - j_i|c_l^* < c_i \leq nb - mc] + Pr[nb - mc < c_i]$$
$$E[-e_i^*|nb - mc < c_i]]) + (N-2)(Pr[c_i \leq c_l] + Pr[k_l \leq k_l^*]E[Pr[k_c \leq k_c^*|n,m]$$
$$\left.Pr[c_l^* < c_i \leq nb - mc]])(Pr[\beta = b]b + Pr[\beta = -c](-c))\right\}. \tag{1}$$

Each period each government is paired with a partner government with whom it must decide whether to cooperate or defect. The governments each draw a cost of compliance. The first half of the continuation value characterizes the costs and benefits to parties in a potential dispute. If $c_i \leq c_l^*$, a government

---

[44] This upper bound is assumed for convenience; a government being punished cannot draw a cost that would cause them to deviate from punishment path. Relaxing this assumption would simply require defining punishment path to be a fixed number of periods of punishment rather than a fixed duration of punishment. See Carrubba (2009) for this alternative specification.

complies. A complying government pays $E[c_i|c_i \leq c_l^*]$. A government partnered with a complying government receives b.

With the expected probability $Pr[k_l \leq k_l^*]E[Pr[k_c \leq k_c^*|n,m]Pr[c_l^* < c_i \leq nb - mc]]$, a government defects, is brought to court, is ruled against (conditional on the realized observations), and complies with the judgment. A complying government pays the expected judgment $E[-j_i|c_l^* < c_i \leq nb - mc]$. A government partnered with a complying government receives b.

With the expected probability $Pr[k_l \leq k_l^*]E[Pr[nb - mc < c_i]]$, a government defects, is brought to court, and exerts enough effort not to be punished for ignoring an adverse ruling conditional on realized observations. The government pays the expected effort cost $E[-e_i^*|nb - mc < c_i]$. Note that the continuation value has double expectations. The inner expectations are over the realization of c_i. The outer expectation is over the realizations of n and m.

The second half of the continuation value characterizes the costs and benefits associated with being a third party to a potential dispute. Each time a government complies in expectation ($Pr[c_i \leq c_l^*] + Pr[k_l \leq k_l^*]E[Pr[k_c \leq k_c^*|n,m]Pr[c_l^* < c_i \leq nb - mc]]$), a third-party government receives a benefit b with probability $Pr[\beta = b]b$ and pays a cost $-c$ with probability $Pr[\beta = -c]$. Assume $Pr[\beta = b]b + Pr[\beta = -c](-c) > 0$ to help ensure that cooperation is net beneficial in expectation.

Note that $CV > 0$ holds for $E[Pr[nb - mc < c_i]]$ sufficiently small because under all other conditions the continuation value is positive for j, which is sufficiently small by definition ($nb - mc \geq c_i$).

The continuation value from punishment path play is:

$$CV_p = \frac{\delta - \delta^t}{1 - \delta}(E[-c_i] + (N-2)(Pr[c_i \leq c_l] + Pr[k_l \leq k_l^*] \\ \times E[Pr[k_c \leq k_c^*|n,m] Pr[c_l^* < c_i \leq nb - mc]])(Pr[\beta = b]b \\ + Pr[\beta = -c](-c))) + \delta^t CV]. \qquad (2)$$

For t periods ($\frac{\delta - \delta^t}{1-\delta}$), the government being punished cooperates every period of its punishment ($E[-c_i]$), other governments do not cooperate with it, and it participates as a third party, filing briefs in the same way as on equilibrium path (($N-2)(Pr[c_i \leq c_l] + Pr[k_l \leq k_l^*]E[Pr[k_c \leq k_c^*|n,m] Pr[c_l^* < c_i \leq nb - mc]])(Pr[\beta = b]b + Pr[\beta = -c](-c)))$.

Complying with judgments

When $c_l < c_i \leq nb - mc$ a government obeys an adverse judgment if:

$$-j_i + CV \geq CV_p \qquad (3)$$

Because $j_i = j + c_i$, equation (3) simplifies to:

$$j \leq CV - CV_p - c_i \qquad (4)$$

To show that condition (4) can be met, we must establish that $j > 0$ can hold. We know:

$$CV - CV_p = \frac{\delta - \delta^t}{1 - \delta}(Pr[c_i \leq c_l^*](b) + Pr[k_l \leq k_l^*](E[Pr[k_c \leq k_c^*|n, m]$$
$$\times Pr[c_l^* < c_i \leq nb - mc]E[b - j_i|c_l^* < c_i \leq nb - mc]$$
$$+ Pr[nb - mc < c_i]E[-e_i^*|nb - mc < c_i]])$$
$$+ E[c_i|c_i > c_l^*]). \qquad (5)$$

Equation 5 always is positive. To see why, first note that $E[c_i|c_i > c_l^*] = E[-c_i|c_l^* < c_i \leq nb - mc] + E[c_i|nb - mc \leq c_i]$. Using this fact, and reorganizing terms in equation (5), we get equation (6):

$$CV - CV_p = \frac{\delta - \delta^t}{1 - \delta}(Pr[c_i \leq c_l^*](b) + Pr[k_l \leq k_l^*](E[Pr[k_c \leq k_c^*|n, m]$$
$$\times Pr[c_l^* < c_i \leq nb - mc]E[b + c_i - j_i|c_l^* < c_i \leq nb - mc]$$
$$+ Pr[nb - mc < c_i]E[c_i - e_i^*|nb - mc < c_i]])$$
$$+ (1 - Pr[k_l \leq k_l^*]E[Pr[k_c \leq k_c^*|n, m]Pr[c_l^* < c_i \leq nb - mc]])$$
$$\times E[c_i|c_i > c_l^*]). \qquad (6)$$

Because j^* can be arbitrarily small and $b > 0$, $E[b + c_i - j_i|c_l^* < c_i \leq nb - mc]$ can always be positive, and because $e_i^* \leq c_i$ when $nb - mc < c_i$, $E[c_i - e_i^*|nb - mc < c_i]$ is never negative. Because all other terms are always positive, $CV - CV_p > 0$.

To complete the proof, note that the largest value of c_i for which j must be paid in equilibrium is $c_i = nb - mc = (N - 1)b$. Thus, for $CV - CV_p > (N - 1)b$ condition (4) can be met, which holds for δ and t sufficiently large.

Also note that punishment path is subgame perfect as long as the punishee accepts its punishment, $-c_i + CV_{p(t-1)} \geq CV_p$. We know CV approaches infinity as δ approaches 1 (given $E[Pr[nb - mc < c_i]]$ sufficiently small from previously), while the punishment phase approaches a constant (given the endogenous cut points are independent of δ, which is shown later). Thus, for δ sufficiently large punishment path is subgame perfect for any $c_i \leq \bar{c}$. The punisher's play is trivially a best reply.

Issuing judgments

The court wants to maximize the probability of compliance whenever it rules against a government. Thus, j must meet condition (4) for any $c_i \leq nb - mc$. Because $max(nb - mc) = (N-1)b$, $j^* \in (0, CV - CV_p - (N-1)b)$.[45]

Court rulings

The court rules against a government if $EU_c(\neg gov) = Pr[c_l^* < c_i \leq nb - mc|c_i > c_l](1) - (1 - Pr[c_l^* < c_i \leq nb - mc|c_i > c_l])k_c \geq EU_c(\text{for gov}) = 0$, which implies $k_c \leq k_c^* = \frac{Pr[c_l^* < c_i \leq n^*b - m^*c|c_i > c_l^*]}{1 - Pr[c_l^* < c_i \leq nb - mc|c_i > c_l]}$.

Government effort in defense

Effort separates government types when $Pr[k_c \leq k_c^*|n,m](-j_i^*) + CV \geq -e_{n,m}^* + CV \Rightarrow e_{n,m}^* \geq Pr[k_c \leq k_c^*|n,m](j_i^*)$. Governments with cost $c_i \leq \frac{e_{n,m}^*}{Pr[k_c \leq k_c^*|n,m]} - j^* = \frac{Pr[k_c \leq k_c^*|n,m](j^* + n^*b - m^*c)}{Pr[k_c \leq k_c^*|n,m]} - j^* = n^*b - m^*c$ are worse off mimicking the separating signal and offer $e_{n,m}^* = 0$. All other governments are best off offering the minimal separating signal $e_{n,m}^* = Pr[k_c \leq k_c^*|n,m](j^* + n^*b - m^*c)$.

Third-party government briefs

A government files a brief against a government if $EU_g(oppose|\beta = b) = Pr[nb - mc < c_i \leq (n-1)b - mc|c_i > c_l^*](b) - \varepsilon \geq EU_g(\neg file|\beta = b) = 0$ $\forall n > 0, m \geq 0$. This condition holds for ε sufficiently small, $\varepsilon \leq Pr[nb - mc < c_i \leq (n-1)b - mc|c_i > c_l^*]b \ \forall n > 0, m \geq 0$. A government files a brief for a government if $EU_g(support|\beta = -c) = Pr[nb - mc < c_i \leq nb - (m-1)c|c_i > c_l^*](0) - \varepsilon \geq EU_g(\neg file|\beta = -c) = Pr[nb - mc < c_i \leq nb - (m-1)c|c_i > c_l^*](-c) \ \forall n > 0, m \geq 0$. This condition holds for ε sufficiently small, $\varepsilon \leq Pr[nb - mc < c_i \leq nb - (m-1)c|c_i > c_l^*]c \ \forall n > 0, m \geq 0$. For $\beta = 0$, the government is strictly worse off filing for $\varepsilon > 0$.[46]

---

[45] Note that j could be indexed by n and m, but nothing in the solution other than the upper boundaries on j would change. Thus, for parsimony, j is left as an unconditional value.

[46] Note that there is no collective action problem for this condition because each government has a unilateral incentive to file a brief. Larger collective action problems could arise, but these are substantively uninteresting and broadly empirically unlikely given the low cost of filing briefs for governments.

Litigants bringing cases

A litigant brings a case if $EU_l(litigate) = E[Pr[k_c \leq k_c^*|n, m]Pr[c_f^* < c_i \leq nb - mc|c_i > c_f^*]]j^* - k_l \geq EU_l(\neg litigate) = 0$, which implies $k_l \leq k_l^* = E[Pr[k_c \leq k_c^*|n, m]Pr(c_i \leq nb - mc|c_i > c_f^*)]j^*$.

Government compliance with regulations

A government complies if $EU_g(comply) = -c_i \geq EU_g(defect) = Pr[k_l \leq k_l^*]$ $(E[Pr[k_c \leq k_c^*|n, m]Pr[c_f^* < c_i \leq nb - mc]E[-j_i|c_f^* < c_i \leq nb - mc] + Pr[nb - mc < c_i]E[-e_i^*|nb - mc < c_i]])$ and defects otherwise. Define $c_f^* = Pr[k_l \leq k_l^*](E[Pr[k_c \leq k_c^*|n, m]Pr[c_f^* < c_i \leq nb - mc]E[-j_i|c_f^* < c_i \leq nb - mc] + Pr[nb - mc < c_i]E[-e_i^*|nb - mc < c_i]])$.

Each condition matches the assumed behavior in the on-path continuation value. Next, we demonstrate that this system of equations yields a unique equilibrium.

By the Kakutani (1941) fixed-point theorem, we know a solution to this system of equations exists. The solution is also unique. There are three cost terms (one of which is a vector) for which we must demonstrate a unique cut-point, k_l, $k_c(n, m)$ and c_i. To prove this claim, we establish that the difference in expected utilities between choices meets the single crossing property requirements (the difference can change signs as a function of the cost term, and it is monotonic in the cost term).

First, consider $EU_l(litigate) - EU_l(\neg litigate)$. This difference is positive for $k_l = 0$ and negative for k_l sufficiently large. It is also strictly monotonically decreasing in k_l (all endogenous probability terms are independent of the realized value of k_l).

Second, consider $EU_c(\neg gov) - EU_c(for\ gov)$. This difference is positive for $k_c(n, m) = 0$ and negative for $k_c(n, m)$ sufficiently large. It is also strictly monotonically decreasing in $k_c(n, m)$ [all endogenous probability terms are independent of the realized value of $k_c(n, m)$].

Finally, consider $EU_g(comply) - EU_g(defect)$. This difference is positive for $c_i = 0$ and negative for c_i sufficiently large (recall for δ arbitrarily approaching 1, $\bar{c}$ can be arbitrarily large). It is also strictly monotonically decreasing in c_i. To see why, note that the government pays c_i with certainty if it complies and only probabilistically if it does not. Further, the probability it pays c_i is decreasing in c_i ($Pr[c_f^* < c_i \leq nb - mc]$), and all other endogenous probability terms are independent of the realized value of c_i. Thus, the difference must be strictly monotonically decreasing in c_i.

Predictions

Prediction 1: A court is more likely to rule against a defendant government the more briefs filed against the government and the fewer filed in support of it.

   Proof: The probability with which the court rules against a defendant government is $Pr[k_c \leq k_c^*]$, where $k_c^* = \frac{Pr[c_l^* < c_i \leq n^*b - m^*c | c_i > c_l^*]}{1 - Pr[c_l^* < c_i \leq n^*b - m^*c | c_i > c_l^*]}$. Because k_c^* is increasing in n and decreasing in m, the prediction follows.

Prediction 2: Court rulings against governments are less likely to change government behavior the more briefs filed in support of the government and the fewer filed against it.

   Proof: Conditional on a ruling against the defendant government, the probability the ruling is obeyed is a function of how likely the defendant government was to draw a cost for which it would obey an adverse ruling. The probability the government acquiesces is $Pr[c_i \leq n^*b - m^*c | c_i > c_l^*]$. Because this probability is increasing in n and decreasing in m, the prediction follows.

3

Putting the theory to the test

Evaluating the hypotheses in the European Union

In Chapter 2, we presented a theoretical model that explains how a court can facilitate government compliance with an international regulatory regime. The model demonstrates how courts can mitigate intergovernmental collective action problems exacerbated by variable, privately known costs of compliance with the regime's rules. This finding holds even though a member-state government can have an extremely strong incentive to defect from the regime's rules (and evade an adverse court decision), and even though the court has no direct means of enforcement.

The remainder of the book focuses on the empirical relevance of the model. As described in the introduction and presented in Table 1.1, the key components of the theoretical model are descriptively consistent with the political and institutional context of many international regulatory regimes. Put differently, our theoretical model does not depend critically on unusual assumptions regarding the process of adjudication or the underlying compliance problems faced by international regimes. As a result, we consider the model a plausible explanation for how a court can contribute to the performance of a variety of international regulatory regimes. The implications of our theoretical model therefore should apply to many of these settings.

That said, we are unaware of any study that has tested our model's predictions. Some studies provide suggestive evidence. For example, Kono (2007) evaluated whether the performance of preferential trade agreements (including those described in our table in the first chapter) has depended on the type of dispute resolution mechanism (or dispute settlement mechanism, DSM). Specifically, he found that the agreements that included a third-party review of disputes (and, to a lesser extent, standing tribunals) were more successful in liberalizing trade than were agreements lacking such a provision.[1] But, as Kono (2007) argues, this impact of DSM design could be the result of several factors, not necessarily the specific argument advanced in our theoretical model. More directly related to our model, Busch and Reinhardt (2007) execute a test of the influence of third-party briefs on rulings by an international court (the WTO appellate body). They show that the presence of third-party briefs in favor of the complainant increases the likelihood of a pro-complainant ruling. This is generally consistent with the Political Sensitivity Hypothesis. But, although suggestive, this evidence is not a direct test of the hypothesis. It does not, for example, speak to whether the number and balance of third-party briefs influence rulings, as our hypothesis specifies. Similarly, past studies have examined the effectiveness of rulings by international courts. For example, several studies have examined whether pro-trade rulings, in general, expand trade (e.g., Gabel et al. 2012). But none of those studies considered the conditional effect specified by the Conditional Effectiveness Hypothesis.

Consequently, the remainder of the book presents an original empirical analysis of the two predictions from our model. Specifically, we evaluate them in one particularly important setting: the European Union (EU).

I. THE EUROPEAN UNION AND THE EUROPEAN COURT OF JUSTICE

a. *The theoretical model and the European Union*

Among international regulatory regimes, the European Union (EU) is a particularly attractive venue in which to test the predictions of our theoretical model. First, it is a substantively important example – arguably the EU is the preeminent international organization in the world. Second, the key theoretical assumptions discussed previously apply well in this setting. And third, the historical record of the EU provides rich data for testing the predictions of the model.

Most scholars would agree that the EU is one of the most important, and fully realized, international organizations in the world. The EU is the current manifestation of the European Economic Community (EEC), created in 1957 by the Rome Treaty. As initially conceived, the EEC provided for the gradual elimination of all barriers to the movement of goods, capital, labor, and services among France, West Germany, Italy, Belgium, the Netherlands,

---

[1] Kono (2007) shows that, on average, trade liberalization is greater in regimes with third-party dispute resolution and with standing tribunals, although the effect of standing tribunals is statistically insignificant.

and Luxembourg. The EEC also provided for a Common Agricultural Policy that would regulate production of and commerce in the agricultural sector. Finally, the EEC established a common external trade policy.[2] The member states wanted the EEC to be the foundation for peace in Europe after World War II and the basis for economic recovery and growth (Hitchcock 2002a).

Over time, both the policy and geographic scope of the EEC grew. The EEC merged with the European Coal and Steel Community (ECSC) and European Atomic Energy Community (Euratom) to form the European Communities (EC) in 1965. Subsequent treaty revisions (the Single European Act, the Maastricht Treaty, and beyond) again reorganized the EC as part of a larger structure (the European Union), with additional policy responsibilities, including regional development, international development, environmental policy, social policy, health and safety standards, and monetary policy, among others. Concurrently, the membership expanded dramatically: Denmark, Ireland, and the United Kingdom (1973); Greece (1980); Portugal and Spain (1986); Austria, Finland, and Sweden (1995); Cyprus, Estonia, Latvia, Lithuania, Malta, Poland, Hungary, the Czech Republic, Slovakia, and Slovenia (2004); Bulgaria and Romania (2007); and Croatia (2013).

The EU includes an elaborate set of supranational governing institutions.[3] The European Commission is the executive arm of the EU, the European Parliament and European Council of Ministers constitute a bicameral legislature, and the Court of Justice and Court of First Instance constitute the EU's judicial arm (discussed further later). For many, this constellation of institutions is now better thought of as a political system sharing many important characteristics of a federal state than as a traditional international organization (Hix and Hoyland 2011a).

Most observers see the European experiment as a success. First, the EU has achieved its diplomatic goals. No member state has engaged in a militarized dispute with another member state since joining the union. In fact, the EU won the Nobel Peace Prize for this accomplishment. Second, the EU has created a large, highly prosperous common market. Scholars believe the EU and its policies are directly responsible for this success. For example, Eichengreen and Vazquez (2000: 107) analyzed the effect of EEC membership on trade among the member states. They found a large effect and concluded that this "supports the notion that the institutions of European integration solved commitment

---

[2] The treaties also called for a common transport policy and the creation of a European Social Fund.
[3] The Maastricht Treaty created an EC "pillar" consisting of the European Communities and the newly created authority in Economic and Monetary Union. This pillar was eliminated in further treaty reforms (post-2000), after the period of our study.

and coordination problems hindering the expansion of growth." Similarly, Mattli (1999) describes the EU as a particularly successful integration process as compared to other historical efforts toward economic and political integration, particularly in the resolution of collective action and coordination problems endemic to such efforts.[4] Third, the policy mandate of the EU has only grown over time. The European Union now has an expansive regulatory mandate covering a variety of policy domains. Understanding the EU's success, particularly its ability to implement the regulatory structure necessary for a well-functioning common market, is thus an important substantive question in its own right.[5]

The EU is not just a good case to study because it is substantively important. It is also a good case to study because the two key components of the theoretical model discussed previously, the nature of the regulatory regime's policy domain and the institutional role of the Court, nicely map onto the EU.

First, the EU is an international regulatory regime in charge of policy domains that suffer from our model's fundamental collective action problem. Most importantly, the EU's founding and still primary policy mandate, economic integration, involves exactly the type of strategic dilemmas captured by our theoretical model. To any one member state, the abolition of barriers to the free movement of goods, capital, labor, and services by *other* member states is beneficial. But eliminating such barriers is typically politically costly, creating a collective action problem in the completion of a common market. Further, the costs of compliance vary over time and situation, enough so that at times cooperation may be both undesirable (in aggregate) and unsustainable. The environmental, social, consumer protection, and other standards that have become part of the EU policy mandate since its inception suffer from the same challenges (as illustrated in Chapter 2). Thus, the EU's regulatory domain is replete with the kinds of policy dilemmas that form the basis for our theoretical model.

As with our model, there is no quick fix to the collective action dilemmas. The EU has no strong, independent, supranational authority with the sufficient capacity to ensure government compliance with its laws.[6] Instead, the

---

[4] Historically, the only comparable success story is the transformation of the thirteen American colonies into a continent-spanning US common market.

[5] Note that the EC was a part of the European Union until the Treaty of Lisbon, signed in 2007, reorganized the institutions and political competencies of the EU. Because our study focuses on only the pre-2001 period, we refer to the EU in its pre–Lisbon Treaty form. And, in particular, we focus on only the EC component, which constitutes the key areas of economic integration and the key institution (the ECJ) for our purposes.

[6] The roles of the European Commission and the European Court of Justice are discussed in more detail later. In brief, although we see these bodies as important actors that affect

member-state governments are ultimately responsible for the implementation, application, and enforcement of EU laws (Krislov, Ehlermann, and Weiler 1986). And, although the treaties generally do not provide for retaliatory sanctions, member governments have at their disposal a variety of economic and political means by which to impose costs (punishment) on one another.[7,8] Consequently, compliance by member-state governments with EU law is critical for the success of the EU. And, given the underlying collective action problem, it is no surprise that compliance problems persist (e.g., Börzel et al. 2010; Falkner et al. 2005; Krislov, Ehlermann, and Weiler 1986).

Second, the EU has a central dispute settlement mechanism – the European Court of Justice (ECJ)[9] – that operates consistent with the central tenets of our theoretical model. First, the ECJ is a regularly available and identifiable location for dispute resolution. More precisely, it is a permanent court with exclusive competence to hear cases over EU law.[10] The Court consists of full-time judges who are appointed for fixed, six-year terms. Although officially judges are appointed jointly by the member states, in practice each member-state government proposes one judge, who then is approved by common accord.[11] The judges are assisted by a professional staff, including a set of independent legal experts (more on this in Chapter 4).

---

compliance with EU law in substantively important ways, we do not see them as capable of enforcement independent of member-state government willingness to back their decisions.

[7] The European Coal and Steel Community Treaties do provide for retaliatory sanctions, but they have never been used (Hartley 2007: 317).

[8] Punishment, in the theoretical model, involves a government denying the benefit of cooperation to another government. For example, this could involve disruptive action in diplomatic or legislative settings. It could also involve derogations from treaty obligations that are not explicitly sanctioned by the treaty. At various times, EU members have employed both of these tactics. For example, consider the behavior of the British, French, and German governments during the mad cow disease crisis of the 1990s. The Germans and French imposed restrictions on British beef that went beyond EU-specified limits ("Roasting for Germans over British Beef Ban," *Daily Mail*, June 29, 1994, 11; "French Play for Time over Beef Ban," *Guardian*, October 9, 1999, 9). The UK government adopted a diplomatic strategy designed to disrupt EU legislative business ("The British Strike Back at Europe on Beef Ban," *New York Times*, May 22, 1996, A7).

[9] The ECJ was recently renamed the Court of Justice of the European Union. We maintain the ECJ acronym because it applies to the name of the court during the period of our study.

[10] The treaty prohibits member-state governments from appealing to any other body to resolve disputes about the treaty (Dehousse 1998: 18). Note that the focus of our book is the highest court of the EU. The European Court of First Instance (now the General Court) is a lower jurisdictional instance of the European Court of Justice (now Court of Justice of the European Union).

[11] This means that the size of the Court has increased with the membership. The Court always has an odd number of judges, however. Thus, when the EU had an even number of members, one member state appointed two judges.

Third, parties with a vested interest in member-state government compliance can pursue an allegation before the Court. In the EU, standing to bring suit before the ECJ is quite broad, at least by the standards of international DSMs. First, EU institutions, member-state governments, and (in a more limited capacity) private parties can bring actions directly to the Court. These direct actions are in contrast to preliminary references, which are discussed subsequently. The most common form of direct action is an enforcement action against a member-state government for failure to fulfill its obligations under the treaty and secondary legislation.[12] Such actions can be brought by a member-state government or by the Commission, which is a supranational EU bureaucracy with a professional staff. The second most common direct action is an action for annulment. These are cases brought by EU institutions, member-state governments, and private parties challenging an act by an EU institution.[13] The Court's interpretation of standing for annulment actions has privileged applications from member-state governments and key EU institutions over private parties (Hartley 2007: 343). Other forms of direct action are rare.[14]

Questions of EU law also can be brought to the Court via preliminary references. If a question over interpretation of EU law is deemed material to the resolution of a domestic judicial proceeding, the presiding domestic judge can request a preliminary ruling from the ECJ over proper interpretation of the relevant point (or points) of EU law. Upon receiving the ECJ's ruling, the presiding court disposes of the case. Standing to bring suits that generate preliminary rulings is dictated by the rules of the domestic court of origin. The preliminary ruling system has become a powerful tool for private litigants to defend their rights under EU law, including challenging member-state noncompliance with EU law.[15]

Fourth, in both direct actions and preliminary references, third-party governments can signal their position on each case, and these signals are observable to the Court and to a defendant government during the proceedings. Specifically, third-party governments can participate in the judicial proceedings by submitting written briefs that take positions on legal questions raised in the

---

[12] These are based on Articles 258–260 TFEU (Treaty on the Functioning of the European Union; Articles 169–171 TEU [Treaty on European Union]).
[13] These are based on Article 263 TFEU (Article 173 TEU).
[14] These include challenges for inaction by an EU institution (failure to act) under Article 265 TFEU (Article 175 TEU) and administrative actions.
[15] Not all ECJ cases involve a question of member-state compliance. Later we carefully distinguish cases on this criterion in our empirical analysis.

case. In direct actions, these briefs are called interventions, and the intervening government formally becomes a party to the case. In preliminary references, these briefs are called observations because third-party governments typically cannot serve as formal parties to the domestic case at issue in preliminary rulings.[16] In both settings, the position of the third-party briefs is observable to the parties in the case. Those parties then have an opportunity to respond to the briefs in their arguments before the Court.[17]

Fifth, the ECJ reviews all materials in the case and issues a single published ruling (no dissents, no concurrences) that both states the proper interpretation of EU law and provides a rationale for that interpretation. Although decisions are made by majority rule, no information about the level of agreement on the Court is provided. In direct actions, the ECJ provides a declaratory ruling on each legal issue in the case. In preliminary references, the ruling answers the question of EU law but does not address directly the controversy before the national court. That said, the ECJ's interpretation of EU law generally implies how the legal issues in the national case touching on EU law should be resolved.

Sixth, consistent with the assumptions of our model, the Court generally pursues an agenda distinct from that of the member governments. Most practitioners and academics agree that the members of the Court prefer an expansive interpretation of EU law – an "integrationist" agenda – that typically favors EU rules over national laws, particularly when national laws inhibit the completion of a robust internal market (e.g., Alter 2001: 53; Edward 1996: 67; Hartley 2007: 76; Rasmussen 1986a).

Finally, if a ruling goes against the defendant, the Court cannot independently enforce it. This is clearly the case in preliminary rulings. Where a preliminary ruling disfavors the defendant in the original national court case, the ECJ has no way of compelling the national judge to follow its ruling or, even if it is followed, to ensure the defendant complies.[18] The ECJ also cannot enforce direct action rulings. An infringement ruling against a member state in an enforcement action indicates what must be done to come into compliance,

---

[16] The ECJ does not have the authority to grant that status to a member-state government because the case is from a national court whose rules determine the parties to the case.

[17] Because of time constraints governing the written procedure, the parties may only respond during the oral arguments. The key point is that, returning to the theoretical model, the ECJ does allow a defendant government to adjust its effort to the distribution of third-party briefs on the legal issue in question.

[18] See Vanberg (2005), Staton (2010), Staton and Moore (2011), and Carrubba and Zorn (2010) for discussion and evidence of how national courts confront compliance issues.

but the ruling does not usually specify a punishment and does not make any provision for enforcement. The one exception in terms of punishment is an action under Article 260 (ex 171 TEU [Treaty on European Union]), whereby the ECJ can impose a financial penalty on the defendant member-state government. This procedure does not figure prominently in our study because it was introduced only in 1993. And, more importantly, the ECJ can no more enforce compliance with an Article 260 (ex 171 TEU) ruling than any other ruling.

In short, the European Union is a compelling venue to test our predictions because it is a substantively important international regulatory regime with an underlying policy and institutional structure that nicely map onto our theoretical model. But these attributes alone are not sufficient for our purposes. We also need a setting with reliable and consistent data. Fortunately, the EU is attractive on this front as well. First, the ECJ has issued a large number of rulings involving government litigants when compliance was an issue. This supply of rulings is critical to testing both predictions. Second, the ECJ publishes all of its rulings, which include a summary of the case and the position of any third-party briefs on the legal issues in the case.[19] This record is consistently reported in the *Report of Cases Before the Court*. Thus, the relevant information for testing the predictions is publicly available. This, of course, is a great value to us, but it also ensures that other scholars can fairly easily revisit our analysis and challenge, revise, and supplement our coding and findings.

Third, the ECJ's process of adjudication allows us to examine our first prediction while controlling for important confounds. In particular, our study faces a common problem in the empirical study of judicial decision making: how to distinguish the hypothesized influence on rulings from the balance of the legal merits in the case. From a traditional legal perspective, we should expect judges on international courts to base their rulings on the quality of legal arguments on both sides of the case. This poses a problem for our study because the balance of third-party government briefs in a case could plausibly correlate with the balance of the merits. Consequently, we would ideally test our first hypothesis in a context where we can identify a control for the balance of the legal merits. Such contexts are rare.[20] Fortunately, the ECJ setting

---

[19] The actual content and organization of this published information have changed over time. We discuss this in more detail in the next section.
[20] Perhaps the World Trade Organization (WTO) is one such context. Busch and Reinhardt (2006) present an impressive effort to capture the balance of the merits given the limited observable attributes of disputes. However, we consider the ECJ context as significantly better. We are concerned that the relevant measures available for the WTO adjudication body cases (e.g., the legal complexity of the case) are not sufficient to comprehensively capture the

affords an unusually good measure of the balance of the legal merits, which we describe in Chapter 4. This is another key advantage of the EU context for testing our model of an international court.

In sum, we expect our theoretical model to provide a plausible explanation for how the ECJ contributed to the success of the European Union as an international regulatory regime. As a result, we would expect the two predictions of the model to hold in that context. We devote the remainder of the book to evaluating these expectations.

b. *The theoretical model, its predictions, and the literature on the ECJ*

We are hardly the first scholars to conjecture that the ECJ has contributed to the success of the European Union. Indeed, the ECJ is among the most studied international dispute resolution mechanisms, let alone courts, in the world. Thus, before testing our predictions, we briefly compare our model, its assumptions, and its predictions to related theoretical and empirical work on the ECJ. We also discuss whether and to what extent the tests of our predictions distinguish between our arguments and extant arguments about the role of the ECJ in European integration.

Our model is built on a number of assumptions. In particular, we assume an underlying collective action problem in which governments can choose to comply with EU law or not. If governments do not comply, we assume they can be taken to court, third-party governments can take positions on the case, and the defendant government can choose how hard to work to defend itself. The Court then issues a ruling, and the government can decide whether to acquiesce to an adverse Court decision. We also assume that a noncompliant government can be punished only by other member states. Finally, the Court issues rulings aware of the strategic context in which it is embedded.

Several of the critical first principles of this argument appear in the existing literature, but the argument itself is unique. In terms of commonalities, a variety of scholars agree that government noncompliance is possible and that the ECJ contributes to the performance of the EU by facilitating the monitoring and enforcement of EU law (e.g., Garrett 1992: 557; Mattli 1999: 100; Pollack 2003: 160). Some scholars also have noted that enforcement of ECJ decisions ultimately is in the hands of the member states. For example, Hartley (1988: 315) concludes that when a member state ignores an infringement ruling

---

balance of the legal merits. And we consider the measure of the legal merits available at the ECJ superior. See Chapter 4 for our description of that measure.

the matter passes outside the realm of the law and becomes political. In such a situation, coercion of the Member State by the Community is hardly practical; this is inevitable in view of the basic political nature of the Community. Only concerted action by the other Member States – or a compromise solution – will bring the violation to an end.

Also, we are not the first to argue that the ECJ considers how governments will respond (or have responded) to its decisions when ruling on a case (e.g., Obermaier 2009: 170–3).[21] Thus, the notion of government compliance issues, the idea that the ECJ can help moderate them, and the suggestion that the ECJ is aware of its strategic context are not novel to the existing EU literature.

That said, our argument is not simply derivative of this literature. The closest match to our model in the ECJ literature is a theoretical account proffered by Garrett, Kelemen, and Shulz (1998).[22] Like us, they argue that governments may not acquiesce in adverse Court rulings and that other EU governments may or may not support the litigant government if it chooses to evade a ruling. Thus, several of our key primitives can be found in their argument. However, beyond these foundational elements, our theories substantially diverge. First, their argument starts with the ECJ disposing of a case; it does not model the microfoundations for why the governments joined the EU or created a court, nor does it endogenize the case generation and litigation process. Second, governments choose whether to support the litigant government through secondary law and treaty revision rather than to retaliate for unsanctioned noncompliance, as in our model. These differences are both theoretically and empirically salient.[23] For example, as demonstrated in Chapter 2, what happens before the Court issues a ruling is critical to what one infers from the theory. Further, as we will discuss in Chapters 5 and 6, threats of treaty revision and secondary legislation generate different empirical predictions than the two generated from our model.[24]

Our empirical analysis of ECJ decisions, both the hypotheses we specify and the data we employ to evaluate these hypotheses, is also novel. A great body of empirical research has evaluated ECJ rulings in settings where government compliance is at issue (e.g., Conant 2002; Obermaier 2009; Panke 2010; Stone

---

[21] We discuss the events described by Oberrmaier (2009) more in the next section. Ritter (2005: 761) makes a more general claim about the Court's sensitivity to the interests of governments.
[22] See Chapter 2 for discussion of related arguments outside of the ECJ literature.
[23] Their model is best thought of as a stylized soft rational choice argument, because the model itself is not solved in the paper.
[24] Specifically, threats of treaty revision and secondary legislation cannot account for the systematic evidence we report.

Sweet and Brunell 1999). Scholars have also investigated how individual third-party briefs relate to decisions by the Court (e.g., Kilroy 1999; Stone Sweet 2004). And several scholars have investigated how rulings by the Court relate to outcomes (e.g., trade) plausibly influenced by those rulings (e.g., Stone Sweet 2004). But no empirical study has posited our specific predictions or presented empirical evidence directly assessing these predictions.[25]

What are the implications of our tests for existing arguments about the role of the ECJ in European integration? In testing our predictions, we do not claim to be testing *the* explanation for how a court can facilitate compliance with an international regulatory regime; rather, we are evaluating *an* explanation. We suspect that the ECJ may contribute in multiple ways, and finding evidence consistent with our predictions does not automatically imply other explanations are wrong. Indeed, our account may simply complement alternative explanations. For example, Alter and Vargas (2001a), Slepcevic (2009a), Conant (2001), and Panke (2010) all share our assumption that the Court cannot expect voluntary compliance by member-state governments and that compliance varies with conditions surrounding the ruling.[26] They differ from us in terms of the character of those conditions; for example, Conant (2001) focuses on the distribution and resources of organized domestic political interests. Empirical evidence in support of our predictions says nothing directly about the quality of these other explanations.

Further, our analysis does not speak to the extensive and fascinating research documenting and explaining the volume, origin, and character of cases before the ECJ. In particular, an impressive body of research has examined how domestic interests and courts over time dramatically increased their engagement with the ECJ through the preliminary reference procedure. This had important effects on the policy areas adjudicated before the Court, the opportunities for the ECJ to interpret EU law and develop legal doctrine, and the volume of cases before the ECJ (e.g., Alter 2000; Burley and Mattli 1993; Stone Sweet and Brunell 1998a). Our analysis does not engage these issues. The two predictions of the model are predicated on adjudication of cases involving alleged violations of treaty obligations, but the evolution of the legal system is exogenous to our model (i.e., we do not attempt to explain this process).

---

[25] Our analysis builds off of Carrubba, Gabel, and Hankla (2008). That article examines very similar (but not exactly the same) relationships to those described in prediction 1, but only for a more limited time frame than we examine here.

[26] We discuss in more detail later our definition of *compliance*, which is similar to what some authors refer to as "implementation" of a ruling. Some authors use *compliance* to indicate only that the parties adhere to the ruling in the instant case. We do not use that definition.

That said, other extant explanations differ fundamentally from ours in their assumptions about the authority of ECJ rulings, and we therefore attend carefully to whether and how our predictions comport with them. In particular, several scholars have argued that, in addition to generating a large number of cases for ECJ adjudication, the preliminary reference system has significantly limited the threat of noncompliance with the Court's rulings. The basic argument is that the ECJ's development of the doctrines of direct effect and the supremacy of EU law over national law empower national courts to enforce the ECJ's interpretation of EU law through national court rulings (e.g., Burley and Mattli 1993; Tallberg 2002a: 622; Weiler 1991). Thus, when issuing preliminary rulings, the ECJ enjoys the authority of national court rulings. One can read this argument to imply that the ECJ faces weaker compliance concerns with its preliminary rulings than in direct actions or, in the extreme, that compliance is not an issue in preliminary rulings.[27] Obviously, this argument – particularly the extreme version – conflicts fundamentally with one of the key assumptions of our theoretical model (i.e., that noncompliance concerns influence ECJ decision making).[28] Consequently, evidence regarding our predictions likely has direct implications for the validity of this alternative argument. We pay particular attention to it in the empirical analysis of the Political Sensitivity Hypothesis (see Chapter 5). We should also note that, to the extent this alternative argument holds, an evaluation of our predictions in the ECJ context presents a particularly difficult test for our theory.

II. DATA: THE ECJ DATABASE PROJECT, 1960–1999

To test the two predictions of the model, we created an original and extensive database on ECJ rulings from 1960 to 1999.[29] These data (the ECJ

---

[27] As we discuss later, how and whether such claims comport with our argument depend, in part, on some definitional issues regarding what constitutes member-state compliance.

[28] Although our study is weighted toward the earlier period (1960–99), related claims that the contemporary ECJ is an unusually powerful international court have the same implication for our study: they imply that the ECJ context is a difficult test of our model.

[29] Other scholars have assembled databases (not all publicly available) that capture some of the information in our database, but we are unaware of any other database that covers the years, rulings, and ruling-related information assembled in the ECJ Database Project. For example, Stone Sweet and Brunell (1999) have assembled an impressive and publicly available data set describing characteristics of preliminary references, including the referring nation, the date, and the issue area. But their data set does not provide any information about the disposition of the ruling, the presence and position of third-party briefs, or several other factors relevant to our study. Others have assembled data sets that code similar information to ours for a subset of rulings defined by time period, policy area, or importance (Jupille 2004; Kilroy 1999; Stone Sweet 2004). For example, Stein (1981) presented and evaluated information on the

Database Project) are publicly available at http://polisci.emory.edu/home/people/carrubba_ecjd/index.html, where we provide a full description of the coding protocol and composition of the database. The information about rulings was extracted from the official publication of the Court, *Report of Cases Before the Court*.

We begin by providing a general description of the data set created from this database and used in this study. One purpose is to introduce important details of the assembly and coding of data for the testing of the two predictions of our model. Our discussion is also designed to provide the reader with a general overview of the data set. This overview includes information about the judicial process that is not directly necessary for the ensuing tests and that may be valuable for the reader beyond the purposes of testing our predictions. Following this general description of the data set, we specify the scope of our theoretical model. That is, we identify which sets of rulings are pertinent to our theoretical predictions. The subsequent chapters then execute empirical tests of the two hypotheses.

a. An overview of the data set

The data set is organized around ECJ published judgments.[30,31] The broadest level of information we coded is the "general case characteristics."[32] This information includes the case number, the judgment title, the date the judgment was rendered, and the identity of the plaintiff and of the defendant. The last two are categorical variables, indicating whether the litigant was a private litigant, a national government, an administrative agency, the Commission, the European Parliament, the Council of Ministers, or some combination of those actors working in concert.[33] We also coded the chamber hearing the case

---

disposition of eleven "constitutional" rulings and included information on the position of third-party governments and other relevant actors. But none of these is as comprehensive as the ECJ Data Project in terms of years, rulings, and supplemental information (e.g., position of important nonlitigant parties on each ruling, such as the Advocate General). In addition, several are not publicly available.

[30] Based on a postcoding audit, we found that coders missed coding a very small number of judgments (fewer than ten).

[31] The ECJ also publishes orders and opinions, which are not included in our data set. Often the Court issues orders in the process of hearing a case (i.e., interim orders). The Court can be asked to render a preliminary opinion on such matters as an international agreement. We ignore orders and opinions because they typically do not comport with the theoretical scope conditions of interest here.

[32] The database sheet containing this information is labeled as such.

[33] We coded the litigant as a national government if a member of the cabinet or the government itself was party to a suit; otherwise, we coded the litigant as an administrative agency.

(i.e., whether it was heard by the plenum or one of the numbered panels of judges), the number of judges who heard the case, and the treaty article under which the case arose (e.g., whether it was an enforcement action, an action for annulment, or a request for a preliminary ruling).[34] For preliminary rulings, we included the referring nation and court, as well as the date the referral was made.

All remaining information was coded at the within-case legal issue level. For each case, a set of legal issues is raised when the case is put on the Court's docket. Litigants raise the legal issues they believe, if disposed of, favor their preferred outcome. Third-party briefs may simply respond to those issues, or they may raise separate ones that might be dispositive. If the case is a preliminary ruling, the referring court raises its own set of legal questions that it believes will help resolve the dispute appropriately. The Advocate General (AG), upon reviewing all of this material, may use his/her opinion to reframe or otherwise offer up other relevant legal issues. And, finally, the Court writes an opinion at the end of which the Court enumerates each of the legal issues it is disposing of in deciding the case. For each judgment, we coded each legal issue the Court identifies and disposes of at the end of the case.[35] Because we were ultimately interested in how the Court decided cases, this was the most appropriate metric. It was also the easiest method by which to ensure intercoder reliability because the Court's disposition of the case is clearly bolded and enumerated at the end of the opinion. We define the Court's decision on each legal issue as a "ruling," meaning one judgment can involve more than one ruling.

All remaining information was coded based on these enumerated legal issues. For each legal issue, the position of the Court, the Advocate General, and any third-party briefs was recorded.[36] The positions were coded

---

[34] We attempted to code an issue area variable but for a variety of reasons found it difficult to make such distinctions consistently based on the Court documents. As such, we recommend that scholars rely on the issue area coding provided by Stone Sweet and Brunell (1999). We also attempted to code the Judge Rapporteur for a number of years but found that this information was not as systematically available as we would have liked.

[35] Sometimes these legal issues are individually enumerated and sometimes they organize them hierarchically (e.g., there may be two legal issues with one of the legal issues having two parts). Coders were instructed to code only by the individually enumerated legal issues unless the subparts were clearly identifiable as distinct issues in and of themselves. See the codebook for further details.

[36] Information about the position of third-party interveners on the legal issues in the case is reported directly in "the report for the hearing." The location of the report for the hearing was provided in the "facts and issues" section of the judgment until 1986 (with the exceptions of 1984 and 1985). From 1986 to 1994, the report for the hearing was published in its own section prior to the judgment (Edward 1995). For the post-1993 period, we relied on the information

as either for plaintiff or for defendant.[37] For each brief, we also coded its source.

In sum, the database consists of every judgment rendered by the Court from 1960 to 1999, coded at the level of the individual legal issue. We should note that coding at the level of the legal issue was critical for our purposes because the Court makes decisions by legal issue and other actors (i.e., the AG and the third-party briefs) agree or disagree with the Court by legal issue. It is not uncommon for a case consisting of multiple legal issues to have the Court and these other actors agree on the disposition of some issues and not others. As such, aggregating up to the case level would have lost valuable information as well as added unnecessary noise to the coding when multiple legal issues were involved in the case.

b. *Descriptive statistics*

Before proceeding to the test, we present some basic descriptive statistics regarding the database as a whole. We primarily present these statistics to provide an overview of ECJ activity for those unfamiliar with the Court. We focus on a few key attributes of the data: who participates in cases under the various judicial procedures, under what procedures the cases tend to be brought, who weighs in on the case, how legally complex the cases are, and who tends to win. For all of these statistics, we focus on the three key judicial procedures discussed in detail earlier: infringements, annulments, and preliminary rulings.

Figure 3.1 presents the breakdown of litigant identity for annulments and preliminary rulings.[38] Infringements are omitted because the Commission is always the plaintiff and a member state is always the defendant. In terms of annulments, private litigants and EU institutions each bring some actions, but

---

provided in the Advocate General's opinion and the judgment by the ECJ, both of which were routinely published in the Report of Cases before the Court. These sources are inferior to the report for the hearing in that they do not have a specific section dedicated to summarizing the positions of third-party interveners. However, these two sources usually reference and describe third-party briefs on the legal issues as part of their analysis of the case (Mortelmans 1979: 583–4).

[37] Our coding protocol on these variables changed somewhat across the database (Access) files. Originally, we only coded the position of the Advocate General relative to the plaintiff and then coded whether the Court and third-party briefs agreed with the AG's position. However, we discovered that in some cases the position of the AG was unclear on some legal issues, but the positions of the Court or third-party briefs were not. As such we later added variables to capture Court and third-party brief agreement with the plaintiff directly.

[38] The unit of analysis here is a legal issue in a judgment.

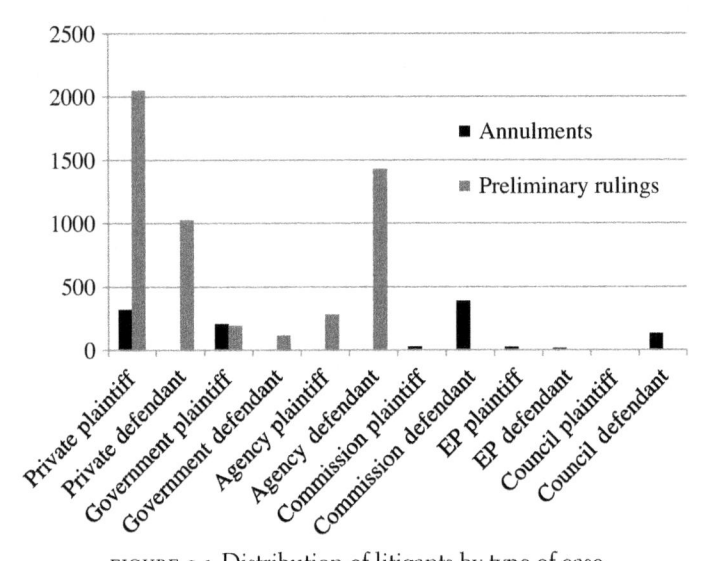

FIGURE 3.1 Distribution of litigants by type of case

the most common plaintiff is a member-state government. The Commission, primarily, or the Council, secondarily, is the defendant in these cases. In terms of preliminary rulings, the litigants are the parties to national cases. This includes private parties and subnational agencies, with national governments also regularly involved both as plaintiffs and as defendants. On rare occasions, EU institutions are involved in these cases. In sum, governments are common litigants in all three types of cases, but private litigants certainly gain access to the court as well.

Figure 3.2 presents the distribution of judgments over time by the three key procedures of interest. As shown, the ECJ regularly used all three procedures; there are no gaps over time in the use of a procedure. Further, consistent with aggregate numbers reported by the Court, our data show that the ECJ increased the number of its rulings over time, and the bulk of that rise is due to a dramatic increase in the number of preliminary rulings. Figure 3.3 provides a breakdown of judgments in preliminary rulings by referring nation. As shown, preliminary references arise in all countries; however, there is some unsurprising disparity. Larger, more populous, and more economically prosperous countries tend to have more preliminary rulings. Even so, across the board, preliminary rulings have increased steadily over time, consistent with Figure 3.3. Thus, all three procedures have been used over time, preliminary rulings are made in all the member states (though proportional to the size of the state), and the use of all these procedures has increased over time, especially preliminary rulings.

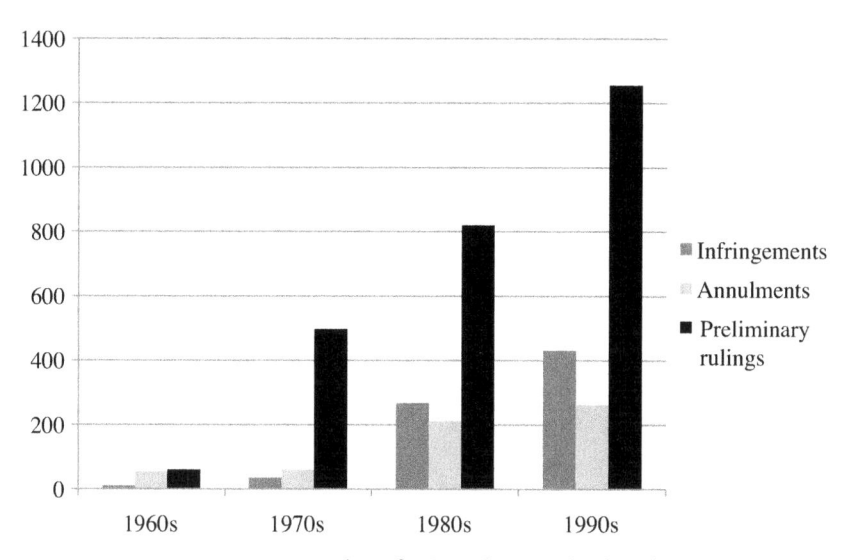

FIGURE 3.2 Number of ECJ judgments by decade

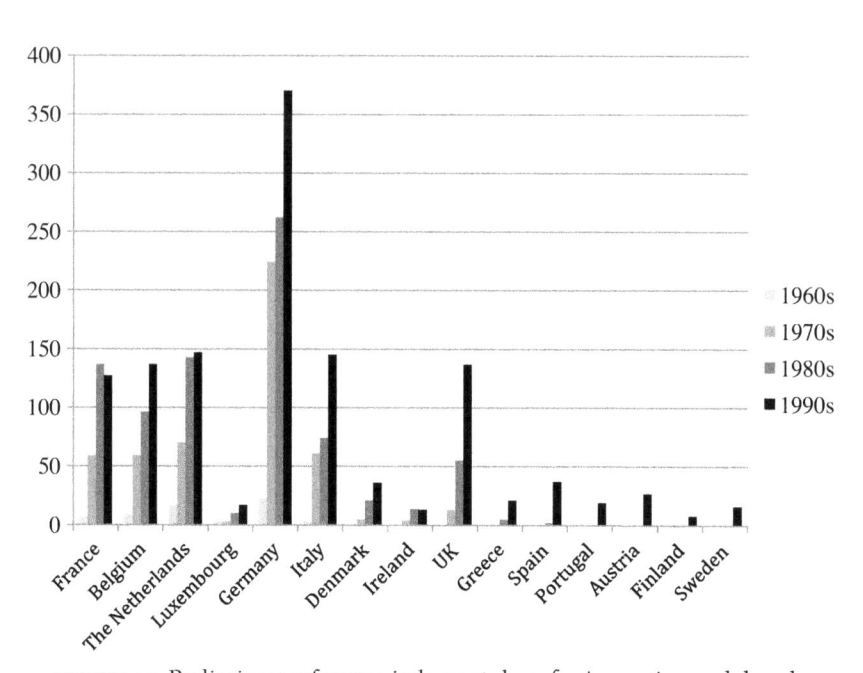

FIGURE 3.3 Preliminary reference judgments by referring nation and decade

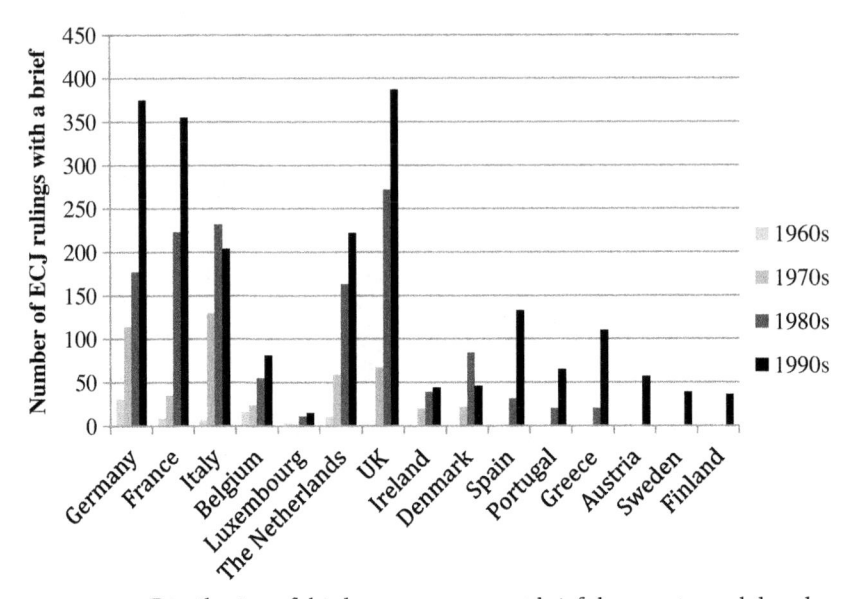

FIGURE 3.4 Distribution of third-party government briefs by country and decade

Many of these preliminary references involve multiple legal issues, which is much less common in direct actions. In our data set, almost half of preliminary rulings involve more than one legal issue, and occasionally they have three or more. Direct actions feature more than one legal issue in 10 percent to 20 percent of the cases. This variation in the legal complexity of the cases reinforces the importance of coding our data by legal issue rather than at the case level.

Figure 3.4 presents the distribution of third-party briefs across member states by decade.[39] Several patterns are worth highlighting. First, the largest member states – Germany, France, Italy, and the United Kingdom – historically tend to make the most third-party briefs. The Netherlands has also been highly active. Second, all of the member states get involved at times. Finally (not shown), whereas member-state governments tend to weigh in on behalf of defendants more often, they do regularly intervene on behalf of plaintiffs as well. In sum, we observe briefs being filed predominantly by the larger member states, but all countries participate to some degree. And, although there is a modest tendency toward filing for the defendant, governments regularly file on behalf of plaintiffs as well.[40]

---

[39] The unit of analysis here is the legal issue.
[40] It is important to note that this description also generally pertains to the distribution of briefs on rulings with a government litigant. Those are the rulings at issue in the ensuing empirical analysis.

Data: *the ECJ Database Project, 1960–1999* 75

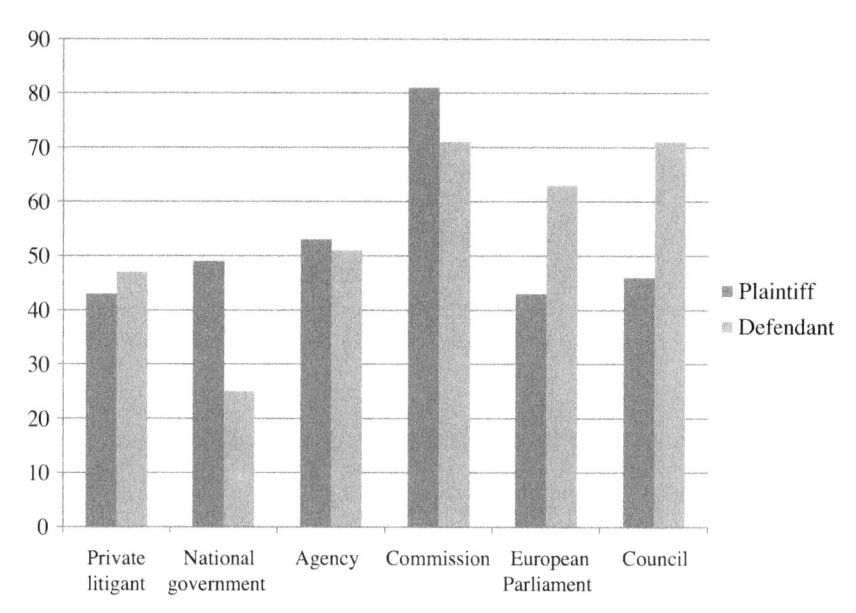

FIGURE 3.5 Litigant success (percentage of favorable rulings) before the ECJ

Overall, in 2,437 of 6,222 rulings on infringement, annulment, and preliminary ruling cases in our database, governments made at least one third-party brief. That translates to slightly more than 39 percent of the rulings. Breaking the numbers down, roughly 8 percent of infringements, 11 percent of annulments, and 49 percent of preliminary rulings have at least one third-party brief.

Finally, Figure 3.5 shows how frequently rulings have favored various types of actors. EU institutions do the best on average in court, private litigants win just under 50 percent of the time, and governments have mixed success. Governments are slightly more likely to win when they are the plaintiff than some other litigants and much more likely to lose when they are defendants. The governments' poor performance as defendant is driven by the fact that governments almost always lose infringement cases, which also explains why the Commission is much more likely to win as a plaintiff than any other litigant is.[41]

---

[41] This bias toward the Commission under infringements is not particularly surprising. Infringement cases start with the Commission notifying a member-state government of a failure to fulfill its obligations. Following that notification is an extended back-and-forth between the member-state government and the Commission. Only if the Commission believes its demands

Put together, these figures support the general impression that the EU has a robust legal regime. These descriptive statistics also show a system that certainly appears to be keeping government behavior in check. However, as Carrubba (2005) showed, inferences from this evidence must be cautiously drawn. We could observe governments regularly being brought to Court and ruled against (and regularly complying with those decisions), even if the Court is sensitive to threats of noncompliance. The analysis in the next three chapters examines whether, as depicted in our theoretical model, the risk of noncompliance, as indicated by the balance of third-party government briefs, factors in the decisions made by the Court and shapes the effectiveness of the Court's rulings.

III. THE THEORETICALLY RELEVANT DOMAIN OF RULINGS

Our theoretical model implies two hypotheses that are predicated on a court ruling on cases involving a threat of noncompliance. Thus, to identify the domain of ECJ rulings to which the model applies, we must define concretely when the potential for government noncompliance with an ECJ decision may arise. This, in turn, requires defining what we mean by compliance with EU law and when issues of government compliance with EU law may arise before the Court. We define member-state compliance with EU law as the promulgation of community norms within their national territory. This typically requires implementation, application, and enforcement by national institutions (Krislov, Ehlermann, and Weiler 1986). Compliance can require a state to take action or refrain from action (Steiner 1993: 3, 21).

ECJ rulings interpret EU law by indicating or at least implying what a member-state government must do or not do to comply with the obligations laid down in the treaties and the secondary legislation. ECJ rulings often have broad policy implications, including requiring changes to national law or administrative practices (Steiner 1993: 4). Thus, a threat of noncompliance with a ruling is a threat by a government whose actions are at issue in a case to obstruct or fail to implement the promulgation of the norm defined by the ECJ. This use of the term *compliance* is consistent with several studies of compliance with ECJ decisions (e.g., Beach 2005; Kilroy 1999; Krislov, Ehlermann, and Weiler 1986; Obermaier 2009; Steiner 1993) and the literature on judicial politics in the international arena (Staton and Moore 2011: 559).[42]

were not sufficiently met, and it thinks it can win the case, will the Commission actually bring the case to Court.
[42] The term *compliance* is also used by scholars to describe other aspects of the response to a court ruling. For example, some scholars use the term to indicate that the losing party obeyed the

We now turn to identifying rulings by the ECJ in which member-state government compliance with EU law is at issue. Recall that cases arrive at the ECJ through essentially one of two routes: direct actions and preliminary references. Among direct actions, the most obvious rulings involving compliance are enforcement actions brought against member states for failure to fulfill their obligations under the treaty or secondary legislation.[43] The European Commission almost always initiates such actions, and thus the member-state government is the defendant. These rulings are the most descriptively consistent with the adjudication process described in our theoretical model.

Member-state government compliance can be at issue in another form of direct action: annulment actions. Specifically, some annulment cases challenge an action (e.g., a Commission decision) that depends on a national government for implementation. This is particularly relevant in annulment actions brought by a national government against the Commission or the Council. Historically, most of these cases have involved EU agriculture or competition policies (Bauer and Hartlapp 2010), both of which often rely on national government implementation. For one, member states are intricately involved in the administration of the Common Agricultural Policy. For example, in *France* v. *Commission* (Case C-366/88), the French government challenged a measure adopted by the Commission that obliged national officials to cooperate with Commission officials in specific aspects of supervising and monitoring the European Agricultural Guidance and Guarantee Fund. Clearly, the effectiveness of this measure depended fundamentally on the actions of the member-state government.[44] Similarly, member-state governments are central to the execution of Commission decisions on state aid.

---

immediate requirements of the ruling (e.g., payment of a fine), leaving aside any broader policy implications of the ruling (Alter 2000: 507). This is a more narrow definition than the one we employ here. Other scholars use *compliance* with a ruling to indicate that a lower court in a judicial hierarchy faithfully followed the rulings/precedent of superior courts (e.g., Westerland et al. 2010). This issue is relevant in preliminary references to the ECJ, though Nykios (2003) provides evidence that national courts regularly do implement ECJ rulings. To the extent that national governments respond to their national courts' rulings by implementing the broad policy implications of the rulings (i.e., promulgation of the norm defined by the ruling), lower court compliance would imply government compliance in the context of preliminary rulings. However, as we discuss further later, Conant (2002) and others provide compelling evidence that decisions by national courts do not routinely translate into government compliance as we define the term. The broader literature on the judicial impact of domestic courts also indicates that governments often ignore, obstruct, or otherwise fail to implement the broader policy changes implied by a ruling (Canon 1991). Thus, we do not equate national court compliance within the judicial hierarchy with member-state government compliance with an ECJ ruling.

[43] These are based on Articles 258–260 TFEU; Articles 169–171 TEU.
[44] Of course, some annulment cases do not involve government compliance. This is particularly true when private litigants or EU institutions bring annulment actions.

A Commission determination that a state aid is invalid (i.e., in breach of competition policy) requires the national government to terminate the current subsidy and desist from erecting a substitute policy. In particular, member states are responsible for the recovery of state aid that the Court deems unlawful (Jestaedt, Derenne, and Ottervanger 2006). Thus, annulment rulings can involve government compliance.

Not all annulment rulings involve member-state government compliance. Annulment actions can involve one EU institution challenging an act of another institution or a private litigant challenging the act of an EU institution. In these settings, government compliance is less commonly relevant to implementation (e.g., see *Partie Ecologiste 'Les Verts'* v. *European Parliament* [Case 294/83]). Consequently, we expect compliance to be much more commonly at issue when a national government initiates the annulment action than when such an action is brought by an EU institution or a private party (which is rare).

Similarly, member-state compliance with EU law can be at issue in preliminary references when the implementation of the ruling requires government compliance. According to Alter (2000: 491), the original intent of the preliminary reference system was to provide domestic litigants with a means by which to challenge EU law. But through the doctrines of direct effect and supremacy, the ECJ and national courts transformed this procedure into a vehicle for national litigants to invoke EU law to challenge national law in national courts. As a result, preliminary rulings provide the Court with opportunities to evaluate whether and to what extent national governments are meeting their obligations to the EU. In turn, the rulings articulate what the Court understands to be the appropriate actions by member-state governments under EU law. In such cases, preliminary references involve member-state compliance.

As with annulment rulings, not all preliminary rulings necessarily involve member-state compliance. Indeed, some studies suggest a sizable share of preliminary rulings do not engage national law or practices (Alter 2000: 500). But some clearly do, and that is often indicated by the presence of the government as a litigant in the case.

Having established the types of cases in which member-state government compliance with EU law is likely at issue, we can now address whether the ECJ can face a threat of noncompliance with its rulings in these situations. Noncompliance is generally possible in enforcement actions against member-state governments. As described previously, all of these entail a national government being brought to the ECJ by the Commission for a failure to fulfill obligations. Generally, this charge is made either because a government has not transposed a directive into national law in a timely fashion or because the Commission deemed the law incorrectly or inadequately transposed. Whatever the specifics, the government allegedly is not in compliance with EU law. If the Court rules against the government (an infringement ruling), it is up to the government to correct the error. Prior to 1993, if the government procrastinated in following the prescribed remedy, the only recourse for the Commission was to bring repeat cases.[45] Post-1993, the Court could also impose a fine for continued noncompliance. However, payment of this fine, like compliance with the initial ruling, is entirely in the hands of the national government.[46] Moreover, such cases are very rare in the time period of our study. Thus, as Weiler (1991: 2420) and Dehousse (1998: 48) highlight, the threat of noncompliance is generally present for infringement rulings against a member state.

Not surprisingly, member-state governments sometimes fail to comply, at least in part, with infringement rulings (Chalmers 2005: 453).[47] For example, Panke (2007: 851) finds that the majority of enforcement actions against Germany for its failure to transpose directives in social policy and environmental policy from 1978 to 2000 was met with partial or complete noncompliance by the German government.

Noncompliance is also possible in annulment actions involving member-state governments. As in enforcement actions, the ECJ has no means by which to compel member states to implement its rulings. And the member states often have domestic political and economic incentives to obstruct the ECJ's rulings. This is most apparent in rulings invalidating state aid. The inherent conflict of interest for member-state governments that both grant and are charged with recovering state aids raises an obvious concern with the implementation of Commission decisions requiring recovery. According to a comprehensive survey of the enforcement of state aid rulings, member-state compliance with

---

[45] As Panke (2007) describes, this strategy could be paired with a complementary strategy of domestic litigants bringing repeat cases through the preliminary ruling system as well. However, as described in Panke (2010: 261), seeing repeat preliminary rulings was generally an indication of continued noncompliance with an infringement ruling.

[46] As discussed earlier, the Treaty on European Union in 1993 introduced a new procedure (Article 171 TEU) whereby the Commission could pursue a member state before the ECJ for failure to comply with a previous infringement. In such cases, the ECJ can do more than issue a declaratory judgment; it can specify sanctions. Here, too, the ECJ has no way to enforce its rulings. In any event, such rulings are rare in our data set, and thus we focus on the typical enforcement actions, which do not specify any penalty.

[47] For a nice example of how a national government can meet the letter of a ruling but completely ignore the broader policy implications of that ruling, see Rasmussen (1986a: 362–3). The Danish government lost an infringement ruling that determined its spirits law created a tax environment that discriminated against imports. The government eliminated the policy in question and erected a new tax environment that re-created the protectionist policies.

such decisions is particularly problematic after an ECJ ruling confirming the Commission decision – that is, when the member-state government loses an annulment action (Jestaedt, Derenne, and Ottervanger 2006: 538).

For a clear illustration of a threat of noncompliance in an annulment action, consider the conventional account of the annulment action brought by the United Kingdom against the Council regarding the Working Time Directive.[48] The directive in question defined minimum rest periods and maximum weekly working hours. At the time, the United Kingdom enjoyed an exception from EU social policies and considered this one such policy. However, the Council had adopted the measure under a treaty article that both applied to the United Kingdom and allowed the Council to decide without the support of that state. In 1994, the UK government brought an action to annul this directive on the grounds that it had been adopted with the wrong legal basis.

The Advocate General opinion in the case, issued prior to the ruling, advised the Court to find that the directive was valid. In response, the UK government publicly announced that it would not implement the directive if the Court followed this recommendation. Pollack (2003: 333) described the context thus:

> Yet the defiant mood of John Major's government, and the significant financial and political costs likely to be imposed by an adverse ECJ ruling, posed a non-trivial risk of overt non-compliance by the UK. This possibility of noncompliance was highlighted, moreover, by the British government's reaction to the preliminary opinion of Philippe Leger, the Advocate General in the case, on 12 March 1996.

Finally, we turn to noncompliance with preliminary rulings. We assume that national courts cannot ensure the compliance of their governments with their rulings. Consequently, preliminary rulings also face a potential noncompliance problem, since national courts ultimately articulate the preliminary rulings in their judgments.

This assumption about national courts is consistent with two streams of research on judicial politics. First, the general literature on the impact of judicial rulings supports the assumption. Primarily focused on the study of domestic courts, judicial impact studies have long recognized that court rulings may fail to gain compliance from the parties to the case. And even with compliance in this narrow sense, compliance by the government (our concern here) with the broader policy effects of the ruling can be limited because of bureaucratic and political resistance in implementation (Canon 1991).

---

[48] Case 84/94. For further description, see Nicol (2001a), Pollack (2003), and Beach (2005).

More recently, scholars studying national court decision making come to the same conclusion. These scholars find that domestic judges (at least on high courts) appear to adjust their rulings as a result of credible threats of government noncompliance with their judgments. For example, Vanberg (2001a, 2005) derives a theory of government–court relations that shows that if the domestic public is either unaware of the implications of a court's ruling or unsupportive of the court's position, the government can credibly threaten to evade the court's decision. As a result, the court is more likely to defer to the government's position in those cases. He finds support for his theory by looking at evidence from the German Constitutional Court. Carrubba and Zorn (2010) extend Vanberg's argument to the United States. Again, they find supportive evidence, this time showing that the Supreme Court tends to defer to the US government when evasion is more likely. Finally, Staton (2006, 2010) extends and elaborates on Vanberg's argument as well, this time applying it to Mexico. Thus, across a variety of countries, including a founding member state of the EU, there is robust evidence that threats of national government noncompliance can affect domestic court decisions.

These national court studies suggest that preliminary rulings in response to questions from national courts should face the risk of government noncompliance. Conant (2002: 16) makes this point explicitly when discussing preliminary rulings by the ECJ:

> If supranational legal authority has become functionally equivalent to domestic legal authority, traditional limits on judicial power must be addressed in accounts of the ECJ. In particular, judicial policy impact cannot be assumed.

Furthermore, Conant (2002) persuasively demonstrates that governments can, under fairly general conditions, "contain justice" by limiting, if not neutralizing, the effect of ECJ preliminary rulings with a variety of tactics ranging from simply ignoring the ruling to evasion.[49] Conant (2002: 69) concludes, "If a national measure is the subject of a preliminary ruling, therefore, compliance with an individual judgment is typically followed by business as usual. The national administration is unlikely to introduce broader changes in policy." Alter (2000) and Slepcevic (2009a) reach similar conclusions. Specifically, Alter (2000: 507) argues:

> Just because the ECJ decides in favor of the plaintiff challenging national policy, one should not assume that the government will change its policy. The government may simply compensate the litigant while leaving the legislation in effect and administrative policy unchanged. Or it can change the language

---

[49] Also see Panke (2007) for evidence of variation in compliance with infringement proceedings.

of a national law to technically comply with the decision, without significantly changing domestic policy.

Finally, anecdotal evidence indicates that the ECJ is sensitive to member-state government noncompliance in its preliminary rulings.[50] For example, Obermaier (2009: 170–3) describes how the ECJ adjusted its jurisprudence on patient mobility in the face of member-state noncompliance. The ECJ issued two rulings in 1998 (*Kohll* and *Dekker*) that concluded national laws requiring patients to obtain prior authorization for medical services delivered outside their home country violated EU law.[51] The national governments in question, as well as many governments that submitted amicus briefs on these cases, were opposed to these rulings. Not surprisingly, the rulings were met with widespread noncompliance (Obermaier 2009: 84) and a threat of continued noncompliance. In response, the ECJ significantly altered its position in subsequent rulings to satisfy the concerns of the member-state governments (Obermaier 2009: 170).

Thus, we assume in our empirical analysis that preliminary rulings by the ECJ also face potential problems with members-state government compliance. That said, as discussed in the previous section, we are aware that some scholars expect compliance concerns to be significantly lower in preliminary rulings than in direct actions. If so, this has potentially important empirical implications for the extent to which we should find evidence consistent with our predictions across these two types of rulings. We therefore are careful to examine this consideration in evaluating the robustness of our findings.

In sum, the purpose of this section was to identify ECJ rulings to which our predictions should apply, and we use the procedure and presence of government involvement in the case to define that set of rulings. We evaluate the prediction on infringement rulings, which result from enforcement actions and always have a defendant member-state government; annulment rulings that involve a government litigant (always a plaintiff); and preliminary rulings where the national government is a litigant in the original case in national court.

Our theoretical model can be read narrowly or broadly in terms of the contexts to which it applies. The most direct and narrow application to the

---

[50] Another example of the Court responding to a threat of noncompliance involves the *Sheep Meat* case (C-232/78). France blatantly ignored the adverse ruling in that case. In a subsequent related enforcement action, the Court changed positions and refused to grant an interim order against France. Hartley (2007: 316) explains this turnaround as follows: "One suspects that the Court, knowing that any order it gave would be ignored, decided that it would be better to save what was left of its tattered authority by refusing the order."

[51] Cases C-120/95 and C-158/96.

ECJ setting would be to consider only rulings where a member-state government is a defendant, which is the explicit assumption of the formal model in Chapter 2. This would include infringement rulings and preliminary rulings with a defendant government in the national case, but it would exclude annulment rulings and preliminary rulings in which the government is the plaintiff. In that setting, the prediction our theoretical model implies is that the threat of noncompliance by the defendant government is more credible the less opposition the government anticipates from other governments. Thus, the more support from third-party governments for the defendant government's position, the less likely the Court is to believe the government will comply and therefore the less likely the Court is to rule against the government.

A broader application of the theoretical argument would include annulment rulings and preliminary rulings in which a member-state government is the plaintiff. In other words, the focus would be on rulings with a government litigant, not only a government defendant. As discussed previously, one can justify this based on the relevance of national government compliance to ECJ rulings when the government is a plaintiff (e.g., in an annulment action).[52]

In our empirical tests of the predictions, we consider both the narrow and the broad application of the prediction to the ECJ. The first test maps onto the model and its predictions as closely as possible. That is, we consider only rulings with a government defendant. The second test generalizes to a wider set of conditions under which threats of noncompliance should be present.

Before concluding, we briefly return to the two hypotheses. Figure 3.6 presents a simple description of the relationship between the disposition of ECJ rulings and the balance of third-party government briefs.[53] The bars represent, for the narrow and broad sets of rulings pertinent to our theory, the percentage of pro-plaintiff rulings. This simple figure presents suggestive evidence supporting our theoretical argument. First, and most obviously, it appears that the ECJ is more likely to rule for the plaintiff as the balance of third-party government briefs becomes more supportive of the plaintiff. That is consistent with the Political Sensitivity Hypothesis.

Second, Figure 3.6, particularly the dark gray bars, provides some insight into why the Conditional Effectiveness Hypothesis predicts that we should see rulings cause significant change in substantive outcomes (e.g., trade), yet empirical evidence to date finds no consistent significant effect. Recall that

---

[52] We exclude actions brought by governments that likely do not involve compliance issues, such as actions brought against the Commission for failure to act (Article 175 [EC] actions). Such rulings are relatively rare (e.g., our data set included three rulings on actions for failure to act).
[53] We exclude briefs from a litigant government or from the government of the country of origin of a preliminary ruling.

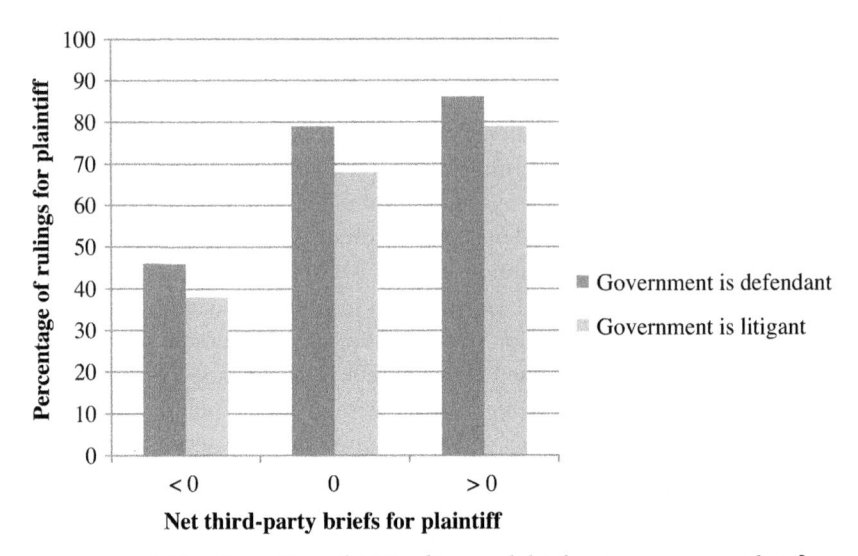

FIGURE 3.6 The disposition of ECJ rulings and third-party government briefs

our second hypothesis states that the effectiveness of a ruling is conditional on the balance of third-party briefs; as that balance moves to support a ruling against a government, that ruling is more likely to be effective. This is not what past empirical studies of effectiveness have examined. Figure 3.6 shows why this might be important to understanding and estimating the impact of rulings. When a government is a defendant (the dark gray bars), the ECJ rules against the defendant both when that ruling enjoys the net support of third-party governments and when it does not.[54] According to our theory, we would not expect all of these rulings to have the same impact; the impact should be greater when the pro-plaintiff ruling is also supported by the third-party briefs. Thus, if one were to estimate the average impact of ECJ rulings, one could find little or no impact in general. Yet, the evidence could still support our theoretical argument because the theory predicts effectiveness to be conditional on third-party support.

Of course, Figure 3.6 provides suggestive evidence at best. A proper test of the two theoretical predictions requires a much more careful analysis. In Chapter 6, we focus on testing the second prediction, the Conditional Effectiveness Hypothesis. However, we first turn to developing and executing a test of our first prediction, the Political Sensitivity Hypothesis. One important

---

[54] Recall that the presence of rulings against the defendant in both contexts is consistent with our theory, which predicts that such rulings are decreasingly likely as third-party support for the government increases.

concern in designing that empirical test is to distinguish the hypothesized effect on rulings from other potentially confounding explanations. We are concerned that the relationship suggested in Figure 3.6 could reflect other attributes of rulings that are associated with the balance of third-party briefs. In particular, the balance of briefs could simply indicate the balance of the legal merits (which litigant has the stronger legal case). Thus, in Chapter 4 we identify and validate a measure that captures the effect of the legal merits on ECJ rulings. In Chapter 5, we then test the Political Sensitivity Hypothesis and challenge the robustness of that hypothesis in light of a variety of alternative explanations, including the legal merits.

4

Preliminary considerations

Designing a control for the legal merits

Our first hypothesis states that the Court is more likely to rule against a defendant government as the net number of third-party briefs filed against the defendant government increases. Before bringing our data from the European Court of Justice (ECJ) to bear on that claim, we first develop a strategy for controlling for a prominent alternative explanation: the Court rules based on the balance of the legal merits in the case.

When the ECJ decides a case, it reviews previous decisions (case law), treaty articles, and secondary legislation relevant to the concrete controversy in the case (Hartley 2007: 71–4; Mattli and Slaughter 1995: 187). Although these texts do not always point unequivocally toward a particular resolution of the case (after all, cases often arise because the appropriate interpretation of these texts is ambiguous), they help define the legal merits of each litigant's position. The ECJ has a variety of reasons it might care about the fidelity of its rulings to this corpus; to list just a few, the judges sincerely may value doing their jobs "right," they instrumentally may see it as a way to retain the support of the legal community, and/or they may value a coherent and consistent legal system (Burley and Mattli 1993; Mattli and Slaughter 1995). To the degree these factors matter, we would expect the ECJ's decision to reflect the legal merits of the case.

The balance of the third-party government briefs may also reflect the legal merits of the case. That is, member states may be more likely to file briefs on the side with the best legal argument.[1] To list just two possible reasons, member states might be interested in supporting the "right" interpretation of the law, or they might find it easier to make arguments (and therefore are more likely to file briefs) when their preferred position is supported by the

---

[1] In fact, Everling (1984a: 227) claims that briefs are influential on rulings because they effectively convey the merits of a legal position.

legal merits. In either case, we would generally expect to find both the Court's rulings and the balance of member-state briefs in support of the side of the case with the stronger legal merits (Pollack 2003: 199).

As a result, the legal merits could explain some and potentially all of the coincidence between the position supported by member-state briefs and the position favored by the ECJ's ruling. In terms of statistical estimation, ignoring the legal merits therefore may introduce omitted variable bias. If true, the effect of third-party government briefs on ECJ rulings should decrease (and potentially disappear) once we control for the litigant's position with the strongest legal merit.

Accounting for the role of legal principles in judicial decision making is a longstanding concern in the study of judicial politics. This concern has particular relevance to American judicial behavior scholars interested in understanding how much ideology and strategic considerations drive judicial decision making (e.g., Segal and Spaeth 2002). To that end, they have sought to distinguish evidence of ideological and strategic behavior from evidence for the legal model, which holds that judges apply the law "objectively, dispassionately, and impartially" (e.g., Segal and Spaeth 1993: 33).[2]

The most common approach used to control for the legal model is to directly quantify the legal quality of each side's argument. For example, in examining search and seizure cases, scholars quantify the intrusiveness of the search to measure the likelihood the search should be deemed inadmissible (Segal and Spaeth 2002: 314). Similarly, in death penalty cases scholars have quantified legal characteristics of the case that are supposed to influence the likelihood a death penalty is reversed on appeal (George and Epstein 1992). More recently, Bailey and Maltzman (2011) quantified the role of precedent,[3] legislative deference, and judicial doctrine in Supreme Court justice votes through an innovative identification strategy involving bridging observations to Congress.[4]

This approach is particularly useful when one is studying a substantive subset of cases (e.g., search and seizure) or one is interested in examining how

---

[2] Specifically, the legal model argues that cases are decided on the basis of (1) the plain meaning of the relevant laws, (2) the relevant precedent, and, when necessary, (3) the intent of the politicians responsible for these texts (Segal and Spaeth 2002).

[3] An alternative way of trying to measure the influence of precedent (Segal and Spaeth 1996; Spaeth and Segal 1999) is cogently discussed and dismissed in Bailey and Maltzman (2011: 55–8).

[4] This last approach reflects a change in the US judicial politics literature as it moves away from testing among competing models – the "legal model" versus the "attitudinal model" versus the "strategic model" – and toward studying how legal considerations interact with ideological and strategic considerations in a justice's calculations (Lax 2011).

a particular legal characteristic (e.g., stare decisis) influences legal decision making. However, we cannot use it here because we are interested in looking at all cases decided by the ECJ across a broad range of substantive areas of law. Furthermore, we want to control jointly for all legal factors that might influence the ECJ's decisions, not a specific legal characteristic or subset of characteristics.

An alternative approach is to control for the legal merits of a case by including the position adopted by a third-party legal expert on the case. For example, the US Solicitor General (SG) is not a member of the Supreme Court but submits amicus briefs on a large number of cases before the court. Scholars contend that in so doing the SG is a valuable agent of the court, providing expert analysis of the legal merits of the cases and, as a result, having substantial influence on the judgments of the court (for summary, see Bailey, Kamoie, and Maltzman 2005: 73). Given the frequency of SG amicus briefs and the attention to the legal merits in these briefs, one might consider using the SG's position on a legal issue in a case as a control for the legal merits.

In this chapter, we pursue this second approach to constructing a control for the legal merits in cases before the ECJ. Specifically, we propose a measurement strategy based on a third-party analysis of the cases before the ECJ: the published opinion of the Advocate General (AG).

Before proceeding, a word of caution is in order. Our confidence in a third-party position as a proxy for the balance of the legal merits depends on several characteristics of the third-party analysis of the case. Ideally, we would like to find a third-party source that (1) has the necessary legal expertise to discern and evaluate the legal merits, (2) has a motivation to provide an assessment of the legal question based on those merits, and (3) lacks an incentive to take a position on the legal issue based on factors other than the legal merits. Applied to the preceding SG example, these conditions obtain to varying degrees. Although experts generally agree that the SG possesses a high level of legal proficiency and serves in part as an agent of the court, the SG is appointed by the president explicitly to advocate for the executive branch (Bailey, Kamoie, and Maltzman 2005). Not surprisingly, scholars find that the SG position on a case to some degree reflects the policy interests of the president (Bailey, Kamoie, and Maltzman 2005). Thus, the value of the SG as a proxy for the legal merits depends on whether one can easily isolate these political considerations from the analysis of the legal merits in the positions taken by the SG.

We encounter a similar issue with the Advocate General. As we discuss in more detail later, the AG is generally considered a legal expert, writes thorough legal analyses of the legal questions in each case, and provides a published advisory opinion to the ECJ. This is the explicit duty of the AG, who is an officer of the Court, not (as is the case with the SG) an appointed advocate for any political institution, member state, or other interested party. Thus, the AG's analysis plausibly fulfills conditions (1) and (2) and is not explicitly mandated to violate (3). That said, AGs are not perfectly inoculated from potential conflicts of interest. AGs do not enjoy life tenure, their opinions are named and published, and home governments may have an interest in and ability to influence the AGs' opinions through their impact on AGs' future career opportunities. Thus, political considerations may enter an AG's analysis of the case and shape the position presented in the published opinion. We devote considerable attention in this chapter to identifying such considerations, isolating any such effects, and adjusting our measure of the legal merits to minimize their influence. In brief, we find only a highly conditional and limited political influence on the AG.

The rest of the chapter proceeds as follows. First, we review the role of the AG in some detail. We start by describing the AG's office and the character of AG opinions. Then we review the conventional wisdom that the AG's opinion consists of a careful treatment of all legal issues in the case and the resulting proposed ruling represents the balance of the legal merits. We finish by contrasting this apolitical depiction of the AG with a straightforward principal–agent argument based on the appointment procedures for the AG position. Unlike the apolitical story, this argument suggests that AGs should be responsive to the interests of their home governments at least under certain conditions.

Second, we look for evidence consistent with this political argument. Critically, we first identify the context within which a potential conflict of interest arises, and then, within that context, we evaluate the AG's responsiveness to home government pressure. Only with both of these pieces of evidence can we draw well-reasoned conclusions about the extent of political influence on the AG's opinion. We consider a variety of possible models of AG responsiveness to home government political pressure to help ensure that we successfully identify and isolate any home government influence on the AG's position.

Finally, we perform an indirect test of the underlying assumption that the AG opinion, in the absence of political influence, reflects the balance of the legal merits of the case. If the ECJ rulings and AG positions are a function of the legal merits on each side of the case, they should correlate positively, which they do. This correlation should weaken when the AG's position deviates from the merits as a result of political influence. We test this claim, which provides some circumstantial evidence for our underlying assumption.

We conclude the chapter by considering how best to use the AG as a control for the merits. Based on our findings, we develop alternatives that vary in terms of how they manage avoiding contamination due to political influence. The following chapter then implements these alternative strategies in a reanalysis of the bivariate relationships in Chapter 3.

I. THE ADVOCATE GENERAL

The role of the Advocate General at the ECJ was inspired by the commissaire du gouvernement at the French Conseil d'Etat (Dashwood 1982: 205; Ritter 2005: 751)[5] and is defined by the EEC Treaty in 1957 (Article 166) thus:

> It shall be the duty of the Advocate-General, acting with complete impartiality and independence, to make, in open court, reasoned submissions on cases brought before the Court of Justice, in order to assist the Court in the performance of the task assigned to it.

The AG, as a member of the Court, is not an advocate for a litigant in the case or a third party, such as a public institution or organization. Furthermore, no European Union (EU) institution or national government exercises authority over the AG during the AG's term.

When a case arrives at the Court, it is assigned to a judge rapporteur, who is one of the judges at the ECJ, and to one of the Advocates General. Advocates General are typically not assigned to cases in which their home government is a litigant. They are also almost never assigned to preliminary rulings originating from their home states (Tridimas 1997: 1356).

The assigned AG is charged with reviewing all case materials, including briefs submitted by national governments and by EU institutions, and developing an answer to legal questions raised in the case. The AG does this in isolation from the judge rapporteur and the members of the Court who will ultimately decide the case. At the end of the oral procedure, and immediately before the Court deliberates on the case, the AG reads his/her opinion in open court. The opinion and the name of its author are typically published along with the ruling.

The AG does not participate in the Court's deliberations and is not consulted after reading the opinion. As Dashwood (1982: 211) describes it, "Once the

---

[5] The role is common in Civil Code systems, where Advocates-General exist. Common law systems do not have an analogue. It should not be confused with the positions of Solicitor General or the Attorney General in the US courts.

opinion has been read the case disappears behind the wall of secrecy that surrounds the Judges' deliberations which, you will remember, the AG does not attend."

Originally, two AGs served at the ECJ, one from France and one from Germany. Over time, with the expansion of membership in the European Community (EC; and then the EU), the number of AGs increased significantly. Currently, there are eight Advocates General. The governments of France, Germany, the United Kingdom, Italy, and Spain each appoint one AG. The other three positions rotate among the remaining member states. During the period of our study, the number of AGs varied from two to nine, with France, Germany, the United Kingdom, and Italy retaining the power to nominate one AG and with the remaining positions rotating among the other member states.

The AGs are appointed by common accord of the member states. According to the EC Treaty, they are "chosen from among persons whose independence is beyond doubt and who possess the qualifications required for appointment to the highest judicial offices in their respective countries or who are jurisconsults of recognized competence."[6] In practice, they are typically selected from national judiciaries, senior civil servants, and academics (Tridimas 1997: 1352). Some AGs have had significant political experience. For example, Advocate General Lenz had a clear political career in the Christian Democratic Union party and served in the Bundestag in West Germany. In any event, Brown and Kennedy (2000: 74) conclude that the variety of professional backgrounds generates differences in style, but not substance, of the opinions written by AGs.

An AG's appointment is for six years. For AGs from member states that retain control over nomination of an AG position, this term is renewable. For the other AGs, it is not directly renewable, although an AG could be reappointed when the rotation returned the nomination to the AG's home government. The six-year terms are staggered so that AG terms overlap only partially. Once in office, an AG cannot be removed from office by his/her national government until the end of the term.

Figure 4.1 presents the names and terms of all of the AGs who served from 1960 to 1999, the period of our study.[7] The figure shows that, as expected, AGs

---

[6] Consolidated Version of the Treaty Establishing the European Community, Article 223, *Official Journal* C 325.

[7] Data used in this chapter regarding the names, nationality, ages, and dates of service for the Advocates General were assembled from the *Official Journal of the European Communities*, Series C (various years), the *Synopsis of the Work of the Court of Justice of the European Communities* (various years), and Burrows and Greaves (2007).

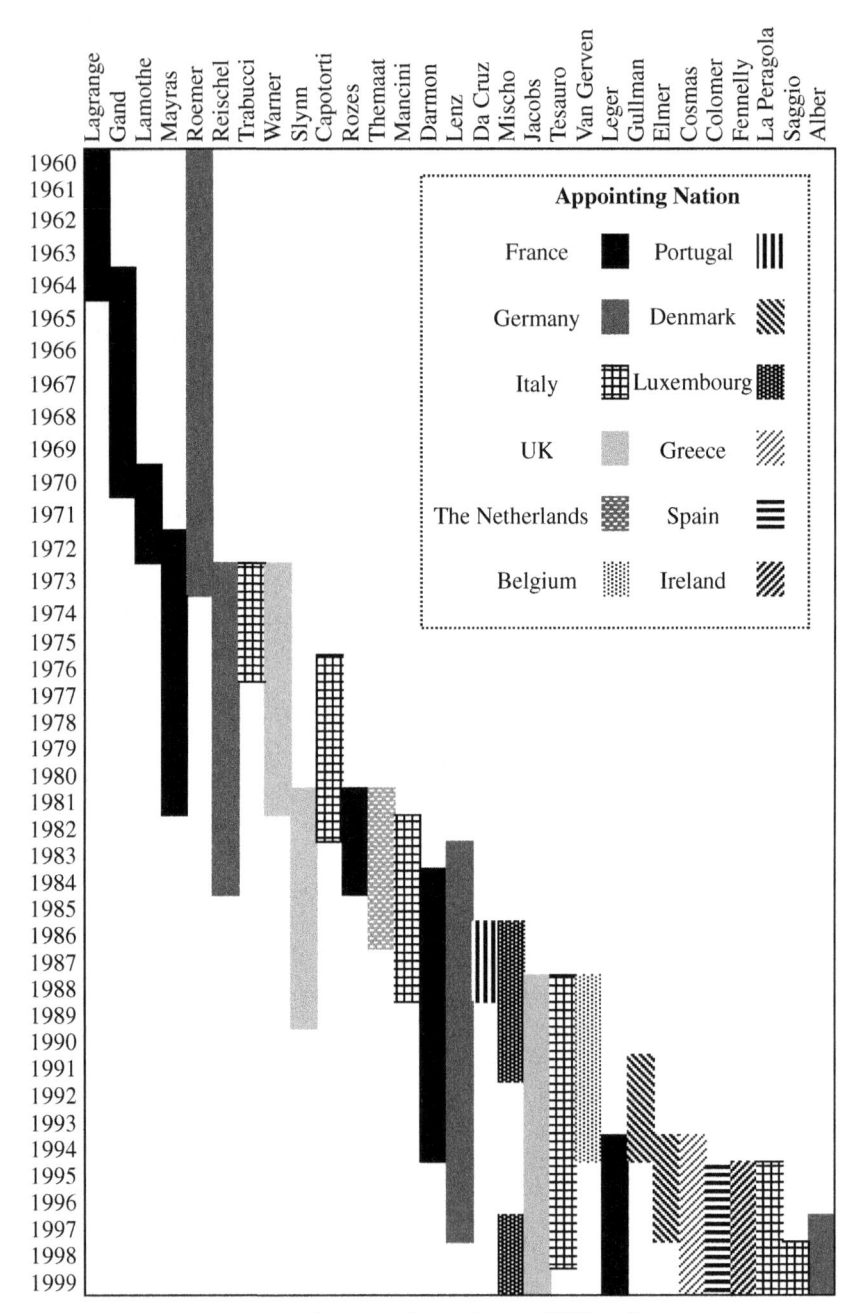

FIGURE 4.1 Advocates General at the ECJ, 1960–99

from the larger member states often enjoy multiple six-year terms, whereas the AGs from the smaller member states do not. We also see a fair amount of variation in the length of terms among AGs from the same country.

a. *The AG as legal advocate?*

A strong case can be made that the Advocate General is a legal expert helping the ECJ make good law. This view is grounded first and foremost in a perception of the AG's position as meeting the three criteria described previously: the AG (1) has the necessary legal expertise to discern and evaluate the legal merits, (2) has a motivation to provide an assessment of the legal question based on those merits, and (3) lacks an incentive to take a position on the legal issue based on factors other than the legal merits. The AG selection process meets the first criterion. As described, the AG is selected from national judiciaries, senior civil servants, and academics. Further, the same standards and protections are set out in the treaties to select AGs as to select other justices of the Court. Although they come from varied backgrounds, scholars widely considered these individuals to be well qualified for the job. Brown and Kennedy (2000: 67) describe the AGs as "professorial Chairs of Community law," and Dashwood (1982: 212) points out that (particularly in the early days) the AGs have provided expert legal analysis of Community law to judges who were not always familiar with that area of law.

The second and third criteria are met by the nature of the position. As also described previously, once appointed, AGs' professional responsibility is solely to the Court; they are not advocates for litigants or third parties, direct communication between governments and AGs is forbidden, and no one has authority over them while they fulfill their tenure. Thus, the design of the office is such that AGs should be able to fulfill their formal role at the Court.

Of course, just because the position is designed to ensure that the AG consistently produces high-quality legal briefs that can be of use to the Court does not mean it succeeds. But expert observers of the AG, in fact, see this system functioning as designed. First, Brown and Kennedy (2000: 71) see the AGs as having internalized their institutionally designed mandate; the authors state: "The advocates general often regard it as one of their principal functions to remind the Court of its previous case law and to emphasize the virtue of a consistent and harmonious development of law." Note, in contrast, the same view is not consistently held of the Court. According to Ritter (2005: 760), the ECJ, but not the AG, "can be suspected of sometimes yielding to non-legal considerations." Interestingly, Ritter (2005: 761) identifies member-state compliance as one of the "non-legal considerations" that do not figure in the AG's opinion but that may influence the ECJ rulings.

Second, the consensus is that the AG does in fact produce very high-quality legal opinions. AG opinions involve a full analysis of the relevant case law, treaty articles, and secondary legislation related to the controversy at hand (Brown and Kennedy 2000: 62; Dashwood 1982: 207; Ritter 2005; Tridimas 1997). Their analyses generally engage all possible dimensions of the legal question and all arguments found in the submissions of the litigants and amicus briefs. As Dashwood (1982) describes, AGs must dispose of every legal issue raised in a case because the Court might not follow them on any given issue (Dashwood 1982: 208). Further, the AG opinion also considers the academic "doctrine," which captures the reception of past rulings by the academic and legal communities (Lasser 2009a: 122). As a result, the opinions tend to be extremely comprehensive accounts of the legal merits associated with each side of a case, and these exhaustive legal analyses are the bases for the rulings proposed in the opinions' conclusions (Jacobs 2000).

Again, in contrast, the ECJ rulings are terse, often significantly shorter than the AG's opinion. Brown and Kennedy (2000: 68), comparing the ECJ rulings with the AG's opinion, conclude, "The Court's judgment by contrast, is less free and less full, usually setting out only those propositions which are necessary to its decision, and often not seeking to justify or substantiate them." Dashwood agrees, stating that the Court engages in a policy of "judicial self-restraint," "confining its judgments to the issues necessary to dispose of a given case" (Dashwood 1982: 208). The ECJ also produces less elegant and consistent reasoning. This appears to be a result of the collective effort involved in building a sufficient coalition to support a ruling. According to Dashwood (1982: 213–14), " the resulting judgments have the look of documents produced by a committee. The search for consensus, both as to the decision and as to the steps leading to it, inevitably entails fudging some issues and occasional incoherence in reasoning."

Given the high quality of the AGs' briefs, it is hardly surprising that these briefs are perceived to be useful to the Court. First, scholars see the AG's opinion as a major factor in the Court proceedings. Previous AG opinions are cited routinely by litigants before the Court (Ritter 2005: 757). And, even more importantly, the AG opinion often structures the considerations of individual judges and the discussion among the judges (Dashwood 1982; Jacobs 2000: 21). As Judge Lecourt, then president of the ECJ, stated, "Although the AG may not be present at the deliberations, his voice is not silent" (Dashwood 1982: 211).

Second, the ECJ rulings frequently concur with the AG's opinion (e.g., Hartley 2007: 52; Jacobs 2000: 22).[8] The actual rate of agreement is difficult to gauge because the ECJ could agree with the AG's position but perhaps differ in its justification. That said, Dashwood (1982: 212) placed the "received wisdom" at 70 percent agreement between the AG and the Court.[9] In the 84 rulings from the first half of 1996, Tridimas (1997: 1362) estimated that 88 percent were in agreement with the AG's opinion. And, in our data, we find the AG position and the ECJ ruling coincide on 86 percent of the legal issues.[10]

In sum, the conventional wisdom is that AGs provide opinions based on very careful, and thorough, legalistic assessment of the merits in the case, and these opinions are useful to the Court in identifying and resolving the legal merits of an argument. Most observers do not consider the possibility that other factors, such as political pressure, could influence an AG's opinion. Some even go so far as to explicitly dismiss this possibility. For example, Dashwood (1982: 209) states, in reference to the possibility of AGs favoring their home government's interests, that there is not even a "whiff of suspicion of bias."

b. *The AG as a political actor?*

Observers of the Court tend to dismiss the possibility that criterion (3) is violated – that is, that the AG lacks an incentive to take a position on the legal issue based on factors other than the legal merits. However, the institutional setting does not fully insulate the AG from potential political pressure. This fact arises from an important distinction between Court decisions and AG opinions. The judgment of the Court is signed by all of the judges assigned to the case (through chambers), whether or not they in fact agree with the decision or its rationale.[11] There are no dissenting or concurring opinions published by the Court. Thus, it is impossible to identify with certainty the position of any one judge on a ruling. But, because the position of the AG is

---

[8] Given that AGs and judges on the Court are generally drawn from a common set of jurists, it should be no surprise that they evaluate the legal merits on similar grounds.

[9] Although he (Dashwood 1982: 212) thought the rate was lower while he was at the Court.

[10] Some scholars interpret this agreement as evidence that the AG's opinion influences the Court's ruling. Demonstrating such an influence is complicated. In particular, to do so requires an argument and/or evidence about the counterfactual – that is, how the Court would rule without an AG opinion. For our purposes, the question is beside the point. Because the AG's opinion is a careful treatment of the legal issues based on the merits, the most plausible source of influence of that opinion would be to persuade the Court to rule for the side the AG considers favored by the legal merits. As a result, any observed correlation due to influence would also reflect the balance of the legal merits.

[11] The Court reaches judgments by majority rule.

publicly disclosed during the Court proceedings, one can identify a specific AG's position.

This exposure potentially leaves the AG vulnerable to political pressures (e.g., Brown and Kennedy 2000: 71; Solanke 2008–9: 104). The canonical principal–agent framework can be used to help clarify why. The AG's home member-state government, the principal, appoints an AG, the agent. The AG then issues a series of publicly observable opinions. At the end of the AG's tenure, the home government has the opportunity to influence the AG's future career prospects. Exactly which tools are available to the home government depends on the specific AG. Recall that the AGs from France, Germany, Italy, Spain, and the United Kingdom can be reappointed. Indeed, several AGs from these countries have served for multiple terms. For these AGs, the potential political threat is clear: reappointment could hinge on the government's assessment of the AG's opinions.

The same basic political considerations apply to AGs from the smaller member states, even though they cannot serve successive terms as AG (Solanke 2008–9).[12] These AGs may find the support of their home government valuable to their post-AG career goals. This might involve appointment to a judicial position in the national setting, to a government office, or to a position on an international court. For example, Nial Fennelly, an Irish AG, was appointed to the Supreme Court of Ireland after his term at the ECJ. Of course, these sorts of appointments are also of potential interest to AGs from the large member states.[13] For example, Jean-Pierre Warner, the first British Advocate General, left the ECJ to become a judge at the High Court of Justice's Chancery Division and received a customary knighthood upon that appointment. And Federico Mancini was nominated by the Italian government to be a judge at the ECJ following his term as Advocate General. Thus, through their power to nominate or appoint AGs to future positions, national governments may be instrumental to the career ambitions of AGs from all member states (Solanke 2008–9). If AGs value those prospects, they have an incentive to tailor their opinions to please the home government.

In sum, the descriptive literature on the role and historical behavior of the Advocates General typically portrays them as careful legal analysts, helping the Court evaluate the legal merits of its cases. Furthermore, this literature offers

---

[12] That is not to say they cannot be reappointed at a later date. Jean Mischo, from Luxembourg, served as an AG from 1986 to 1991 and then from 1997 to 2003. In the intervening years, he served in the Ministry of Foreign Affairs of Luxembourg.

[13] As Solanke (2008–9) and Kenney (1998) note, even in the large member states, reappointment as AG may not be a possibility given national traditions of balancing regional, linguistic, or party interests.

no evidence of political influences on AGs' opinions.[14] That said, we do not consider the case closed regarding political influence. For one, because AG opinions are disclosed publicly, the AG is exposed, at least in theory, to the possibility of political pressure. In addition, no previous study has developed or tested for specific manifestations of such political influence.[15] This issue is critical to our present effort to design a control for the balance of the legal merits on cases before the ECJ. If the AG is responsive to political pressure, then the high correlation between AG opinions and ECJ decisions may be a function, at least in part, of something other than agreement on the legal merits of a case.

In the remainder of the chapter we specify and test a number of theoretical expectations for how political pressure might influence AG opinions. We take an expansive approach to this testing. Rather than specify and test a specific principal–agent relationship, we test for a variety of ways in which the AG, as the agent, *might be* responsive to the home government, as the principal. The purpose of this approach is to help ensure that we do not miss a plausible way in which the AG is being responsive.[16] We want to inoculate against a variety of ways in which political pressure might be exerted, not test for a specific argument over how political pressure is being exerted.

II. HYPOTHESES

In this section we develop testable hypotheses about when AG opinions might be sensitive to political pressure. For all of these hypotheses, several necessary conditions must hold. First, the home government must consider the case salient to its interests. Second, the AG from the home government's country must be assigned to the case. Finally, the AG must be able to discern the interest

---

[14] For example, Brown and Kennedy (2000: 71) raise the possibility of political influence but conclude they do not see evidence to that effect.
[15] One exception is Solanke (2008–9: 99), which develops a fairly specific concern over whether AGs act independently of the interests of the member state when career goals depend on assistance from the member-state government. However, Solanke (2008–9) does not present specific hypotheses or provide relevant evidence.
[16] The disadvantage of this approach is that we are no longer rigorously testing a theory. For example, if we find a plausible unconditional relationship between political pressure and AG opinions but we do not find one or two of the plausible conditional relationships (e.g., the AG is not as responsive when he/she is about to retire), we cannot conclude that the relationship exists and it must be unconditional. If the "theory" were playing baseball, we would have given it several extra swings at the plate with which to try to get a base hit. As such, from this evidence we can conclude only that an unconditional relationship is *possible*. Of course, all one can ever do with empirical evidence is not falsify a theory. However, this is certainly still weaker evidence than is not falsifying a precise prediction.

of the home government. This may be obvious in some instances – for example, when that government is a party to the case – but not necessarily otherwise.

If these conditions obtain, an AG with an interest in pleasing the home government has an incentive to write a favorable opinion. The following hypotheses describe plausible conditions under which a career-minded AG, when exposed to home government pressure, might be responsive.

We begin with an unconditional hypothesis. If AGs expect their reappointment or other career opportunities to depend on consistent and unwavering support for the preferred position of their national government, then AGs should always respond to their home government's interests when writing opinions.[17] Hypothesis 1 follows.

Hypothesis 1: The AG's opinion will reflect the AG's home government's preferences whenever those preferences are revealed.

This hypothesis presumes that all AGs, on average, equally value satisfying the preferences of their home governments. But AGs could vary systematically in the value they attach to gaining favor with their home government depending on their career objectives and on their expectations of the relevance of current rulings to their future career goals. Accordingly, we develop two sets of conditional hypotheses.

First, personal attributes of the AG can shape how an AG evaluates the future career benefits controlled by the home government. The more an AG values those future career benefits at the time of the opinion, the stronger the AG's incentive to be responsive. A number of factors could influence the value of future career benefits, but perhaps the most obvious and important is the age of the AG. Certainly, at a more advanced age, when the AG is approaching retirement, the value of future career goals should be comparatively small. In contrast, young AGs may have many years of professional life ahead and would see their current behavior as an investment in achieving future career goals. Thus, the sensitivity of the AG to the home government's interests should decrease with the AG's age.

This relationship would hold in general across the term of the AG. In principle, the AG is always potentially a candidate for a job where the home government has influence.[18] Indeed, several AGs have resigned from the ECJ

---

[17] A variety of other reasons for this relationship might exist. For example, the AG might be interested in supporting home state interests independent of whether the national government expresses an interest. We are agnostic on which specific story motivates hypothesis 1. What is critical is simply that we evaluate this possibility and account for it if necessary when we use the AG as a proxy for the legal merits.
[18] One could argue that there could be stronger incentives near the end of an AG's term (as we discuss later) and that the age-related effect hypothesized here should be conditional on

in the middle of their terms to accept prominent national positions. For example, Simone Rozes resigned as AG after only two years to become the first president of the Cour de Cassation in France. Thus, if AGs are only responsive because of threats to their career goals, AGs have an incentive to attend to their home government's interests at all times. But if age has the expected effect, their responsiveness to those incentives should weaken as retirement approaches. This expectation is hypothesis 2.

Hypothesis 2: The younger the AG, the more likely the AG's opinion will reflect its home government's preferences whenever those preferences are revealed.

Second, attributes of the home government may also influence the value an AG attaches to satisfying the home government's interests. For one, the home government may systematically differ over time in the attention it devotes and salience it attaches to an AG's opinion. As Bernhard and Sala (2006) argue in a different context, the principal (home government) in such a relationship may discount past behavior and place heavy weight on the agent's (AG's) behavior proximate to reappointment. Home governments typically wait until very late in the term to even consider the appointment issue and often delay the decision as long as possible (Solanke 2008–9). Thus, the saliency of AG opinions to the home government's actions regarding the AG's career is likely higher at the end of the AG's term than at the beginning. This is particularly relevant to AGs because the vast majority of them complete their terms. For AGs appointed in the pre-2000 period, more than 75 percent of the terms were served to completion.[19] As a result, just as Bernhard and Sala (2006) found in their study of US Senators, we might expect the agents (the AGs) to be more sensitive to the principals (home governments) at the end of the term and adopt more responsive opinions than adopted earlier in their terms.[20]

Hypothesis 3: The closer to the end of the AG's term, the more likely the AG's opinion will reflect its home government's preferences whenever those preferences are revealed.

Finally, the identity of the government – and its ideological interests related to AG rulings – may change over the course of the AG's term. In particular, the current principal (the party or coalition in government) may not be the principal at the end of the agent's (AG's) term. A sophisticated AG might

---

the year of the term. We have investigated that and not found any systematic evidence that responsiveness related to age is stronger at the end of the AG's term.

[19] We selected this range of years because it is the period for our study of ECJ decision making.

[20] Bernhard and Sala (2006) show that senators are more likely to moderate their behavior to respond to constituency opinion near the end of their six-year term.

take this into consideration when responding to the interests expressed by the current home government. If so, the AG's sensitivity to the current government's opinion on a case would reflect the AG's evaluation of whether the party or parties currently in power will be in that position at the end of the AG's term. This assessment would be a function of how much time remains in the AG's term and the staying power of the incumbent government. So, then, in contrast to hypothesis 3, this means that, even at the beginning of a term, an AG may be highly attentive to the incumbent government's interests if the AG believes control of the government will not change hands before the end of the term. And near the end of the AG's term, an AG may place low value on satisfying the incumbent government if the fall of the incumbent is imminent. In short, if AGs are sufficiently foresighted, their responsiveness should depend on their assessment of the likelihood the current government will be in a position to influence their career goals at the end of their term.[21] This expectation is hypothesis 4.[22]

Hypothesis 4: The more likely the incumbent government is to be in office at the end of the AG's tenure, the more likely the AG's opinion will reflect its home government's preferences whenever those preferences are revealed.

Empirical evidence of political influence on AG opinions

Before examining these four hypotheses, we first return to the general conditions that must hold for the hypotheses to apply to an AG opinion. Recall that these conditions in effect define the potential scope of the political influence we are attempting to discover. The conditions are that the home government (1) considers the case at issue relevant to its interests, (2) expects the AG from the home government's country to influence the case outcome through its opinion, and (3) can communicate that interest to that AG.

AG case assignment rules limit substantially the applicability of these conditions to AG opinions. As mentioned previously, AGs are normally not assigned to direct actions (e.g., infringement or annulment cases) involving their home government or to preliminary reference cases from their home country

---

[21] This is essentially the same general argument made by Helmke (2002) in the context of judicial behavior in Argentina. Helmke (2002) argues that judges with unsecure tenure are more likely to make anti-government rulings as it becomes clear the incumbent government is likely to lose power.

[22] An especially sophisticated AG might both anticipate how strongly he/she cares about future career goals and how likely the current government is to survive to reappointment. We checked for this possibility in some robustness tests but found nothing conclusive. Because of the multiplicity of interaction terms in the analysis that arises from these hypotheses and the null results, we do not report that analysis.

(Tridimas 1997: 1356). Thus, AGs typically do not write opinions on cases in which their home governments might directly care about the outcome of the case. And, therefore, AGs will rarely be assigned to the cases their home governments consider salient (conditions 1 and 2).

Of course, conflicts of interest might arise in direct action cases involving another member-state government or a preliminary reference from another member state. Although not a directly affected participant, a home government might take an interest as a third party to the case, depending on the issue and the government in question.[23] We would observe this interest when a home government submits an amicus brief. These also are instances that fulfill condition (3): the position of the home government is observable by the AG. Because AGs consider these briefs before writing their opinions, the brief can act as a very effective, and legal, way of the home government informing the AG of its interest and preferred outcome. This is not a trivial point because direct communication between governments and AGs is in violation of the norms of the Court. Consequently, we expect the necessary conditions for the political influence hypotheses to obtain when we observe an amicus brief from the AG's home government.

Before proceeding, note that a "home government brief" – that is, a brief submitted by the AG's home government – occurs in only 6 *percent* of the legal issues in our data set. For the vast majority of rulings (94 percent) in the period of our study, the scope conditions for political influence on the AG's position are not met. This shows that the opportunities for conflicts of interest are severely curtailed by the institutional rules of the ECJ. This initial finding is highly encouraging for the prospects of using the AG as a control for the legal merits. We now turn to testing the hypotheses for those relatively rare cases in which the scope conditions do obtain.

III. MEASUREMENT AND TESTS

To test these hypotheses, we examine the position of the Advocate General on legal issues answered by the ECJ in all of the cases from 1960 to 1999. An

---

[23] The relevance to a government of ECJ rulings involving other member-state governments or litigants in court in another member state is ambiguous. ECJ rulings are binding on the parties to the case, and national courts may rely on these rulings to guide their judgments in future related cases. But the possibility of a broader (*erga omnes*) impact on courts and litigants in other member states is simply that, a possibility. There is no obligation on domestic courts to apply past ECJ rulings in similar future cases. See Conant (2002: 65–9) for a careful discussion of these points. Consequently, even ECJ rulings on legal issues of interest to a third-party government may not be salient to that government's interests.

opinion of the Advocate General was published on virtually all of the rulings in the data set.[24] We coded the opinion on each legal issue as to whether it was in favor of the plaintiff or the defendant in the case. This resulting dummy variable is called *AG Opinion for Plaintiff*.

All four hypotheses are conditioned on the AG's home government at the time of the case having a preference on the outcome of the case. As described previously, we use an AG's home government brief on a legal issue as an indicator of that government's interest in the outcome of the case and by implication what position the home government would prefer the AG take. For each ruling, we code each home government brief as for the plaintiff or for the defendant. The resulting dummy variable is called *Home Government Brief for Plaintiff*.[25] These two variables are sufficient for testing hypothesis 1. A positive relationship would be consistent with the hypothesis.

To test hypothesis 2, we created a variable that indicates the age of the AG in the year of the ruling. The variable, *Age (centered)*, is normalized so that zero indicates the average age of AGs in the observed set of rulings and higher ages represent older AGs.[26] This variable is interacted with the position of the AG's home government (*Home Government Brief for Plaintiff*). If hypothesis 2 holds, the position of the home government brief should be positively related to the AG's position on the legal issue, and this effect should decrease as the age of the AG increases. This means the interaction term should have a negative coefficient.

To test hypothesis 3, we created a variable called *End of Term*. This variable is coded 1 for AG opinions on rulings in the last year of the term of appointment and 0 otherwise.[27] We then interact this variable with *Home Government Brief for Plaintiff*. If AGs are more sensitive to home government briefs at the end of their term, the interaction term should be positive.[28]

Testing hypothesis 4 requires an explicit model of how an AG forecasts the likelihood the incumbent government survives to the end of the AG's term. To

---

[24] In a few instances, we encountered cases without an AG opinion or in which the AG's identity was missing.
[25] The identity of the AG is typically provided with each ruling by the ECJ.
[26] We discerned the age of the AGs and connected AGs to their home government based on biographical information provided in the *Synopsis of the Work of the Court of Justice of the European Communities* (various years) and in Burrows and Greaves (2007).
[27] Note that some AGs are appointed as replacements and serve the remainder of the original AG's term. That means some AGs hold office only in the last year of a term.
[28] One could also operationalize this with a continuous variable capturing each year in the term. We have done that. The results of that analysis support the same conclusion as the analysis presented here.

create such a measure, we first need to define "the government." Although the nomination process for the AG is not well documented (Solanke 2008–9),[29] all appointments are ultimately made by the national executive.[30] Thus, we treat the party controlling the national executive, the party of the prime minister, as the key actor affecting an AG's career goals.[31] By implication, we evaluate whether AGs adapt their behavior to a home government amicus brief based on the likelihood the current prime minister's party will be in office at the end of the AG's term in office.

Next, we define how the AG evaluates the likelihood the current prime minister's party will endure until the end of the AG's term in office. Forecasting political survival is a difficult task, particularly in this setting. Most importantly, the maximum term of an elected government in the member states is less than the term of an AG. Consequently, the forecast must anticipate the electoral cycle and the outcome of elections. This cycle is not always fixed. In some EU countries, the sitting prime minister can call elections before the end of the maximum term. As a result, the timing of such elections can be difficult to anticipate. And to make matters even more complicated, the prime minister's party could change without an election as a result of parliamentary bargaining after, for example, a vote of no confidence. Thus, particularly early in an AG's six-year term, the AG might realistically expect to observe more than one election and a wide array of events (e.g., economic shocks, international crises, or political scandals) that would threaten the survival of the current government before the end of the AG's term.

We have no strong empirical or theoretical guidance on the exact model AGs would use to forecast government survival. But we cannot test hypothesis 4 without specifying such a model. To help ensure that we do not miss evidence consistent with political influence, we consider two such models. One model is a comparatively simple, retrospective calculation, whereas the other is a more sophisticated evaluation.

---

[29] Anecdotal accounts indicate that specific public officials (e.g., the finance minister) have approached potential candidates for AG or that the prime minister approached particular candidates about the job (Kenney 1998: 258; Solanke 2008–9: 103).

[30] This process is consistent with the role of national governments (the executives) in judicial and political appointments within the EU as well as throughout international courts and organizations.

[31] This is a simplifying assumption. Some EU national governments consist of coalitions of political parties. It is possible that certain ministries enjoy some autonomy from the prime minister for appointments. As a result, there may be instances when the prime minister's party is not directly responsible for a relevant appointment or nomination. But detailed information regarding ministerial appointment powers across all member states is not available. Thus, we cannot make such distinctions in our empirical analysis.

The first model is effectively an inductive exercise in forecasting based on observed past political experience in that country. The model assumes the AGs consider the political history in their country since the end of the Second World War or the transition to democracy (whichever was most recent) up to the date of their opinion. AGs forecast in the following way. First, they calculate the length of time between when the current prime minister's party took office and when their term as AG concludes. This defines the survival question: how likely will the current government stay in office for this period or longer? Second, the AGs examine the history of tenures of past prime ministers' parties in that country and determine the share of those tenures that endured for as long as the time period from the first calculation (i.e., the survival question). For example, consider a scenario in which a new AG and prime minister enter office in 1960 and the government had changed the prime minister's party every five years since 1945. In this scenario, the survival question is how likely the government will survive for six or more years (the term of the AG). The AG then calculates the share of the past tenures of prime ministers' parties that had reached six years. The answer is zero. Thus, this model would assign a zero to the likelihood the current prime minister's party would be in office at the end of the AG's term. In contrast, if this same AG were in his/her sixth year in office with the same political history, the AG would place 100 percent probability on the survival of the prime minister's party. All governments up to that point would have survived at least one year.[32] Importantly, in the calculation of past tenures of prime ministers' parties, we do not consider elections as necessarily defining the end of the term of a party holding the prime minister's office. If the same party continues in office after an election, we consider the prime minister's party as remaining in office.

Based on this simple retrospective forecasting model, we create the variable *Expected Government Survival (retrospective)*, which ranges from 0 to 1 and increases as the estimate of survival to the end of term increases.

The second forecasting model assumes a more sophisticated appraisal of the prime minister's party's survival prospects. In contrast to the first forecasting model, this one assumes the AGs make causal inferences about the survival of the home government. The AGs consider particular political factors (e.g., the size of the coalition government) and economic conditions (e.g., inflation rate) as influential on the survival of the prime minister's party in government and adjust expectations of survival on the current status of those factors. The

---

[32] We use life table survival rates to calculate these probabilities. Details of the calculations are presented in the technical appendix at the end of the chapter.

weight the AGs put on those factors in their forecast is a function of how these factors had historically related to observed survival in the home country and neighboring countries. Thus, this model is more sophisticated than is the simple forecasting model for the fact that it relies both on causal arguments about survival and observed history of the survival of prime ministers' parties across several countries.

In terms of the causal model of survival, we draw on the rich literature in comparative politics that has examined the survival of governments in advanced industrial democracies. This literature identifies institutional factors (e.g., electoral rules), structural attributes (e.g., size of the winning coalition), preferences (e.g., policy preference diversity in the coalition), the bargaining environment (transaction costs), and critical events (e.g., scandals) as significant determinants of cabinet survival (for a summary, see Strom, Mueller, and Bergman 2008). A variety of studies have estimated the impact of these factors on cabinet survival, using survival analysis statistical models (for a summary, see Laver 2003). This research provides a theoretical basis for forecasting cabinet survival as well as empirical estimates of the relative importance of these different determinants. For example, Bernhard and Leblang (2006) use an empirical model borrowed from these studies in order to study how the expected stability of the government affects financial markets.

However, this literature does not directly serve our purposes because typically a cabinet is defined as terminated by an election, the resignation of the prime minister (even if replaced by someone else from the same party), or a change in the partisan composition of the cabinet (Laver 2003: 26). We, in contrast, are interested in a model that forecasts the endurance of the prime minister's party, which could survive any of the aforementioned events defined as terminal for the cabinet. Empirically, this turns out to be a significant distinction. Many governments that terminate by the standard survival criteria actually endure in the sense that the same prime minister's party remains in power after a new cabinet in formed. For example, Damgaard (2008: 309) found that 40 percent of the 407 cabinets in his data set for postwar Europe were led by the same prime minister as the previous cabinet. Thus, we cannot simply borrow a statistical model of cabinet survival from this literature and then calculate survival probabilities based on the remaining term of the AG and the relevant contextual information surrounding the incumbent government.

Instead, we construct our own statistical model of survival of the incumbent prime minister's party based on a subset of the factors used to account for government survival as defined in the traditional literature. In selecting explanatory variables, we could not simply borrow the usual suspects from the literature on cabinet survival. As Damgaard (2008) shows, many of the common predictors of cabinet survival account only for technical terminations, which often do not involve a change in the parties in government. Terminations resulting from intracoalition conflict are less common but much more relevant for our purposes. That is, when the bargaining environment, economic conditions, or institutional setting is more likely to cause interparty conflict, we expect the party of the prime minister to be at risk of change. Subsequently, we identify the factors relevant to this sort of conflict, drawn primarily from the analysis in Strom, Mueller, and Bergman (2008).

First, we expect the prime minister's party to be more likely to survive when the coalition of support for the government is stable. This is a function of the distribution of policy preferences among parties in the government. Specifically, we expect the prime minister's party to stay in power longer when it leads a government with policy incentives for staying together: the coalition is a minimum connected winning coalition, the bargaining power of the median party is high, and the coalition includes a core party.[33] Second, we expect survival to be a function of the bargaining environment. The prime minister's party should face greater risk of losing power as the dimensionality of the issue space increases and if the parliamentary party with the greatest bargaining power is not part of the government.

Third, we expect the type of electoral system to affect the duration of the tenure of the prime minister's party. As Powell and Vanberg (2000: 392) show, majoritarian and proportional representation systems differ in how changes in electoral preferences translate into changes in the parties in power. In particular, they show how, via the disproportionality generated by single-member districts, small shifts in voter preferences can translate into dramatic swings in the fortunes of political parties. Proportional representation systems, in contrast, should show much less volatility in party seat shares in response to small electoral shifts. Consequently, we would expect lower risk to the prime minister's party's survival from one election to the next in proportional representation systems.

Fourth, we expect the likelihood of survival of a prime minister's party to increase with the number of days until an election must be called. Lupia and Strom (2008: 75) argue that a coalition's value to its members decays as it approaches the formal limit on its tenure. Finally, we expect the survival of the prime minister's party to depend on macroeconomic conditions. Specifically, survival should be inversely related to the level of inflation and unemployment.

[33] A "core" party is stable because its ideal point is a core point in the two-dimensional legislative policy space (Schofield 1993).

The technical appendix to this chapter provides further justification for the selection of these factors and description of their measurement.

In this forecasting model, the AGs use the status of these factors in the domestic setting, based on the historical impact of these factors on government survival in west European postwar democracies, to estimate the survival prospects of the incumbent government. It is important to note that this model of AG forecasting is not meant to imply that AGs are conscious of this specific theoretical literature or actually conduct statistical analyses of survival data from multiple countries. The causal arguments capture basic intuitions that a sophisticated observer of domestic politics in western Europe would plausibly hold. For example, journalists and political commentators can appreciate that some parties are positioned such that they are attractive coalition partners or that the policy basis for coalition bargaining is more or less complex. And a nonexpert observer could certainly appreciate the differences in the historical experiences of different cabinets (e.g., contrast the stability of the Christian Democratic Union governments in Germany in the 1950s with the rapid turnover of governments in Fourth Republic France) and use that to draw inferences about how institutional factors might influence stability.

To translate these causal arguments into specific expectations about the likely survival of the prime minister's party to the end of the AG's term, we first estimate a statistical model (survival model) that regresses the tenure of past prime ministers' parties on the factors described earlier. Specifically, we amended the best currently available data set of cabinet survival and relevant covariates – the Comparative Parliamentary Data Archive (Strom, Mueller, and Bergman 2008) – by replacing the dates of cabinet origin and termination with the dates of origin and termination of the tenure of the prime minister's party in each country in the postwar period. This data set consists of cabinets of seventeen western European countries (including all of the EU member states in our study) from the end of World War II to 2000.[34] The statistical inferences are therefore based on the average effects of these variables (e.g., the inflation rate) on the prime minister's party's survival across these countries and over time.

For each AG in each year of his/her term, we estimate a survival model only for the cabinets in the data set that had been in power or were holding power up to that year. Thus, the estimated effects of these factors on survival estimates are restricted to only the history that the AG could have observed. For each model, we then generate the predicted baseline survival for the

---

[34] Greece, Portugal, and Spain enter the data set after democratization in the 1970s, and France enters the data set with the Fifth Republic.

108 Preliminary considerations: designing a control for the legal merits

TABLE 4.1 *Summary Statistics*

	Mean	Standard deviation	Min.	Max.
Advocate General Opinion for Plaintiff	0.51	0.50	0	1
Home Government Brief for the Plaintiff	−0.01	0.25	−1	1
End of Term	0.17	0.38	0	1
Expected Government Survival (retrospective)	0.41	0.37	0	1
Expected Government Survival (sophisticated)	0.77	0.26	0.01	1
Age (centered)	0	6.39	−15	16

Comment: N = 7,188.

national attributes of the AG's nation. This provides survival rate estimates for all possible lengths of tenure. We select the rate that corresponds to the days left in the AG's term and assign that to the AG as the likelihood the prime minister's party will survive in office to the end of the AG's term.[35] The resulting variable, *Expected Government Survival (sophisticated)*, ranges from 0 to 1 and increases with the likelihood of survival.

To test hypothesis 4 via these two forecasting models, we create interaction terms between each of these forecasting variables and *Home Government Brief for Plaintiff*. The expectation is that the interaction term will have a positive coefficient because the influence of the home government on the AG's opinion should increase with the likelihood the current home government will be in power at the date of reappointment. Table 4.1 reports descriptive statistics on each of the variables used in the analysis.

IV. ANALYSIS

We estimate these hypothesized relationships with probit models of the AG's position on each legal issue. We use the complete data set of ECJ rulings on legal issues from 1960 through 1999 across all procedures.

In both models, we include the net number of government briefs for the plaintiff as a control variable. This variable is defined as the number of government briefs (including the home government, if submitted) for the plaintiff

---

[35] We determine the number of days left in the AG's tenure by counting the days from the midpoint of the year of the AG opinion to the date of the end of term. For a comprehensive description of measurement and analysis used in these forecasts, see the technical appendix to this chapter.

on a legal issue minus those for the defendant.[36] This control is critical, given the empirical concern at the heart of this chapter. Recall that this chapter is motivated by a concern that third-party governments are more likely to submit briefs on behalf of a litigant if that litigant's position benefits from stronger legal merits.[37] We have proposed the AG's position as a control for the balance of legal merits. Thus, we would expect a home government's brief and the AG's opinion to be positively correlated even in the absence of political influence. Consequently, if we simply estimate the bivariate relationship between the AG's position and the home government position, we may overestimate the political influence of the home government. To minimize this problem, we include the net government briefs as a control.[38]

Table 4.2 reports the results of two statistical models, one each for the two different forecasting models employed to test hypothesis 4. The most important finding, and the most difficult to discern from the table, is that we do not find strong support for an unconditional effect (hypothesis 1). That is, we do not find a consistent effect of home government briefs on AG opinions, and under reasonable conditions there is no statistically significant effect. We return to this point later, when we provide a more intuitive interpretation of the substantive and statistical significance of the variables.

Turning to the conditional hypotheses, we find support for hypothesis 4 based on the simple retrospective forecasting model (presented in model 1), but not the more sophisticated forecasting model (presented in model 2). As the AG increases his/her forecast that the current prime minister's party will survive to the end of the AG's term, the AG's opinion is more likely to comport with the position supported by the home government's brief. In that model, we also find support for hypothesis 2. As an AG's age increases, the relationship between the position favored by the home government brief and the AG opinion weakens. We find no support for hypothesis 3.

---

[36] This is not the same measure as the *Third-Party Support for Plaintiff* variable used in Chapter 5. Here, the briefs are not weighted by GDP, and the net calculation always includes a home government brief if one is submitted. We do not weight the briefs because the justification for the measure is that a government (regardless of economic size) is more likely to file for the side favored by the legal merits. We have no reason to believe that some governments are more likely to discern the legal merits correctly, and thus have no rationale for weighting.

[37] Absent that concern, we do not need a control for the legal merits to test the Political Sensitivity Hypothesis.

[38] Of course, we expect it to also communicate critical information about the likelihood of compliance with a ruling against a government, but we expect the AG (unlike the Court) to ignore that information. We discuss this issue earlier in the chapter. In particular, Ritter (2005: 761) argues that concerns with member-state compliance figure in the Court's – but *not* the AG's – consideration of the case.

TABLE 4.2 *Probit analysis of Advocate General opinion supporting the plaintiff*

	Model 1	Model 2
Home Government Brief for Plaintiff	0.330***	0.401*
	(0.111)	(0.224)
Net Government Briefs for Plaintiff	0.150***	0.148***
	(0.020)	(0.020)
Age (centered)	−0.003	−0.004*
	(0.003)	(0.003)
Age (centered)* Home Government Brief for Plaintiff	−0.019**	−0.013
	(0.012)	(0.011)
End of Term	0.024	−0.040
	(0.047)	(0.051)
End of Term* Home Government Brief for Plaintiff	−0.099	−0.101
	(0.165)	(0.185)
Expected Government Survival (retrospective)	−0.141***	
	(0.048)	
Expected Government Survival (retrospective)* Home Government Brief for Plaintiff	0.262*	
	(0.187)	
Expected Government Survival (sophisticated)		−0.123
		(0.074)
Expected Government Survival (sophisticated)* Home Government Brief for Plaintiff		0.053
		(0.299)
Constant	0.110***	0.144***
	(0.027)	(0.056)
N	7,188	7,188

Comment: Robust standard errors reported in parentheses.
***$p < 0.01$, **$p < 0.05$, *$p < 0.10$, one-tailed test.

The substantive interpretation of these results is complicated by the presence of interaction terms. To address this problem, we provide plots of the effect (probit coefficient) of the key variables with 95 percent confidence intervals (Figures 4.2 and 4.3) across the observed range of the condition of interest based on the results in model 1. We see in Figure 4.2 that home government briefs have a positive and statistically significant effect for relatively young to average-aged AGs. However, this relationship declines sharply and falls to zero a few years above the average age of an AG. Figure 4.3 plots the probit coefficient and confidence intervals for the effect of a home government brief for the plaintiff across the range of survival rates generated according to the simple retrospective forecasting model. This figure shows that the impact of

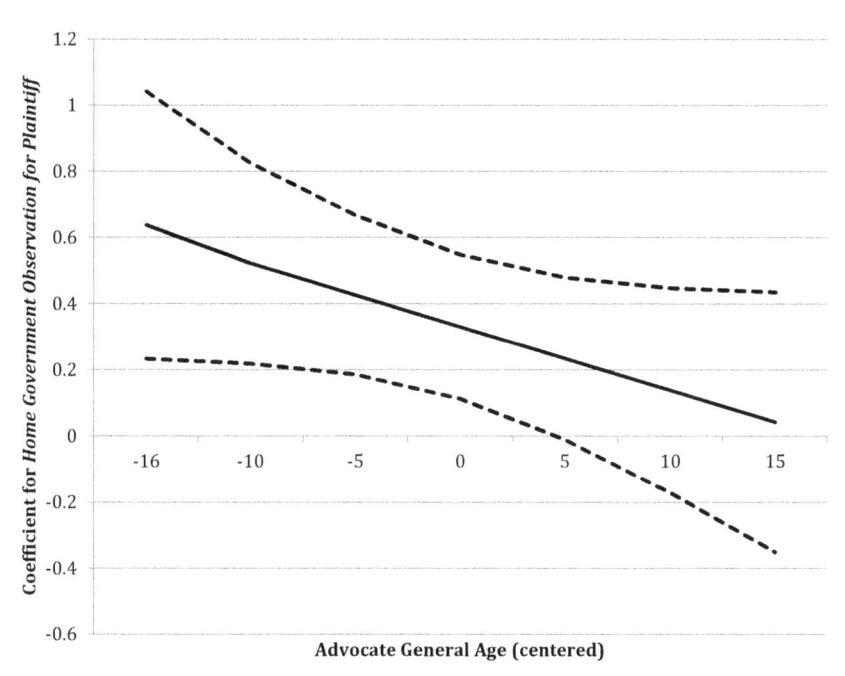

FIGURE 4.2 The effect of the age of the Advocate General on the relationship between the AG opinion and the home government brief

a home government brief on an AG opinion increases with the likelihood of survival. The effect is positive and statistically different from zero across the full range of survival rates. Thus, between these two figures, we show that home government briefs do not have a consistent effect on AG opinions and that, for older AGs, the effect is close to or equal to zero. These findings are inconsistent with hypothesis 1.

What is the substantive impact of a home government brief on the AG's opinion as age and expected survival of the prime minister's party vary? Figure 4.4 helps answer that question.[39] This figure plots the predicted probability of an AG opinion favoring the plaintiff as a function of (1) whether the home government submitted a brief for the plaintiff, (2) the age of the AG, and (3) the likelihood of survival of the prime minister's party. The relevant baseline scenario here is the probability that an AG with average characteristics in terms of age, stage of term, and expected survival of the prime minister's party writes a pro-plaintiff opinion when the home government submits no brief. That probability is 0.51 and is presented in the first row of the figure, along with

[39] Again, these interpretations are based on the results presented in Model 1 of Table 4.2.

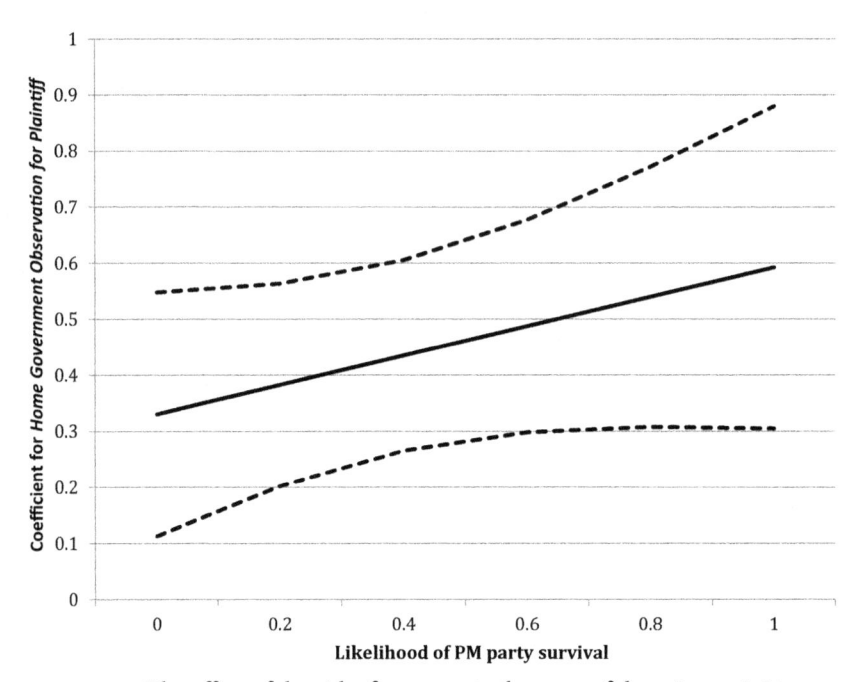

FIGURE 4.3 The effect of the risk of turnover in the party of the prime minister on the relationship between the Advocate General opinion and the home government brief

its 95 percent confidence interval. All else equal, a change from this condition to the home government submitting a pro-plaintiff brief is associated with an increase in the probability of a pro-plaintiff AG opinion from 0.51 to 0.68. The largest total effect of a pro-plaintiff home government brief (i.e., assume the youngest observed AG age and a 100 percent estimated likelihood of government survival) is associated with an increase in the probability of a pro-plaintiff AG opinion to 0.80. At the other extreme, a home government brief for the plaintiff has effectively no impact. An AG with the least responsive characteristics (highest observed AG age and zero likelihood of survival) has a 0.52 probability of finding for the plaintiff when the home government submits a brief for the plaintiff. This probability is statistically indistinguishable from the baseline probability (0.51).

Summing up, the results do not support hypothesis 1. AGs are not uniformly responsive to home government briefs. They are often positively responsive, but the strength of that responsiveness varies considerably and is effectively zero in some contexts. The results do support two conditional hypotheses. Younger AGs are more responsive than are older AGs. Additionally, AGs that forecast that the current prime minister's party will be in power at the end of their

Analysis

[Figure: Forest plot showing probability of pro-plaintiff AG opinion]

- NO HOME GOVERNMENT BRIEF
  - Mean survival, mean AG age
- PRO-PLAINTIFF HOME GOVERNMENT BRIEF
  - Mean survival, mean AG age
  - Minimum survival, maximum AG age
  - Maximum survival, minimum AG age

x-axis: 0.3, 0.4, 0.5, 0.6, 0.7, 0.8, 0.9, 1.0 — Probability of pro-plaintiff AG opinion

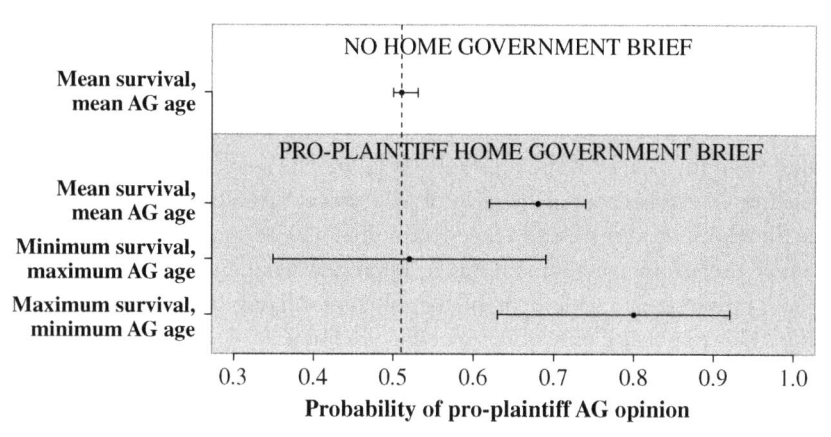

FIGURE 4.4 The relationship between the AG opinion and the home government brief for various combinations of AG age and expected survival of home government

Comment: The figure presents the estimated likelihood of a pro-plaintiff AG opinion (and its 95% confidence interval) for different conditions related to the position of the home government and the AG's personal and political context. The estimates are based on simulations conducted with CLARIFY.

term are more responsive than are AGs that forecast a change in government. Put more generally, the results indicate that the AG is more likely to write opinions supporting the home government's position on a legal issue when the home government is more valuable to the AG's future career goals. Thus, this finding indicates that AG opinions that agree with the position of the AG's home government's briefs can be suspected of political influence when the AG has incentives to be responsive to home government interests.[40]

This is an interesting set of findings in their own right. The AG has typically been depicted as apolitical and unresponsive to the interests of the home government. Even the rare observer who hinted at home government sensitivity had not developed a full argument about this bias or demonstrated any systematic effects. Thus, these results are both novel and substantively interesting for our understanding of the behavior of the AG.[41]

---

[40] Simple agreement between the AG and the home government is not definitive evidence of political influence. As discussed previously, such agreement could also reflect a shared emphasis on the legal merits of the parties to the case. To minimize the chance this latter consideration accounts for observed agreement, we included the control for net government briefs in the regressions. Thus, our analysis implicitly assumes that agreement between AG and home government, after controlling for net government briefs, indicates political influence.

[41] Of course, we must be cautious in this interpretation. As discussed earlier, we have chosen an empirical strategy that helps maximize the chances of finding evidence of political pressure.

That said, the primary reason for this analysis was to identify any home country bias in the AG's ruling so that we could assess the viability of the AG's position as a proxy for the legal merits. Specifically, we were concerned that a home country bias would taint a significant portion of the AG opinions and that this influence would be substantively large. The results do not paint such a picture. In part because of the rarity of AGs serving on cases of direct relevance to their home government, AGs generally do not write opinions on legal issues where their home government has an interest at stake. Furthermore, even in those rare instances with a potential conflict of interest, our results show that the AG is responsive only under specific conditions.

These findings, in combination with the conventional accounts of the AG's opinion, are consistent with a depiction of the AG's opinion as largely a reflection of the balance of the legal merits. However, the findings raise two further empirical questions related to that depiction. First, the results imply that the level of agreement between the AG's opinion and the rulings of the Court should differ depending on whether the AG faces a potential conflict of interest. We elaborate on and test this argument in the next section.

The second empirical question is whether and how to use the AG's opinion as a proxy for the merits in light of the limited but real home country bias. Ideally, we would like to retain as many rulings as possible but also ensure the AG provides a sufficiently good control for the legal merits. In practice, this involves trade-offs between those two objectives. We address these issues in the last section of the chapter.

ECJ–AG agreement and the presence of home government briefs

This chapter is motivated by a concern that the legal merits of a case in part inform the position favored by both the ECJ and the member-state government briefs. The theoretical and empirical analysis in this chapter has focused on determining whether we can use the AG position as a proxy to control for the legal merits. It appears that the answer is yes. All extant evidence indicates that the AG position generally is a reflection of the legal merits, and we find that the AG position rarely is contaminated by political conflicts of interest. Before stopping, we seek one final piece of affirmative, although admittedly circumstantial, evidence to validate the claim that the AG position reflects the legal merits. Specifically, if AGs really are primarily providing high-quality opinions based on the legal merits of the case, and the ECJ decides cases (at least in part) based on the legal merits, we should find systematic patterns of agreement between ECJ rulings and the AGs' opinions. Further, because the ECJ does not have a motive to respond to the AG's home government brief in the way the AG does (and was demonstrated to do), this relationship should attenuate when the AG is responsive to a conflict of interest.[42] Evidence of this conditional relationship would help validate our characterization of the AG opinion as generally a good proxy for the legal merits.

Testing this hypothesis requires identifying "suspect" AG opinions. These are opinions in which the AG agrees with the home government brief. Those are straightforward to identify. Of those opinions, we need to distinguish opinions for which the AG was sensitive to home government interests from those for which the AG was not. The analysis in the previous section provides guidance here. Recall that sensitivity to home government interests should decrease with age and increase with the likelihood of the incumbent government surviving to the end of the AG's term. But the analysis did not provide any strict criteria for distinguishing conditions in which the AG was likely sensitive to the home government's preferences from conditions in which the AG was likely insensitive. To distinguish these conditions, we determine appropriate age and survival values empirically. Specifically, we estimated the effect of home government briefs on AG opinions for subsets of the AG opinions based on the AG's age and the likelihood of government survival. The goal was to use these characteristics to find a subset of AG opinions for which the effect of home government briefs was effectively zero – that is, the AG opinions were not responsive.[43] We then confirmed that the remaining set of AG opinions was responsive to home government briefs and used that subset as the group of AGs we consider sensitive to home government influence.

Table 4.3 presents the results of the analyses on the two subsets of AG opinions. The key difference between the results for the two models is the coefficient for *Home Government Brief for Plaintiff*. In the "sensitive" subset of AG opinions (model 2), the coefficient is positive and highly statistically significant. This is what we would expect. For the "insensitive" subset of AG opinions (model 1), we cannot reject the hypothesis that this coefficient is zero or less at conventional levels of statistical significance.[44]

With this distinction, we can return to the main empirical question: is the level of agreement between ECJ rulings and AG opinions lower for suspect

---

[42] Of course, according to the Political Sensitivity Hypothesis, we expect the ECJ to be sensitive to the balance of third-party government briefs, which could include a home government. But we do not expect the ECJ to pay any special attention to a brief from the home government of the AG compared to the rest of the governments' briefs.

[43] We were conservative in our determination of the set of unresponsive AG opinions, erring on the side of including AG opinions in the responsive set based on their age and the likelihood of government survival. This should make it harder to find the hypothesized effect.

[44] The p value on this coefficient is >0.20 (two-tailed test) and >0.10 (one-tailed test).

TABLE 4.3 *Probit analysis of Advocate General opinion supporting the plaintiff*

	Model 1	Model 2
	Insensitive subset	Sensitive subset
Home Government Brief for Plaintiff	0.177	0.480***
	(0.140)	(0.090)
Net Government Briefs for Plaintiff	0.181***	0.141***
	(0.047)	(0.023)
Constant	−0.021	0.080***
	(0.037)	(0.020)
N	1,657	5,531

Comment: Robust standard errors reported in parentheses.
***$p < 0.01$, **$p < 0.05$, *$p < 0.10$, one-tailed test. The insensitive subset consists of AGs with Age (centered) > 11 or Expected Government Survival = 0. The sensitive subset consists of AGs with Age (centered) < 12 and Expected Government Survival > 0.

AG opinions than for nonsuspect AG opinions? To test this, we created a dummy variable, *Suspect AG Opinion,* which is coded 1 for opinions that agree with the home government's brief and that were written by AGs in the sensitive subset. Two hundred fifty-two legal issues featured an AG opinion that met these conditions. *Suspect AG Opinion* is interacted with *AG Opinion for Plaintiff.* We then regress *ECJ Ruling for the Plaintiff* on this interaction term and its component parts. If the ECJ has lower agreement with "suspect" AG opinions that have potential conflicts of interest, this interaction term should be negative, indicating that suspect AG opinions have a weaker agreement with ECJ rulings than do AG opinions otherwise.

Table 4.4 presents results of a probit model designed to test this hypothesis. The data analyzed are our complete data set of ECJ rulings from 1960 through 1999 across all procedures. Interpretation of the statistical results is complicated because the model includes an interaction term and its component parts.[45] Recall that *AG Opinion for the Plaintiff* is coded 1 when the opinion favors the plaintiff and 0 when it favors the defendant. This means we

---

[45] We include the component parts because this ensures that the interaction effect is capturing the intended effect (Brambor, Clark, and Golder 2006). The models also include a full set of covariates to capture a variety of factors that influence ECJ rulings and could be (at least incidentally) related to the AG's opinion on a legal issue: the position of the Commission, the net GDP weighted number of third-party briefs for the plaintiff, whether a government was a litigant, and an interaction between the net GDP weighted number of third-party government briefs for the plaintiff and whether a government was a litigant in the case. Chapter 5 provides the justification for these controls and a description of their measurement.

TABLE 4.4 *Probit analysis of an ECJ ruling for the plaintiff*

	Model 1
Advocate General Opinion for Plaintiff	1.91***
	(0.05)
Suspect AG opinion	0.21*
	(0.16)
Suspect AG Opinion*	−0.55***
Advocate General Opinion for Plaintiff	(0.23)
Constant	−1.08***
	(0.54)
N	7,187

Comment: The model includes controls for the position of the Commission, the net GDP weighted number of third-party briefs for the plaintiff, whether a government was a litigant, and an interaction between the net GDP weighted number of third-party briefs for the plaintiff and whether the government was a litigant in the case. Chapter 5 provides the justification for these controls and a description of their measurement. Robust standard errors reported in parentheses.
***$p < 0.01$, **$p < 0.05$, *$p < 0.10$, one-tailed test.

have four conditions to consider based on possible combinations of the component parts of the interaction term. We provide a thorough interpretation of these conditions in the technical appendix. The "punch lines," however, are that when AG opinions are not suspect, those opinions strongly agree with the ECJ ruling, but when AG opinions are suspect, the strength of this relationship declines.[46] This change is substantively meaningful, with the ECJ ruling about 25 percent more likely to agree with the AG opinion when the opinion is not suspect.

These results are consistent with the presumption that the AG position typically reflects the legal merits of the case. The AG opinions and ECJ rulings generally agree, but in the relatively rare instances when the AG position is potentially compromised by political influence, that agreement weakens. Thus, this analysis provides some additional circumstantial evidence

---

[46] One possible alternative interpretation is that suspect opinions are less consistent with the legal merits because younger AGs, due to inexperience, are more error-prone in their legal analysis. Because relatively young AGs are in the responsive subset, the interaction effect could be capturing this inexperience effect. To check on that interpretation, we also estimated a model in which we interacted the AG's opinion with the length of the AG's tenure at the Court, which should be a good measure of the AG's experience. That interaction effect does not support the alternative interpretation.

that the AG position, when not influenced by conflicts of interest, can be used as a proxy for the legal merits of the case.

Finally, it is important to note that, although suspect AG opinions had weaker agreement with ECJ rulings than did nonsuspect opinions, they still showed substantial agreement. One can interpret this attenuated relationship to mean that political influence does not completely dominate AG opinions at the expense of the legal merits when AGs face incentives to respond to their home government. The results of the analysis in the previous section are also consistent with this interpretation of the AG opinion. We found that agreement between the AG and the home government was greater when conditions were conducive to responsiveness, but we did not demonstrate that the position favored by the home government was contrary to the legal merits. Thus, in some of those instances, an AG position consonant with that of the home government could reflect political influence and/or the legal merits. Indeed, given that we expect governments to be particularly compelled to submit briefs when the legal merits serve their political interests (see the introduction to this chapter), we would be surprised if this did not happen. Consequently, we should not conclude that, under conditions ripe for political influence, AG rulings always deviate from the legal merits.

V. THE OPINION OF THE ADVOCATE GENERAL AS A CONTROL FOR THE LEGAL MERITS

The practical goal of this chapter was to examine whether the position taken by Advocates General in their opinions could serve as a proxy for the litigant who was favored by the legal merits. This seemed prima facie plausible based on the conventional description of the AG and that AG's opinion. But we were concerned about potential political influences on the AG's opinion that would cause it to divert from the legal merits. Our analysis generally confirms that the AG's opinion is a reasonable proxy for the merits because political influence is typically not a concern. However, we did determine that political considerations likely contaminate the AG's opinion under particular conditions. These conditions are rare; we isolated 252 suspect AG opinions in the data set. Under those conditions, the AG's position may not provide a good control for the legal merits of the case. The question then is how best to account for those conditions.

We propose two alternatives. These alternatives differ along two important dimensions regarding their value as controls. First, we obviously would like to minimize the risk that we include rulings for which the AG opinion deviates from the position favored by the legal merits. Second, we want to retain as many rulings as possible for the analysis of the Political Sensitivity Hypothesis.

The first option would be to ignore the contamination issue. As we showed earlier, only a small fraction of the rulings involve a suspect AG opinion. And, even in those cases, the AG may still write an opinion that comports with the legal merits. Recall, one should not assume that the home government position is typically at odds with the position favored by the legal merits. The effect of any political influence could be to push the AG toward the position favored by the legal merits. Consequently, under this option, our test would likely include some rulings for which we would not have a good control for the legal merits, but the number of such rulings (no more than 252 legal issues) is a very small share of the rulings analyzed in the next chapter.

The second option is to eliminate all rulings involving a suspect AG opinion from our test. This option provides much better insurance against the risk of contamination of AG opinions. But, as discussed in the conclusion to the previous section, this likely includes the elimination of rulings for which the AG opinion reflects the legal merits. In addition, this rule would eliminate rulings of particular importance to the analysis of the Political Sensitivity Hypothesis. Rulings with suspect AG opinions, by definition, involve government briefs (at least from the home government). Such rulings are obviously relevant to the analysis which focuses on the effect of variation in the number and disposition of government briefs.

Ideally, we would find a compromise between these two strategies. However, with no such compromise available and no clear reason to favor one over the other, we employ both strategies. Obviously, we will have much greater confidence in our hypothesis if it survives tests under both approaches to controlling for the legal merits.

VI. CONCLUSION

This chapter provides an important preliminary step in testing our first hypothesis from the theoretical model presented in Chapter 2. Our first hypothesis states that the Court is more likely to rule against a defendant government as the net number of third-party briefs filed against the defendant government increases. We are concerned that the hypothesized relationship could also reflect the balance of the legal merits in a case, with the party favored by the balance of third-party briefs also enjoying a superior position based on the legal merits. Consequently, this chapter focused on developing a strategy for controlling for the balance of the legal merits in a case. Specifically, we examined whether the position of the Advocate General (AG) opinion on the legal issue could serve as a reasonable control.

Our review of the extant literature and our statistical analysis supports the use of the AG's opinion for that purpose. Past studies of the AG, both of the institution and the character and impact of its opinion, indicate that the AG opinion reflects the legal merits of the case. Our quantitative analysis examined whether there were conditions under which the AG's opinion might deviate from that norm. We developed and tested empirically several arguments about why the AG's opinion might deviate from the legal merits and found that when the AG has incentives to respond to the home government's interests and the government takes a position on the legal issue, the AG opinion is likely to concur with the government's position. Such conditions, however, are rare. AGs commonly are not assigned to cases salient to their national governments, and AGs are not routinely politically sensitive to their home governments. Thus, we can safely consider the AG opinion as void of such political influence for most rulings. In the next chapter, we therefore proceed to analyze the Political Sensitivity Hypothesis using the AG opinion as a control for the legal merits. We do this in two different ways, designed to ensure the results are robust to different assumptions about the effect of political influence on AG opinions.

We conclude by discussing an important contribution of this chapter beyond the practical issue of identifying a control for the legal merits. Our discussion and analysis of how AGs' contexts affect their political responsiveness are novel and potentially relevant to a wide variety of other settings. In many democratic political systems, elected officials have the authority to appoint and reappoint a variety of officials whose terms end after that of the appointing officials. For example, the Federal Reserve chairman in the United States is appointed to a four-year renewable term that often concludes after the appointing president must face reelection or has served his final term in office. The leadership of the EU Commission, appointed by EU member-state governments, serves a five-year term that generally ends after at least some of the appointing governments have faced an election. Judges on the Spanish Constitutional Court serve nine-year nonrenewable terms. In all of these instances, appointees have career interests in pleasing the government that will be in power at the end of their term. But this requires forecasting who will hold office at that time. Thus, the incentives to respond to the interests of that current government are similar to those outlined previously with respect to the AG.

We are not the first to address this issue. For example, Helmke (2002) explicitly considers how judges adapt their behavior to the expected survival of the incumbent government. However, to our knowledge, the extant literature provides no theoretical or empirical guidance regarding how to best model this forecasting exercise. Scholars have posited and examined political influences on some of these officials, particularly the Federal Reserve chairman. For example, Chang (2003) demonstrates the effect of the partisanship of the appointing president and Senate on the positions taken by the members of the Fed and on the policies they adopt. Others have argued that Federal Reserve chairmen are sensitive to the interests of the current president and will engage in a political business cycle.[47] But these models do not engage the strategic concerns about the identity of the future appointing government. Thus, the forecasting models developed here are potentially valuable to the broader literature on the responsiveness of appointed officials to the interest of elected officials in democratic systems.

TECHNICAL APPENDIX: THE CODING OF THE ADVOCATE GENERAL'S FORECAST OF EXPECTED GOVERNMENT SURVIVAL

1. *The "retrospective" measure*

The "retrospective" measure is designed to capture the likelihood the party currently holding the position of prime minister in the nation from which the AG was appointed will be in that position at the end of the Advocate General's term. This requires identifying the length of time from the date when the AG wrote the opinion to the end of the AG's term. The term is six years, beginning on the appointment date, which is specified in the following sources: *Official Journal of the European Communities, Series C* (various years), the *Synopsis of the Work of the Court of Justice of the European Communities* (various years), and Burrows and Greaves (2007). We do not know the exact date of the AG opinion, only the year of the publication of the ruling in which it appears. We determine the number of days left in the AG's tenure by counting the days from the midpoint of the year of the AG opinion to the date of the end of term.

We then create a life table for each country and each year. The life table reports how likely that prime minister will survive past future points in time. The life table is generated based on the survival length of prime minister parties in the AG's country from the first post–World War II government up to the year in question. We calculated this with Stata software using the procedure "ltable." The historical data on prime minister party survival are from the Comparative Parliamentary Data Archive (data set: CII-2007Final.dta from

---

[47] See Chang (2003: 6) for a review of this literature.

the website: www.erdda.se/index.php/projects/cpd/data-archive). This data set is created by Strom, Mueller, and Bergman (2008). We modified the data when necessary to reflect changes in the prime minister's party, not changes in government.

Based on the life table, we identified the probability of the current prime minister's party's survival from the beginning of its tenure to the number of days left in the AG's term. Note that this means the starting date for the prime minister's party changes during the term of an AG if there is a change in power. This probability was then assigned to the AG for the year in question.

2. The "sophisticated" measure

The "sophisticated" measure is the same as the retrospective measure in how it determines the days remaining in an AG's term. The key difference is in the forecasting of the expected survival of the party holding the position of prime minister in the country that appointed the AG.

For each year from 1960 to 1999, we estimate a Cox proportional hazard model using data from all of the west European democracies from the end of World War II up to the specific year (i.e., all previous). The data are from the same source as in the retrospective measure described earlier. The hazard model estimates the impact of the following covariates on the duration of the prime minister's party's tenure: (1) macroeconomic conditions (inflation and unemployment at start of tenure), (2) policy stability of governing coalition (whether the government includes a "core" party and whether the government consists of parties that represent a minimum connected winning coalition), (3) the difficulty of the bargaining environment (the number of effective issue dimensions and whether the party with the maximum bargaining power is in the government), (4) the electoral laws (list proportional representation – list PR – or not), and (5) the electoral cycle (the number of days left before an election must be called). See Strom, Mueller, and Bergman (2008) for definition of these variables and their theoretical motivation. We expect duration to be shorter under poor economic conditions, in a difficult bargaining environment, with an unstable coalition, and with majoritarian electoral laws. The covariates generally have the expected effects across the models estimated (e.g., the prime minister's tenure is shorter when the government is not a minimum winning connected coalition).

We use the estimates of the model for each year to forecast the probability of survival of the prime minister's party in each of the member states with an AG in that year. We use the parameter estimates from the model in each year to generate survival probabilities conditional on the actual value of the variables (e.g., whether the electoral system is list PR) for the nation in question. We do this with Stata software and the procedure "stcox" and the postestimation option "gen" to create a variable with survival probabilities. The output provides probabilities of survival for different durations. We select the survival probability associated with the sum of duration of the current prime minister's party and the days left in the AG's tenure and assign that to the AG in that year.[48] We then assign that probability to the AG from that country for that year.

INTERPRETATION OF PROBIT ANALYSIS IN TABLE 4.4

The interpretation of the results presented in Table 4.4 is complicated by the interaction terms, which are the combination of two dummy variables. Recall that *AG Opinion for the Plaintiff* is coded 1 when the opinion favors the plaintiff and 0 when it favors the defendant. This means we have four conditions to consider based on possible combinations of the component parts of the interaction term. When the AG opinion supports the defendant and the AG opinion is not suspect, all three variables are at zero, and so the combined effect of those variables on the likelihood of a pro-plaintiff ruling is zero. When the AG opinion supports the plaintiff and the AG opinion is not suspect, the variable *Suspect AG Opinion* and the interaction terms are at zero, so the combined effect of these variables is simply the coefficient on *AG Opinion for the Plaintiff* (1.91). All else equal, this condition increases the likelihood of an ECJ ruling for the plaintiff relative to a nonsuspect AG opinion for the defendant.[49]

Now we consider the two conditions when the AG opinion is suspect. If the AG opinion supports the plaintiff, then the combined effect is the sum of the three coefficients (1.91 + −0.55 + 0.21 = 1.57). This is smaller than 1.91 and thus is associated with a smaller likelihood of a pro-plaintiff ECJ ruling than

---

[48] The choice of dates is complicated by the fact that we assume the AG opinion date is the midpoint of the year of the ruling. Thus, the duration of prime minister's party cannot be exactly matched to the timing of the opinion. This is particularly problematic if the government changed hands during the year of an opinion. We use the following rule: if more than one government formed before September 1 of a year, then the one that accounted for the plurality of those nine months is the government of record. We chose September 1 because we assume any ruling after that date in that year was actually written before September 1. For setting the maximum number of days before an election, the reference date is the midpoint of the current year.

[49] This difference is statistically significant ($p < 0.01$, one-tailed test).

when the AG opinion is not suspect.[50] Finally, when the AG opinion favors the defendant and is suspect, the combined effect is simply the coefficient for *Suspect AG Opinion* (0.21).[51] This is obviously larger than zero, the combined effect when the AG's opinion for the defendant was not suspect. Thus, all else equal, the ECJ is less likely to rule for the defendant in the presence of a pro-defendant AG opinion when the AG opinion is suspect. Finally, it is important to note that these differences are substantively important. When the AG opinion is not suspect, a change in the AG's opinion from support for the defendant to support for the plaintiff is associated with an increase from 0.14 to 0.80 in the likelihood of the ECJ ruling for the plaintiff.[52] When the AG opinion is suspect, the same change is associated with an increase from 0.20 to 0.69 in the likelihood of the ECJ ruling for the plaintiff. The latter increase is 25 percent smaller than the former, which is what should hold if AG–ECJ agreement is driven by the legal merits.

[50] This difference in the coefficients (1.91 and 1.57) is statistically significant ($p = 0.02$, one-tailed test).
[51] This difference (0.21–0) is statistically significant at $p < 0.10$, one-tailed test.
[52] Predicted probabilities estimated by CLARIFY. All other variables assumed to be at their mean or median (for dichotomous variables).

5

The Political Sensitivity Hypothesis

Third-party briefs and European Court of Justice rulings

We now turn to testing the Political Sensitivity Hypothesis. The hypothesis specifies that the Court should be more likely to rule against a defendant government the more briefs filed against the government and the fewer briefs filed in support of it. As described in Chapter 3, the prediction is not relevant to all of the cases decided by the European Court of Justice (ECJ). In particular, government compliance must be at issue, and government noncompliance with an ECJ ruling must be possible. We defined the domain of cases that fit these criteria in Chapter 3. Within this domain, we can evaluate the prediction on a narrower or broader set of ECJ rulings. The narrower test maps onto the model and its predictions as closely as possible. Specifically, we consider only rulings with a government defendant. The broader test generalizes to a wider set of conditions under which threats of noncompliance should be present. In this chapter we address measurement issues related to testing the hypothesis. We then provide a statistical test of the hypothesis and examine the robustness of the statistical evidence in the face of a variety of alternative explanations.

I. MEASUREMENT

The dependent variable for all of the analyses is the ECJ panel's decision on the legal issue in a case. It is coded 1 if the ECJ decided the issue in favor of the plaintiff and 0 otherwise.[1] The key independent variable is based upon third-party government briefs. A third-party government is defined to be a government that is neither a litigant in the case nor the home government for a case arising through the preliminary ruling system.

---

[1] In very rare cases, the coder was unable to assign a value to the ECJ's position. That ruling was treated as a missing observation.

As described earlier, member-state governments can submit written amicus briefs that discuss proper disposition of the legal issues in a case. We take these written briefs to indicate the preferences of the member-state governments. This is consistent with all past work that has examined the relationship between government briefs and ECJ rulings (Cichowski 2007: 88; Kilroy 1999; Stone Sweet 2004: 43) as well as our model.[2]

We aggregate these briefs to capture the expected amount of support for either litigant. This involves summing the number of briefs for the plaintiff and for the defendant and subtracting the latter from the former, which gives the net third-party government briefs for the plaintiff. Before we sum the pro-plaintiff and pro-defendant briefs, we weight them so as to capture the differential importance of each government brief. To understand why, recall from Chapter 2 that the third parties were identical (each one draws a payoff for compliance b, c, or 0 from a common distribution). But that is clearly not the case in the European Union (EU). Some member states have greater economic and political importance than others do, and those that are more important have a greater impact on whether compliance is mutually beneficial for the EU as whole (i.e., those more important member states' relative costs and benefits, the b and c payoffs, will be larger). Thus, a third-party brief by the more politically and economically important governments should be weighted more heavily in our measure of net third-party briefs for the plaintiff.

We considered a variety of plausible weighting schemes to capture the political economic clout of member states. For example, one could weight by the member state's voting share in the Council of Ministers, gross domestic product (GDP), population, or total intra-EU trade. Here we weight by the log of the member state's GDP.[3] We chose logged GDP for three reasons. First, GDP is a good conceptual fit for the underlying concept we want to measure. The bigger the GDP, the larger the piece of the EU market that member state controls. Second, we can get reliable data for all countries across the period of the study. Trade numbers, for example, are not as consistently available and would need a strategy to deal with missing data. Finally, GDP is very highly correlated with these alternative measures. For example, third-party government briefs weighted by GDP and by voting share in the Council are correlated at over 0.97 in our data. We normalize the net weighted briefs by

---

[2] These studies did not use government briefs to test the prediction we evaluate here. They did examine how ECJ rulings related to the positions of individual member-state governments, the total number of such briefs, and whether the balance of briefs met the legislative threshold in the policy area under consideration.

[3] We log GDP to account for the skew in the distribution of GDPs across member states.

TABLE 5.1 *The effect of government briefs on likelihood of ECJ ruling for the plaintiff*

	Government is defendant	Government is litigant
Third-Party Support for Plaintiff	5.51***	5.27***
	(1.23)	(0.69)
Constant	0.75***	0.42***
	(0.04)	(0.03)
N	1,098	1,808

Comment: Robust standard errors reported in parentheses.
*** $p < 0.01$, ** $p < 0.05$, * $p < 0.10$, one-tailed test.

the sum of the logged EU member states' GDPs for that year to account for the changing size of the EU GDP over time.[4]

The resulting variable, *Third-Party Support For Plaintiff*, has the following properties for the subsets of data we analyze in this chapter. For rulings for which a government is a defendant, the variable ranges from −0.57 to 0.34, with a mean of −0.001 and a standard deviation of 0.048. For rulings with a government litigant, the variable ranges from −0.57 to 0.34, with a mean of 0.001 and a standard deviation of 0.059.

II. THE BASELINE ANALYSIS

The data set for the test of the Political Sensitivity Hypothesis is 1,098 rulings involving a government defendant and 1,808 rulings involving a government litigant. Recall, the empirical strategy is to test this prediction narrowly with the first set of rulings and more broadly with the second, larger set of rulings. Table 5.1 presents the results from two probit models of ECJ rulings. We report robust standard errors, clustered to account for correlation in errors across legal issues in a case. Column 1 presents the results of the narrow analysis.[5] The results are consistent with our expectation. *Third-Party Support For Plaintiff* is positively related to the likelihood the ECJ rules for the plaintiff. The standard error indicates that we can easily reject the hypothesis that this coefficient

---

[4] If we did not normalize by GDP over time, comparisons could be problematic. For example, if Germany's GDP grew between two years, its relative importance in the case could increase or decrease depending on whether the EU's Total GDP grew proportionally by more.

[5] Infringement and preliminary rulings account for 1,085 of 1,098 rulings. The remaining rulings involved cases brought against member states for failure to fulfill obligations via Articles 170 and 171 (EC [European Community]), Article 141 Euratom (European Atomic Energy Community), and Article 95(3) EEC (European Economic Community).

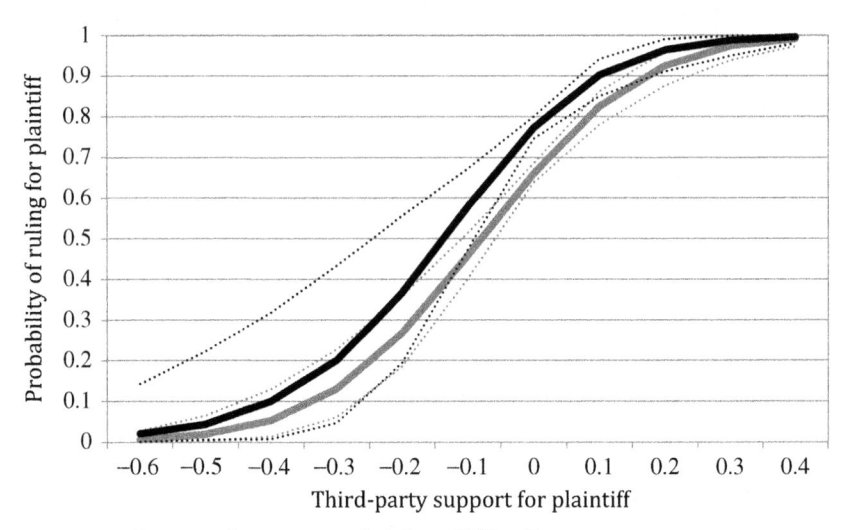

FIGURE 5.1 Impact of government briefs on ECJ rulings

Comment: The figure plots the predicted probability of an ECJ ruling for the plaintiff at different levels of *Third-Party Support For Plaintiff*. The gray line plots this relationship for rulings in which a national government was the defendant. The black line refers to rulings in which a government was a litigant. The dotted lines indicate the 95 percent confidence interval. We used CLARIFY software to generate these predicted values based on the statistical models reported in Table 5.1.

is zero or negative in value. The results of the broader test are presented in column 2 of Table 5.1. This analysis adds 710 rulings to those included in the first analysis as a result of the addition of annulment rulings and preliminary rulings in which the government was the plaintiff.[6] The results from these data are also consistent with expectations: the ECJ is more likely to rule for the plaintiff as the net number of GDP weighted briefs for the plaintiff increases. In the remainder of the chapter, we refer to these findings as the baseline results.

Figure 5.1 illustrates the substantive effect of *Third-Party Support For Plaintiff* on rulings based on the statistical models in Table 5.1. The figure plots the likelihood of a ruling for the plaintiff for different levels of third-party government support for the plaintiff. The x axis of the figure represents the observed range of variation in net weighted government third-party briefs in our data. The figure shows that, moving from the lowest to the highest observed value

---

[6] We exclude actions brought by governments that likely do not involve compliance issues; for example, actions brought against the Commission for failure to act (Article 175 [EC] actions). Such rulings are relatively rare (e.g., our data set included three rulings on actions for failure to act).

of net weighted government briefs for the plaintiff, the probability of a ruling for the plaintiff shifts from 0 to 1.0. This is obviously a dramatic shift. A more modest shift in *Third-Party Support For Plaintiff* – say, from −0.1 to +0.1 – is associated with an increase from 0.45 to 0.83 in the likelihood of a pro-plaintiff ruling. Such a shift represents a change by a medium-sized state (e.g., the Netherlands in 1980) from filing a pro-defendant brief to filing a pro-plaintiff brief.[7] This more modest change has a substantively large impact, nearly doubling the likelihood of a pro-plaintiff ruling. Note that the substantive impact of third-party briefs is very slightly stronger when we include rulings in which a government was a plaintiff or defendant in a case. But once we take the confidence intervals into account, this is not a meaningful difference. That is, the results are similar regardless of whether we consider the narrow or the broader set of rulings.[8]

III. CONSIDERING ALTERNATIVE EXPLANATIONS

The baseline (Table 5.1) results are suggestive of the hypothesized relationship. But, before we reach any stronger conclusion, we first must consider alternative explanations for the patterns observed in our statistical analysis. Our primary focus is on identifying any factor that is both causally prior to our explanatory variable (net weighted government briefs for the plaintiff) and correlated with the disposition of ECJ rulings. We are particularly concerned about one such factor: the balance of the legal merits on the legal issue in question. Pollack (2003: 199) cautions that a positive correlation between the balance of government briefs and ECJ rulings could simply reflect the relative legal strength of each litigant's side in the case. If member-state governments are more likely to submit briefs when their preferred position enjoys the stronger legal argument and the ECJ is more likely to rule for the side with the stronger legal argument, then we would expect to find a positive correlation between the net government briefs and ECJ rulings, even in the absence of the compliance considerations underlying our theoretical prediction. Viable strategies to control for the legal merits are rare in most judicial settings, which means that we typically cannot discriminate between our model's hypothesis and this

---

[7] Recall that the measure of net briefs is the net sum of weighted government briefs. In creating that measure, each nation's brief is weighted by its share of the sum of the logged value of each member state's GDP.

[8] As described in Chapter 3, we generally expect the ECJ to prefer to rule against the litigant government. However, we cannot rule out the possibility that the Court, in rare cases, prefers the government's position. Our model implies that third-party briefs should be unrelated to rulings in such cases. Consequently, to the extent such rulings are in our data set, our statistical analysis likely underestimates the predicted positive relationship between net-weighted briefs and rulings.

alternative interpretation. However, the ECJ setting affords an unusually good test for this confound. In Chapter 4, we carefully developed and validated a proxy for the litigant favored by the legal merits of the case: the position supported by the Advocate General's opinion. In this ensuing analysis, we reexamine the empirical analysis from Table 5.1 in the presence of this control.

We also consider other possible confounds. First, courts often feature important "repeat players" – litigants who appear to influence court rulings because of their frequent participation in cases – and their position in cases could coincide with the balance of third-party government briefs. In the ECJ setting, the key repeat player is the European Commission. A variety of scholars have argued that the ECJ is highly responsive to the European Commission's position on a legal issue (e.g., Stein 1981; Stone Sweet and Brunell 2012a). Indeed, some argue that the ECJ is primarily responsive to the Commission; responsiveness to governmental pressure, once the Commission is taken into account, is marginal at best (Stone Sweet and Brunell 2012a; but see Carrubba, Gabel, and Hankla 2012a). In this chapter we discuss how the Commission's position could confound our analysis, and we look for evidence to that effect.

Second, the compliance problem faced by courts could vary systematically because of differences in the judicial procedure or institutional context of the ruling. For example, in the literature on international courts, compliance is generally considered a less serious problem when the rulings are ultimately articulated through national courts. If so, then any general finding regarding the impact of third-party briefs could hide important and substantively interesting heterogeneity. Our previous analyses assumed the effect of government briefs on ECJ decisions would be independent of the judicial procedure.

Here, we test the appropriateness of this assumption. The literature on the ECJ highlights two ways in which the procedural rules of direct actions and preliminary rulings could affect our analysis. First, threats of noncompliance may be less of a concern on preliminary rulings than on other cases, because these cases are ultimately disposed of by that government's domestic court. Second, threats of noncompliance may be less of a concern on enforcement rulings post-1993, because after that date the member-state governments granted the ECJ the right to issue financial penalties for failures to comply with its rulings. Beyond providing another robustness check on our results, this analysis may also provide a more nuanced view of how courts mitigate compliance problems, in general, and how the authority of the ECJ could evolve over time. For example, if we find that preliminary rulings show no evidence of third-party government influence, it would imply, among other things, that, as preliminary rulings grow in number over time, threats of noncompliance should be of decreasing relevance.

The final concern we must address in testing our first prediction is that the courts could be responsive to third-party briefs for other reasons than our theoretical argument. Specifically, international courts may face threats of legislative override. The member-state governments typically exercise authority over the treaty provisions and secondary legislation that international courts interpret. As a result, if courts value having their rulings implemented, they should be sensitive to whether their rulings will be thwarted by subsequent treaty or legislative revisions. Several scholars have suggested the ECJ is sensitive to this potential constraint on the impact of its rulings (e.g., Wasserfallen 2010). To the extent the balance of government briefs for a litigant captures the strength of the threat of an override favoring that litigant's position, our baseline results can be interpreted through this alternative causal account. We therefore conclude this chapter by attempting to discriminate between this account and our theoretical expectation.

In sum, we investigate a number of arguments over factors that may influence adjudication by international courts, in general, and the ECJ, in particular. For sure, all of these factors are potentially substantively important for understanding the ECJ and its role in the European Union. However, that is not why we are interested in these factors. We are interested in these factors because they may affect the conclusions we draw from the empirical evidence regarding our first prediction. That is, we need to examine them because they are methodologically important; they raise a range of statistical and estimation issues relating to causal inference. The legal merits and the Commission's position raise questions of omitted variable bias. Is the estimated effect of government briefs simply capturing these other factors? The features of the judicial procedure raise questions of generalizability. Is the evidence of sensitivity to third-party government preferences relevant only under certain conditions? And the threat of override raises an issue of causal interpretation. If the Court is responding to the balance of government briefs, is that because of threats of noncompliance?[9]

a. *The legal merits*

The first factor we consider is the legal merits of the case. As discussed in detail in Chapter 4, the legal merits of each litigant's argument may influence

---

[9] That is, we are concerned about interpretation of a causal relationship, defined in the standard Rubin (1974) sense. Consider, for example, a well-designed experiment that establishes that changes in X cause changes in Y. Such an experiment does not provide an interpretation for *why* Y responds to changes in X. The causal interpretation is often a theoretical question, and more than one theory may predict the same empirical causal relationship.

TABLE 5.2 *Controls for position of Advocate General (AG)*

	Government is defendant		Government is litigant	
	All	Subset	All	Subset
Third-Party Support for Plaintiff	4.35*** (1.18)	4.40*** (1.31)	4.41*** (0.79)	4.49*** (0.86)
AG Opinion for Plaintiff	2.16*** (0.12)	2.15*** (0.12)	2.23*** (0.09)	2.24*** (0.09)
Constant	−0.80*** (0.10)	−0.77*** (0.10)	−0.93*** (0.07)	−0.92*** (0.07)
N	1,098	1,070	1,808	1,753

Comment: Robust standard errors reported in parentheses.
***$p < 0.01$, **$p < 0.05$, *$p < 0.10$, one-tailed test.

the ECJ's decision. Further, the member-state governments also may be more likely to file briefs on the side with the stronger legal merits. As such, our baseline results may be a product of omitted variable bias induced by the fact that we did not control for the legal merits.

To account for this possibility, we proposed using the Advocate General's (AG's) position (pro-plaintiff or pro-defendant) on each legal issue as a control for the balance of the legal merits on each legal issue. Recall that the AG writes an opinion after the written stage of the case, and thus the AG views all of the briefs on the case before writing the opinion. Consequently, we would expect any information about the merits conveyed by third-party governments to be captured by the AG's opinion. In the last chapter, we identified two strategies for introducing the AG's position into the models in Table 5.1. The choice of strategy entailed a trade-off over how to account for cases in which the AG's position might be compromised by political incentives (and therefore a weaker control for the legal merits). One option is to discard the rulings when the AG's position might be compromised. This strategy ensures the best possible control for the legal merits but omits some rulings in which third-party governments filed briefs. The other option is to maintain the full set of rulings, albeit with a (potentially small) reduction in the quality of the control.

For robustness we adopt both strategies. In the statistical models, we first add a dummy variable, *AG Opinion for Plaintiff*, that is coded 1 if the AG supports the position of the plaintiff on that legal issue and 0 if the AG supports the defendant's position. The results of these models are presented in Table 5.2. The table also reports estimates of these same models based on only the subset of rulings remaining after eliminating all instances of a suspect AG opinion. Note that we have far fewer observations in this analysis than we did in the analyses in Chapter 4. Most of this decline results from a shift from analyzing all rulings from 1960 to 1999 in Chapter 4 to analyzing only rulings involving a government litigant here.[10]

The results tell a consistent story across all four models. First, the coefficient on the *Third-Party Support For Plaintiff* variable is always positive and highly statistically significant. This is consistent with theoretical expectations; the ECJ is more likely to rule for the plaintiff as the balance of government briefs shifts toward the plaintiff. Second, the position supported by the AG's opinion is also positively related to the position favored by the ECJ, as we would expect if the Court decided cases based, at least in part, on the legal merits. Third, the coefficient for government briefs is smaller than what was reported in the models in Table 5.1, where the AG control was absent. This decrease in the magnitude of the effect of government briefs is consistent with the story motivating the inclusion of this control. We expected a positive correlation between the balance of the legal merits and the balance of government briefs on a legal issue. Consequently, when we include the control for the legal merits, the control variable absorbs some of the positive effect of government briefs reported in Table 5.1.

Finally, it is important to note that these results and interpretations hold regardless of whether we consider only cases in which the government is a defendant or expand to include cases in which a government is a litigant. The results are also insensitive to the exclusion of rulings in which the AG's opinion is suspect.

In sum, the analysis provides strong evidence that the positive effect of government briefs on ECJ rulings is robust to a control for the balance of the legal merits. We next turn to the position of the Commission as a possible source of omitted variable bias.

b. *The Commission's position on the legal issue*

The European Commission is the single most important repeat player in front of the ECJ. The Commission brings enforcement actions against member-state governments. It also appears before the Court as a defendant, most notably in actions for annulment. During our period of study, 30 percent of the rulings involved the Commission as a litigant.[11] The Commission also regularly submits written briefs on preliminary reference cases. In fact, no other single actor participates in as large a share of the ECJ's proceedings.

---

[10] To be clear, the reduction is not due to the elimination of rulings with suspect AG opinions.
[11] Consistent with the definition presented in Chapter 3, we use *ruling* here to indicate a decision on a legal issue in a case.

The Court also frequently sides with the Commission (Carrubba, Gabel, and Hankla 2008; Stein 1981; Stone Sweet and Brunell 1998a: 76). A cursory examination of our raw data confirms this finding; the Court's decision agrees with the Commission's position more than 75 percent of the time.[12] Unsurprisingly, some scholars have concluded that the Commission is a highly influential actor in front of the Court. If true, it is *possible* that not controlling for the Commission's position could cause us to draw incorrect inferences from our baseline results. That is, our analysis may suffer from omitted variable bias due to the exclusion of the position of the Commission.

We are most concerned with omitted variable bias if we have theoretical reasons to suspect something both causes the explanatory variable of interest (*Third-Party Support For Plaintiff*) and correlates with the dependent variable (*ECJ Ruling for Plaintiff*). For example, we described such a concern with regard to the legal merits.[13] However, omitted variable bias may also derive from the exclusion of factors that, although not causally prior to the explanatory variable, are likely correlated with it and the dependent variable.[14] In this second case we must be sensitive to whether the omitted variable under consideration is a consequence of (causally subsequent to) the balance of government briefs. If so, then controlling for such a factor is potentially damaging to the analysis because it introduces bias in the estimates of interest – toward zero, in our context (Angrist and Pischke 2009: 64–5; King, Keohane, and Verba 1994: 182–5). How does the Commission fall within this set of potential concerns? To address this point, we must consider the possible arguments for why the Commission's position is correlated so heavily with the ECJ's position.

There are a variety of possible explanations for why this correlation holds, both with regard to when the Commission is a plaintiff and when it files third-party briefs. The Commission may be favored when it is the plaintiff for at least two reasons. First, the Commission may benefit from its role as a repeat player. Specifically, the Court may defer to the Commission because it is partly dependent on the Commission for setting its legal agenda through the selection of cases for enforcement actions (Conant 2001: 53). Second, the Commission's

---

[12] By *Commission's position*, we mean either the position the Commission holds as a litigant or the position it supported with a brief in a preliminary ruling.

[13] Indeed, Pollack (2003: 199) cautions that a positive correlation between government briefs and ECJ rulings could simply reflect the relative legal strength of each litigant's side in the case.

[14] Of course, with a little imagination, one can create a long list of (perhaps remotely) plausible candidates for inclusion. However, as King, Keohane, and Verba (1994: 182) emphasize, the key here is not to include as many factors as possible; this actually can come at a substantial cost to causal inference. Here, we focus on factors that we expect to be strongly related to ECJ rulings and that scholars interpret as influencing the ECJ rulings in ways that could correlate with *Third-Party Support For Plaintiff*.

success as a plaintiff may be the result of a strategic choice of *which* cases to bring through the infringement procedure for a ruling. If the Commission avoids pursuing member-state governments before the Court when the case is likely to face noncompliance (Falkner et al. 2005: 210; Williams 1994: 396) and the Court is less likely to rule against member states when noncompliance is likely, the Commission would have a high rate of success in infringement proceedings.[15] If either or both of these reasons hold, we would expect to find pro-Commission rulings in enforcement actions.

When the Commission is not a litigant, its written briefs may influence the ECJ in at least three ways. For one, the Commission and the ECJ may share a common agenda to advance European integration, and the Commission's briefs provide the justification for doing that (Cichowski 2007: 44; Stein 1981: 26).[16] Also, the Commission's position, as with the AG's position, may provide a convincing analysis of the legal merits of the case. Finally, the Commission's brief may guide the Court in adopting rulings that will avoid major conflict with the member states. That is, the Commission's position may serve as a bellwether for the Court regarding member-state preferences on the ruling (Mattli and Slaughter 1998; Stein 1981).

Not all of these reasons raise a concern of omitted variable bias with our analysis. That is because only some of these reasons imply that the Commission's position would be positively correlated with the balance of member-state briefs (a necessary condition for omitted variable bias as discussed previously). The clearest argument is probably that the Commission's position reflects the side with the strongest legal merits. As with the AG's position, this could lead the Commission's position to be positively correlated with the balance of member-state government briefs. Of course, even if true, we have already addressed this concern more directly in the previous analysis, where we included a control for the legal merits. But, at least theoretically, this is a plausible motivation for why excluding the Commission's position might generate omitted variable bias.

The other two reasons why the Commission's position might correlate with member-state government briefs are less worrisome in terms of omitted variable bias. Let us quickly review these two arguments. First, if the Commission disproportionately pursues enforcement actions when it expects compliance with a favorable ruling and compliance is more likely when the defendant

---

[15] According to Schepel and Blankenburg (2001: 18), "Its success rate is so high as to make the ECJ look like a kangaroo court – being the baby in the pouch of the mother, it has to follow wherever the Commission goes."
[16] According to Hartley (2007: 73–7), judges are guided by the legal merits and their pro-integration agenda – and are reluctant to challenge the interests of the member states – in deciding a case.

TABLE 5.3 *Controls for position of the Commission*

	Government is defendant		Government is litigant	
Third-Party Support For Plaintiff	3.65*** (1.19)	3.59*** (1.28)	4.04*** (0.74)	3.87*** (0.82)
Commission is Plaintiff	0.86*** (0.20)	0.38** (0.22)	0.88*** (0.12)	0.34*** (0.13)
Commission is Defendant			−0.46*** (0.14)	−0.17 (0.16)
Commission Brief for Plaintiff	0.92*** (0.25)	0.48** (0.28)	0.85*** (0.15)	0.48*** (0.16)
Commission Brief for Defendant	−0.83*** (0.25)	−0.48** (0.28)	−0.73*** (0.14)	−0.37*** (0.16)
AG Opinion for Plaintiff		1.98*** (0.13)		1.99*** (0.09)
Constant	0.09 (0.19)	−0.97*** (0.22)	0.08 (0.12)	−0.92*** (0.12)
N	1,098	1,098	1,808	1,808

Comment: Robust standard errors reported in parentheses.
***$p < 0.01$, **$p < 0.05$, *$p < 0.10$, one-tailed test.

government faces opposing third-party briefs, then we should expect a positive correlation between the Commission's position and third-party briefs. Second, the bellwether role of the Commission could also cause a positive correlation between the position of the Commission and that of the member-state governments' briefs. Indeed, to the extent government briefs capture the balance of member-state preferences on the legal issue, this is exactly what the Commission's brief would be expected to communicate.

These last two reasons actually undermine the justification for considering the Commission's position as a source of omitted variable bias. To the extent they are valid, the Commission's position is causally subsequent to the collective position of the member-state governments on the legal issue. Including the Commission's position in the analysis would then reduce the estimated impact of government briefs on rulings, causing a bias toward zero in the estimate. Thus, including the Commission's position as a control constitutes a conservative test of our hypothesis. In fact, given that our analysis with the AG position already addressed the legal merits, the argument for including the Commission in the analysis is relatively weak. But, for robustness, we report results that include that control.

In Table 5.3, we present the results from probit models that add variables for the Commission's position to the models in Tables 5.1 and 5.2. We include variables for the position of the Commission as a litigant and, when it is not a litigant, the Commission's position on the legal issue indicated in its brief on the case. The expectation is that the ECJ will rule in the direction of the Commission's position. The results show that the ECJ does in fact favor the Commission's position. However, the inclusion of these controls does not eliminate the independent impact of *Third-Party Support For Plaintiff*. It remains positive and statistically significant whether we consider rulings in which a government is a defendant or all rulings in which a government is a litigant.

To assess omitted variable bias more generally, we also estimated models that added the control for the position of the AG to the controls for the Commission. The results of those models are also presented in Table 5.3. Again, even in the presence of controls for both factors, the evidence supports our hypothesis that the ECJ responds to the balance of government briefs. Thus, even with a conservative test due to the ambiguity about whether the Commission's position is an appropriate control, we continue to find strong support for the Political Sensitivity Hypothesis.

The results also indicate that the main impact of adding the AG's position to the models in Table 5.3 is to attenuate the effect of the Commission's position. The decrease in the magnitude of the effect of Commission briefs is much greater (often more than 50 percent) than is the reduction in the size of the coefficient on net government briefs (less than 5 percent). Indeed, for some measures of the Commission's position, the effect goes to zero once the AG's position is included. This is consistent with the argument that the Commission's briefs, in part, capture the balance of the legal merits.

For the central question here – the robustness of our baseline results – this finding provides further reassurance that our estimate of the effect of third-party briefs is not confounded by the legal merits. But it is worth noting that these results may also be of interest to students of the Commission and its role in adjudication by the ECJ. To our knowledge, these are the first results to distinguish between the various interpretations of the positive correlation between Commission and ECJ positions. We return to this point in the conclusion of the chapter.

c. Variation in judicial procedures

The two previous analyses focused on ensuring that our baseline results from Table 5.1 did not suffer from omitted variable bias. However, that is not the only possible concern. The statistical models presented in Table 5.1 assume a constant causal effect of third-party government briefs across all cases. That is the prediction of our theoretical model, and thus we had no theoretical reason to examine whether the substantive impact of the briefs was different across specific subsets of cases. But the impact of government briefs may not be a "general" effect (King, Keohane, and Verba 1994: 92–3). In fact, previous work on the ECJ suggests two substantively important reasons why the threat of noncompliance may systematically vary based on characteristics of the judicial procedure.

Recall that cases reach the ECJ through two mechanisms, direct actions and preliminary references.[17] Scholars argue that the threat of noncompliance should be weaker in preliminary references than in direct actions. Preliminary rulings originate in and are ultimately concluded in national courts, whereas rulings in direct actions are concluded by the ECJ. Because preliminary rulings enjoy the authority of national courts, such rulings may be more likely to be implemented by the national judiciary and enjoy compliance from the relevant government actors as compared to a direct action (Kono 2007: 749; Keohane, Moravcsik, and Slaughter 2000a; Smith 2000; Tallberg 2002a: 622).

Based on this argument, the ECJ should, on average, face much weaker threats of noncompliance when considering a preliminary reference than a direct action. Consequently, the impact of third-party government briefs on Court rulings should be much weaker (and possibly zero) on preliminary rulings than otherwise. This conjecture implies a strong violation of the constant causal effect assumption we made in the baseline analysis.

The second concern involves the introduction of an additional form of enforcement action in the Treaty on European Union (Article 260 TFEU [Treaty on the Functioning of the European Union], ex Article 171 TEU [Treaty on European Union]). Prior to 1994, the Commission had limited options if a government ignored an adverse infringement ruling following an enforcement action. The Commission either accepted that the government would not comply, or it brought follow-up infringement proceedings. With the coming into force of the Maastricht Treaty in 1994, this situation changed. In the Maastricht Treaty, the member states created a new judicial procedure that could be employed if a member-state government did not comply with an adverse infringement ruling. The Commission now can bring the member-state government in question back before the Court, which can impose financial sanctions against a member-state government for failing to comply with a previous infringement ruling.

---

[17] Since 1989, cases also reach the ECJ upon appeal after a ruling by the Court of First Instance. All of those cases originated as direct actions.

TABLE 5.4 *The effect of briefs on ECJ rulings with a government defendant*

	Direct actions	Preliminary rulings	Combined
Third-Party Support for Plaintiff	4.30*** (1.66)	5.11*** (1.44)	4.29*** (1.66)
Third-Party Support for Plaintiff* Preliminary Ruling			0.81 (2.19)
Preliminary Ruling			−0.77*** (0.11)
Constant	0.95*** (0.05)	0.18** (0.10)	0.95*** (0.05)
N	852	246	1,098

Comment: Standard errors clustered by case are in parentheses.
***$p < 0.01$, **$p < 0.05$, *$p < 0.10$, one-tailed test.

If member-state governments feel compelled to pay these financial penalties, the advent of this mechanism would impose a cost for noncompliance that did not exist prior to 1994. Any failure to comply with a ruling could trigger enforcement actions that could ultimately end in a penalty.[18] Consequently, this procedure could have weakened or even eliminated the threat of noncompliance with ECJ rulings after 1994. If true, we should observe a weaker, or no, relationship between third-party government briefs and Court decisions post-1993 as compared to before 1994.

We first examine the possibility that the preliminary ruling procedure dampens threats of noncompliance by reestimating the two probit models presented in Table 5.1 and distinguishing between the effects of third-party government briefs in direct actions and preliminary references. We do this in two ways. First, we estimate the probit models for only direct actions and only preliminary rulings. Second, we estimate a probit model including all rulings with the addition of an interaction term between *Third-Party Support For Plaintiff* and a dummy variable for a preliminary ruling. In the interaction model, we include this dummy variable itself to avoid potential problems with interpretation (Brambor, Clark, and Golder 2006).

Table 5.4 presents the results when we consider only cases in which a government was a defendant (corresponding to the first model reported in Table 5.1). The impact of third-party briefs is positive and statistically significant

---

[18] The Commission can commence an infringement proceeding against a member state that does not comply with a preliminary ruling, and thus this new procedure could deter noncompliance with preliminary rulings as well as direct actions.

TABLE 5.5 *The effect of briefs on ECJ rulings with a government litigant*

	Direct actions	Preliminary rulings	Combined
Third-Party Support for Plaintiff	5.42***	5.38***	5.42***
	(1.17)	(0.81)	(1.17)
Third-Party Support for Plaintiff* Preliminary Ruling			−0.04
			(1.42)
Preliminary Ruling			−0.41***
			(0.07)
Constant	0.58***	0.18***	0.58***
	(0.04)	(0.06)	(0.04)
N	1,102	706	1,808

Comment: Standard errors clustered by case are in parentheses.
***$p < 0.01$, **$p < 0.05$, *$p < 0.10$, one-tailed test.

when we consider only preliminary rulings or only infringement rulings (i.e., the type of direct action with a government defendant). The impact of briefs appears to be slightly bigger in the preliminary ruling context, which is counter to expectations. But this difference is far from statistically significant. The combined results reported in the last column provide a specific test for this difference. The coefficient on the interaction term indicates that the difference in the effect of third-party government briefs across the two sets of rulings is effectively zero. This supports our assumption of a common causal effect of third-party government briefs on ECJ rulings.

Table 5.5 presents the results when we consider cases in which a government was a litigant (corresponding to the second model reported in Table 5.1). Again, we find that the impact on rulings is positive and statistically significant when we consider only preliminary rulings or direct actions. And, just as in the previous results, we find no difference in the effect of third-party government briefs on ECJ rulings across the two types of cases. The coefficient on the interaction term in the last column shows no difference in the effect of government briefs. This again supports our assumption of a common causal effect of net weighted briefs on ECJ rulings across the two types of cases.

Combined, these results provide clear evidence that we have no systematic variation in the causal effect of net government briefs across these two types of cases. This is somewhat surprising, given the expectation in the literature regarding the greater authority of rulings disposed of through national courts. But, as we discuss in the conclusion and in Chapter 6, there may be good reasons to discount such an expectation. Member-state governments often

TABLE 5.6 *Comparison of pre-1994 and post-1993 periods*

	Government is defendant		Government is litigant	
Years	Pre-1994	All	Pre-1994	All
Third-Party Support for Plaintiff	6.05***	4.68**	5.91***	4.16***
	(1.30)	(2.34)	(0.86)	(1.13)
Third-Party Support for Plaintiff* Pre-1994 Period		1.36 (2.68)		1.75 (1.42)
Pre-1994 Period		−0.14 (0.09)		−0.06 (0.07)
Constant	0.71**	−0.85**	0.40***	0.46***
	(0.05)	(0.08)	(0.04)	(0.05)
N	734	1,098	1,226	1,808

Comment: Robust standard errors reported in parentheses.
***$p < 0.01$, **$p < 0.05$, *$p < 0.10$, one-tailed test.

have the incentives, skill, and power to ignore or outright thwart ECJ rulings, even preliminary rulings (e.g., Conant 2002).

Next we evaluate whether the Court is less sensitive to government briefs in rulings post-1993 than in rulings pre-1994. To do so we include an interaction term composed of *Third-Party Support For Plaintiff* and a dummy variable from the pre-1994 period. We also include this dummy variable in the model to avoid problems of interpretation (Brambor, Clark, and Golder 2006). If the creation of penalties for noncompliance with infringement rulings dampened or eliminated the potential for noncompliance, third-party government briefs should have a stronger correlation with ECJ decisions pre-1994; the coefficient on the interaction term should be positive. We estimated the models for the two standard classes of rulings: when a government is a defendant, and when the government is a litigant. The results are presented in Table 5.6 in the second column for each class of rulings. (Later, we discuss the results in the first column.) In both settings, the interaction term is far from statistically significant, indicating that the impact of government briefs does not differ between the two time periods. Thus, the analysis does not provide evidence consistent with the argument that threats of noncompliance on infringement proceedings were curtailed with the introduction of financial penalties.[19]

---

[19] We also estimated the interaction effect with only infringement rulings. The results also easily reject the hypothesis that the effect of government briefs on rulings is weaker in the post-1993 period.

d. *An aside on measurement concerns*

Before we leave the consideration of temporal variation in the statistical results, it is important to raise a measurement error concern that also involves the post-1993 period. Measurement error, particularly regarding the key explanatory variable, can cause serious problems with causal inference. First, systematic measurement error – the consistent over- or underestimation of the explanatory variable for some subset of observations in the data set – can result in biased estimates of the causal effect of the explanatory variable. Second, non-systematic (random) measurement error in the explanatory variable can cause attenuation bias and raise the uncertainty in our estimates of our causal effects. Put simply, this sort of measurement error makes it harder to reject the null hypothesis of no relationship.

We are concerned about both types of measurement error with regard to our key variable: *Third-Party Support For Plaintiff*. We are specifically concerned with measurement error introduced in the post-1993 period. Our concern is due to the change in how third-party briefs were described in the official documents of the Court, published in the *Reports of Cases Before the Court*. In particular, through 1993, the reports included a section that summarized the positions of the third-party briefs on the legal issues in each case. Starting in 1994, this section was removed.[20] Consequently, in the post-1993 period, we relied on the opinion of the Advocate General and the written decision by the Court to determine the position of third-party governments on each legal issue. The AG opinion, in particular, generally discusses the submissions by member-state governments and the Commission (Mortelmans 1979: 583–4).

This change in the source of our information about the positions adopted by third-party governments could introduce error into our measure of third-party support for the plaintiff. First, if the Court or the AG were more inclined to discuss briefs that were persuasive, then we would expect systematic measurement error that would cause a (potentially dramatic) positive bias in our estimate of the causal effect of government briefs on ECJ rulings. Second, the change in the source of information should introduce some nonsystematic measurement error, which would attenuate (i.e., weaken) the estimated effect of government briefs.

---

[20] This section, authored by the reporting judge, remains part of the published records of the Court. A small number are made available at the Court as part of the judicial process of a case. However, the Court stopped publishing it as part of the *Reports of Cases Before the Court*. We are aware based on correspondence with the Court of no publicly available archive that houses these documents, and the Court will make only a very small number available upon formal request.

Depending on which of these two potential sources of error dominates, our baseline analysis could over- or underestimate the true causal effect of government briefs. We do not have any strong theoretical reason to expect one to have a stronger effect. The argument for systematic measurement error is plausible. But, then again, when reading the opinions of the AG and the decisions of the Court, one commonly finds government briefs discussed expressly to dismiss or justify a ruling against that position. In any event, we can settle this account fairly easily with the statistical results reported in Table 5.6.

Recall that the concern with systematic measurement error was that the post-1993 period would feature an upwardly biased effect for net government briefs. Thus, our baseline results could be driven by the rulings in that time period, hiding a weaker (or perhaps no) relationship for rulings from the period without this measurement error concern. This is not what we find. In the pre-1994 period, the effect of government briefs is positive and highly statistically significant. This is true whether we consider only rulings in which a government is a defendant or all rulings in which a government is a litigant. Moreover, as discussed earlier, the results from the models with the interaction terms in Table 5.6 also show no difference in the impact of government briefs across the two periods. This should dispel any concern about systematic measurement error as the source of our evidence supporting the Political Sensitivity Hypothesis.

Next we turn to the potential consequences of random measurement error. Recall that if such error is greater in the post-1993 period, it should lead to attenuation bias and increased uncertainty in our estimates of the impact of net government briefs. As discussed previously, the coefficient on the interaction term is consistent with an attenuation bias: the coefficients on the interaction terms are positive. To assess whether the precision of the estimate is lower in the post-1993 period, we need to compare the coefficient and standard error for each period. The coefficient for the post-1993 period is simply the reported coefficient estimate for net government briefs. For the pre-1994 period, we can use the coefficient and standard error from the model restricted to only that time period (the first column for each set of rulings).[21] The results in both settings show that the precision of the estimate and the size of the effect are smaller in the post-1993 period. This is consistent with the greater random measurement error in that period. But, returning to our primary concern, the evidence still supports the conclusion that the estimated causal effect does not

---

[21] Alternatively, one can sum the main effect and interaction term from the model for the full time period. The sum and standard error are equivalent to the coefficient and standard error from the pre-1994 model.

differ across the two time periods. Thus, in sum, measurement error does not appear to be a source of concern in our analysis.[22]

e. Substantive significance

Before proceeding to the final analysis, it is worth comparing the results from the preceding analyses (Tables 5.1–5.6). Recall that each of the concerns addressed earlier had the potential to weaken or even eliminate the original finding that ECJ rulings responded to the balance of third-party government briefs. We found that our hypothesized relationship survived these challenges: *Third-Party Support For Plaintiff* had a positive and statistically significant effect on ECJ rulings across all models.

One further way to appreciate the robustness of the relationship between government briefs and rulings is to consider the substantive effect of third-party government briefs on rulings across these models. This is not easily assessed from the results reported in the tables because the probit coefficients do not directly convey substantive significance (i.e., the marginal effect of a change in net briefs). Gelman and Hill (2007: 100–3) recommend evaluating the substantive impact of a variable at each observed value of the control variables and then averaging across all of these values to generate a summary of the substantive effect. This is called the average predictive comparison. In the current context, this constitutes estimating the change in the predicted probability of a pro-plaintiff ECJ ruling due to a shift (e.g., from the lowest to the highest observed value) in *Third-Party Support For Plaintiff*, averaged across all observed values of the other variables in the model. We can then compare the impact of a specific shift across the models presented in Tables 5.1–5.6.

We consider two types of shifts: one that captures the maximal observed variation (which varies by context), and one that represents a much more modest shift (−0.2 to 0.2), equivalent to one government of a large economy shifting its brief from pro-defendant to pro-plaintiff. Figure 5.2 presents these average predictive comparisons for the models restricted to only rulings in which a government is a defendant. Figure 5.3 presents the same information for the models that consider all rulings in which a government was a litigant.

---

[22] As a final note, some scholars expected the Court's sensitivity to government briefs to increase in the post-Maastricht period. For example, Dehousse (1998: 167) interpreted the change in the political climate following Maastricht to force the ECJ to be much more sensitive to member-state government preferences over EU law. Our results do not provide support for this argument. We cannot reject the hypothesis that member-state briefs have the same effect on ECJ rulings in both periods.

Considering alternative explanations 145

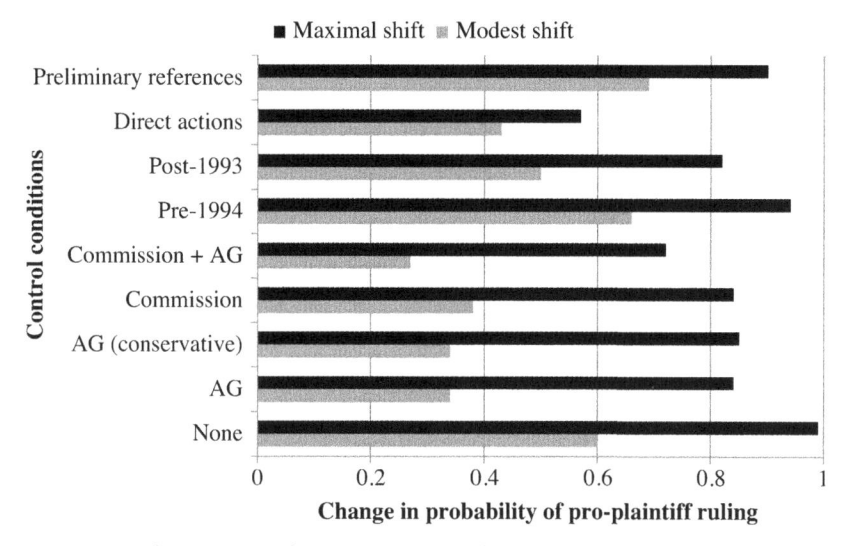

FIGURE 5.2 The impact of government briefs on rulings with a government defendant

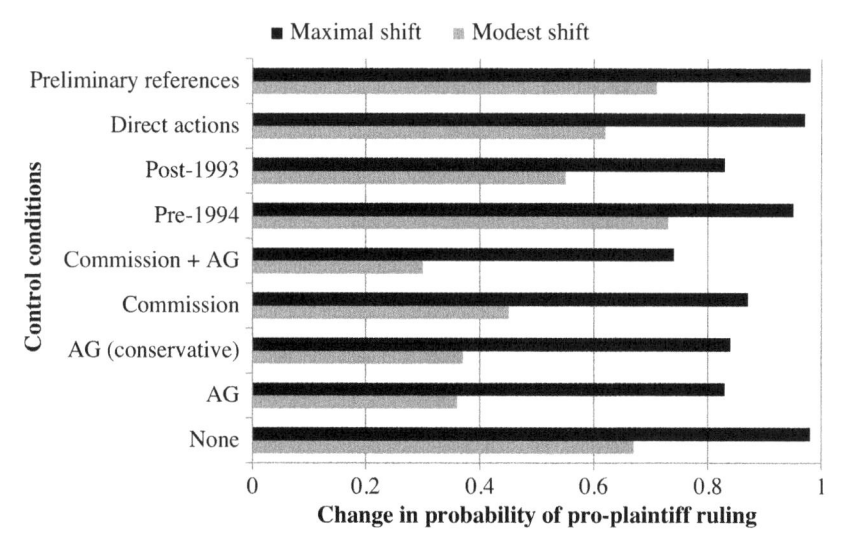

FIGURE 5.3 The impact of government briefs on rulings with a government litigant

The results in both figures tell a similar story. The substantive impact is very similar regardless of the time period or whether we focus exclusively on direct actions or preliminary references. The modest shift in net weighted briefs is associated with a sixty percentage point increase in the likelihood of ruling for the plaintiff. The maximal shift is associated with an almost complete swing in the likelihood of a pro-plaintiff ruling. Once we include controls for the legal merits and the position of the Commission, the substantive impact decreases by about half in the context of the modest shift and by about a quarter in the context of the maximal shift. But even the lowest estimate of the impact of a modest shift is still a thirty percentage point increase in the likelihood of a pro-plaintiff ruling. Thus, the results in Tables 5.1–5.6 are consistent with the Political Sensitivity Hypothesis in terms of direction and statistical significance of the effect, and they indicate this effect is of substantive import.

One way to think about the differences in the substantive effects displayed in the figures is to think of them as defining upper and lower bounds on the actual impact of changes in net government briefs. The models that include the controls for the legal merits and for the Commission's position are a conservative estimate of the substantive effect of government briefs. We discussed this when interpreting the results for the Commission controls. If a control variable is, at least in part, a consequence of the key explanatory variable (i.e., *Third-Party Support For Plaintiff*), then the inclusion of that control can bias our estimate toward zero. We have some concern in that regard for the control for Commission briefs. Thus, the smallest substantive effects in Figures 5.2 and 5.3, which include a control for the Commission's position, may underestimate the true effect.

f. *Threats of override (collective restraint)*

The preceding analyses have examined a variety of omitted variable, generalizability, and measurement challenges to the initial empirical results presented in this chapter (Table 5.1). The results of these analyses increase our confidence in this empirical relationship. However, this evidence, at best, establishes the general relationship; it does not establish an interpretation. That is, the evidence does not directly show or explain *why* government briefs influence ECJ rulings. In Chapter 2, we developed one answer. Our interpretation is that this relationship reflects the ECJ's concern about threats of noncompliance with its rulings. Specifically, we showed that the observed empirical relationship is a logical implication deduced from a theoretical model in which the ECJ is sensitive to compliance with its rulings. The theoretical exercise lends support to our interpretation of the empirical regularity. One of the central strengths of formal modeling is that it ensures that our theoretical intuitions and the hypotheses derived from them are logically consistent (Huber 1996: 14). Thus, we consider our interpretation a theoretically sound, and therefore plausible, explanation for the results.

But we remain concerned that another interpretation might provide a better explanation for the empirical regularities identified previously. In particular, international courts, including the ECJ, could be responsive to third-party briefs because the briefs signal threats by the member governments to amend or override the courts' legal interpretations or even to revise the treaties to limit or weaken the courts' authority. This concern is not unique to the ECJ setting. As Smith (2003) argues, international courts such as the appellate body of the World Trade Organization (WTO) face similar threats and are likely sensitive to them. In the ECJ setting, these threats are commonly referred to as threats of override by the member states; Smith (2003: 75) refers to them as threats of "collective restraint" by the WTO members.

In the EU setting, any ECJ ruling can, in principle, be overturned by the member-state governments. If the ECJ fears such a reaction, then it may temper its rulings to comport with the preferences of the member-state governments.[23] According to Wasserfallen (2010: 1131), the potential for such a reaction can induce the ECJ to balance legal considerations against the concerns of legislative actors and particularly the member-state governments. For instance, Wasserfallen (2010: 1139) describes how the ECJ ruling in *Grzelczyk* (Case C-184/99) anticipated subsequent legislative coalitions by moderating its jurisprudence with regard to student mobility.

Building on the separation of powers literature (e.g., Ferejohn and Weingast 1992), Carrubba and colleagues (Carrubba, Gabel, and Hankla 2008, 2012a) provide a detailed argument for why the ECJ should be sensitive to threats of override and why government briefs in ECJ cases might indicate the credibility of such threats. They contend that the member-state governments form coalitions to pass legislation and to revise the treaties through logrolls. That is, if a subset of governments considers an issue sufficiently important, the governments can trade concessions in other areas in exchange for legislative support from disinterested or otherwise opposed governments. Such logrolls are common in EU legislation (Aksoy 2012).[24] Consequently, Carrubba et al.

---

[23] Maduro (1999: 82–3), analyzing free movement of goods rulings, makes a related argument: that the ECJ interprets EU law so as to reflect the preferences of the majority of the member states. His argument does not involve a threat of override but has the same empirical implications as those we test for later. That is, if that argument holds, we should find an effect of government preferences across all types of cases, and there should be no additional effect when a government is a litigant.

[24] Similarly, Achen (2006a: 293) concludes that the EU legislative process is consistent with an "exchange model" characterized by cross-issue compromises – that is, logrolls.

(2012a) argue override is possible when at least one government wants to revise a ruling. The credibility of such a threat, though, depends on (1) the distribution of preferences among the governments as indicated by briefs submitted on the case and (2) the legislative clout of the governments submitting the briefs.[25] Specifically, they expect the credibility of a threat of override of a ruling to increase with the net number of briefs (weighted by legislative clout) opposing a ruling. As a result, if the Court is concerned with override, the key independent variable, *Third-Party Support For Plaintiff*, may be capturing the Court's responsiveness to threats of override rather than threats of noncompliance.

Before proposing a strategy to distinguish evidence of threats of override from evidence of threats of noncompliance, it is worth noting that several scholars disagree with important parts of the override argument presented by Carrubba and colleagues (Carrubba, Gabel, and Hankla 2008, 2012a). For example, Pollack (2003: 172) and Alter (2001: 201) argue that the difficulty of building appropriate coalitions (among member states and with other institutions) to pass legislation and to reform the treaties severely restricts override opportunities. Also, some scholars assume threats of override are only credible when the number of government briefs clears the Council's supermajority threshold (Kilroy 1999; Stone Sweet and Brunell 2012a). The number of government briefs rarely even approaches that threshold. Obviously, readers who share these objections can dismiss threats of override as an alternative explanation for our results without further evidence or analysis.

For readers willing to entertain the possibility that threats of override could account for our findings, we have designed a further empirical test to distinguish the effect of government briefs due to override concerns from our hypothesis regarding noncompliance. The test is based on the following observation. Threats of override are always present in cases involving EU law. Simply put, any judicial interpretation of EU law can be overturned by member-state governments passing secondary legislation or making treaty revisions. In contrast, threats of noncompliance should not be omnipresent. These threats should be much more likely in cases involving government litigants than otherwise. In Chapter 3, we illustrated how compliance concerns arise when governments are litigants. Here, we expand on that discussion to describe more fully why, in general, we expect compliance concerns, but not threats of override, to be more salient in cases with a government litigant.

---

[25] Carrubba, Gabel, and Hankla (2008) measure legislative clout with the share of weighted votes for each country in qualified majority voting in the Council. This correlates at greater than 0.9 with the national shares of EU GDP.

Consider first direct actions. As discussed in Chapter 3, when a government is a litigant in an enforcement action or an annulment action, government compliance is typically critical to implementation of the ruling. However, a significant share of direct actions does not involve a government litigant, and these rulings are much less likely to feature a threat of noncompliance. Annulment actions can be brought by an EU institution challenging an act of another institution or a private litigant challenging the act of an EU institution. In these settings, government compliance is less commonly relevant to implementation. For example, in *Partie Ecologiste 'Les Verts'* v. *European Parliament* (Case 294/83), members of the French environmental party in the European Parliament (EP) challenged the distribution of campaign resources by the EP authorities. A ruling for or against the EP authorities would not entail any government action to implement. Thus, we would not expect threats of noncompliance to figure in the ECJ ruling. But a ruling in this case could face an override. If the member-state governments disagreed with the ruling, they could attempt to override the ruling through subsequent legislation or treaty revisions.

Private parties can also initiate annulment actions. For example, a firm can challenge the form and outcome of Commission investigations regarding violations of competition rules.[26] Again, the ruling in such a case would not require any specific national government role in implementation, but the impact of the ruling could be nullified by subsequent amendments to competition rules by the member-state governments. Similarly, a successful private party in an annulment action can seek damages through a direct action under Article 235 EC (ex 178 EEC [European Economic Community]) brought against the Commission. The ruling is subject to potential override, but it would raise no issue of compliance by a specific national government. A majority of the direct actions in our data set that do not involve a government litigant involve these types of annulment actions.

Other forms of direct actions also lack threats of noncompliance. The remaining direct actions in our data set predominantly consist of administrative cases involving a dispute between Community institutions and their employees. We also have twenty-nine rulings from actions against Community institutions for failure to act. In both cases, implementation of the ruling does not require action by a national government. And, in principle, the ruling of the Court could be thwarted, at least prospectively, by treaty reform or legislative actions.[27]

---

[26] See, for example, *Dow Benelux* v. *Commission* (Case 85/87).
[27] Some failure to act rulings involve a demand that the Commission initiate infringement proceedings against a member-state government because the plaintiff asserts a violation of

Preliminary rulings also may not involve the national government in the promulgation of the preliminary rulings. We argued in Chapter 3 that preliminary references featuring the national government as a litigant typically do require national government compliance for implementation of the ruling. In such cases, an action by the government or the interpretation of national laws and regulations is generally in question. Thus, we would expect threats of noncompliance to influence the ECJ in those contexts. But this is not necessarily true of preliminary rulings without the national government as a litigant. As Alter (2000: 500) notes, many preliminary references do not involve a conflict between EU and national law and regulations, and thus do not feature a serious national compliance question. Furthermore, cases involving two private parties (a frequent event) are less likely to raise compliance challenges than when a government is a litigant.[28] In short, as with direct actions, we expect threats of noncompliance to figure more prominently in cases with national government litigants than otherwise.

To test whether we can reject the alternative hypothesis that the threat of override is a better causal explanation for our findings, we compare the effect of third-party government briefs on ECJ rulings when the threat of override is present and the threat of noncompliance is absent (or weaker) with the effect when both threats are present. If we find no difference between the two effects or a weaker effect in the presence of a threat of noncompliance, we cannot rule out the alternative explanation. If we find the effect is greater when threats of noncompliance are most salient (i.e., when governments are litigants), the evidence will support our theoretical prediction regarding threats of noncompliance. Put differently, we would not expect the effect of third-party government briefs on ECJ rulings to be stronger when governments are litigants if the relationship between government briefs and ECJ rulings is driven solely by threats of override.[29]

---

community obligations by that government (e.g., *Star Fruit Company SA v. Commission*, Case 247/87). It is not clear how the member states could override a ruling in this context. We therefore have analyzed the data with and without the twenty-nine rulings from failure to act cases. Their exclusion does not alter the conclusions we draw from the analysis presented here, which includes such rulings.

[28] Although the acts in question in these cases may occasionally involve national implementation, we expect both the salience of the act to the national government and the relevance of national implementation to be much lower than when the national government is a litigant.

[29] Note that it is possible cases with government litigants are more salient to third-party governments, and that salience could induce governments to submit briefs. But that would not generate our predicted difference in the impact of the marginal brief on the Court's ruling.

Considering alternative explanations 151

TABLE 5.7 *The effect of briefs on ECJ rulings with a government litigant*

	Direct actions	Preliminary rulings	All rulings
Third-Party Support for Plaintiff	1.41	3.31***	3.05***
	(1.34)	(0.37)	(0.36)
Third-Party Support for Plaintiff* Government is Litigant	3.77**	2.07***	2.17***
	(1.76)	(0.89)	(0.78)
Government is Litigant	1.10***	0.16***	0.56***
	(0.06)	(0.06)	(0.04)
Constant	−0.53**	0.01	−0.15***
	(0.03)	(0.25)	(0.02)
N	2,725	4,474	7,199

Comment: Standard errors clustered by case are in parentheses.
***$p < 0.01$, **$p < 0.05$, *$p < 0.10$, one-tailed test.

g. Analysis

We now turn to testing whether the impact of government briefs is greater in rulings involving a government litigant than in rulings without a government litigant. To do this, we consider all rulings from 1960 to 1999 in our database, which includes more than five thousand rulings without a government litigant. The statistical model is the same as the basic model presented in Table 5.1. However, in addition to our measure *Third-Party Support For Plaintiff*, we also include an interaction with a dummy variable for whether a national government was a litigant in the case. We include the dummy variable itself in the model to avoid potential problems with interpretation (Brambor, Clark, and Golder 2006). We execute separate tests for rulings from direct actions, from preliminary rulings, and for all rulings combined. The key coefficient in the models is on the interaction term because that indicates whether the effect of government briefs when a government is a litigant is different from when a government is not a litigant. If our baseline results were driven by threats of override and not threats of noncompliance, this coefficient should be zero (or negative). If threats of noncompliance influence the ECJ, this coefficient should be positive and statistically significant.

Table 5.7 presents the results of these three probit models. The results are inconsistent with the alternative explanation of our baseline results. The interaction term is positive and statistically significant in all three models.[30]

---

[30] We are not aware of any obvious factors that should cause government briefs to be stronger in influence when a government litigant is present, and thus we do not include any control

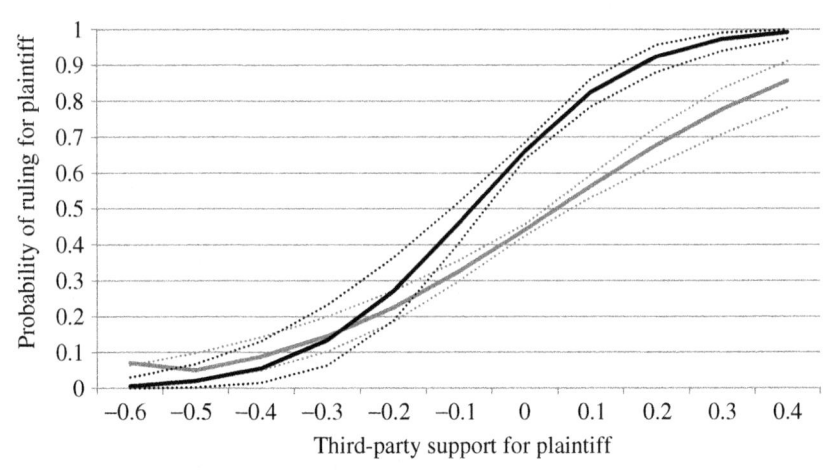

FIGURE 5.4 Predicted probability of ECJ ruling for the plaintiff

Comment: The figure plots the predicted probability of an ECJ ruling for the plaintiff at different levels of *Third-Party Support For Plaintiff*. The gray line plots this relationship for rulings without a government litigant. The black line refers to rulings in which a government was a litigant. The dotted lines indicate the 95 percent confidence interval. We used CLARIFY software to generate these predicted values based on the statistical models reported in the third column of Table 5.7.

This is consistent with our interpretation of ECJ rulings as sensitive to threats of noncompliance.

The substantive effect of a change in the balance of third-party government briefs on rulings with and without a government litigant is presented in Figure 5.4. That figure plots the predicted probability of a ruling for the plaintiff based on the results in the last model (all rulings) in Table 5.7. These results support our theoretical interpretation of our baseline results, as presented in Table 5.1; the impact of briefs is greater when a government is a litigant than otherwise.

It is also interesting to note that the results suggest the impact of threats of override is small. In the context when the threats of noncompliance are least likely to be relevant – when a government is not a litigant in a direct

variables. However, for readers who may identify relevant arguments, we have also estimated these models with the full complement of controls for the legal merits and the position of the Commission used in the previous sections. Their inclusion does not change the results for the interaction term. However, their inclusion does dramatically reduce the substantive effect of government briefs when a government is not a litigant. This casts some doubt on the substantive significance of the threat of override.

action case – the effect of third-party government briefs is effectively zero. In the preliminary ruling cases, this effect increases dramatically both in terms of substantive and statistical significance. But these are cases in which noncompliance could be at issue. Our contention was simply that threats of noncompliance are less relevant in those preliminary rulings than in ones featuring a government litigant.

Finally, these tests offer additional evidence that our measure of third-party government briefs is not simply capturing the balance of the legal merits in each ruling. If that were true, we would not expect to see the differential effect associated with cases in which a government is a litigant. We are unaware of any argument for why the government briefs should more closely track the legal merits when a government is a litigant than when a government is not a litigant. Yet we do find the differential effect.

IV. CONCLUSION

In our initial analysis in this chapter (Table 5.1), we found evidence that ECJ decisions were positively correlated with the weight of third-party government briefs in cases when governments are litigants. This evidence is consistent with the theoretical argument derived in Chapter 2, namely, that an international court can facilitate enforcement of international law, but credible threats of member-state government noncompliance circumscribe its ability to do so. However, based on the literature on international courts and on the ECJ, we identified a number of arguments that could undermine these results.

The first concern was with regard to the legal merits of the case. We employed, based on careful analysis in Chapter 4, the AG's position as a proxy for which litigant had the stronger legal case. The AG's position shows up as a strong predictor of the ECJ's final decision, but, conditional on that, we still find a robust effect for government briefs. Thus, this evidence is inconsistent with the argument that the relationship between third-party government briefs and ECJ decisions is simply a function of the legal merits of the case.

The second concern was with regard to the Commission's position in the case. Scholars have put forward a number of arguments for why the Commission's position might be correlated with ECJ decisions. However, only some of them would cause the Commission's position to also be correlated with government briefs. In fact, most of those arguments actually would make it inappropriate to include the Commission in the analysis. Despite the thin theoretical motivation to include the Commission in our analysis, for the sake of robustness we did so. We found a strong relationship between the Commission's position and ECJ decisions, but this relationship did little to affect the relationship between government briefs and ECJ decisions.

Both of the preceding analyses involved statistical concerns with omitted variable bias. Was the relationship we identified in our baseline results spurious because we had not included a control for a third factor that was actually generating the observed correlation? The third concern we addressed was of a different nature. In our original analysis we assumed a constant causal effect of government briefs. However, for theoretically plausible reasons government briefs might have had a more conditional effect than allowed in the analysis.

First, government threats of noncompliance might not be as credible on preliminary rulings as on other types of cases. The argument is based on the notion that governments are less likely to ignore a domestic court ruling than an international court ruling. We did not find evidence to this effect. This finding is not a complete surprise in light of recent research on judicial politics in the domestic arena. Conant (2002), for example, has argued that national governments frequently evade ECJ preliminary rulings, even though the national judges faithfully communicate those rulings in domestic courts. More generally, several scholars have demonstrated that national high courts struggle with compliance problems similar to those of international courts when they issue a ruling adverse to the interests of national governments (Staton and Moore 2011: 561; Vanberg 2005). Consequently, the ECJ would have an incentive to defer to the balance of third-party briefs in preliminary rulings as well as direct action rulings. This is what we find.

Second, we considered whether the Court's ability to apply financial penalties for noncompliance with infringement rulings after 1993 might have reduced threats of noncompliance in that period. We found no evidence to that effect. The ECJ appears to have been equally sensitive to the balance of third-party government briefs after 1993 as before. Thus, the results support our assumption in the analyses in Table 5.1 that the Political Sensitivity Hypothesis should apply generally to the relevant rulings by the ECJ.

The final concern we addressed in this chapter was one of causal interpretation. Is there an alternative causal mechanism driving the relationship we identified in Table 5.1? We focused on whether the Court might be sensitive to government briefs, not because the briefs indicated the threat of noncompliance, but rather because they indicated the threat of override of the Court's decision through amendment of the EU treaty or secondary legislation. To evaluate this possibility we compared the influence of government briefs on cases with government litigants and cases without government litigants. Consistent with the argument that the Court is responding to threats of noncompliance, we found that the Court was much more sensitive to government briefs when governments were litigants (when threats of noncompliance would be most present) than otherwise.

In sum, in this chapter we considered a variety of reasons why we might need to reevaluate any conclusions we drew from our baseline results. We considered the possibility of omitted variable bias, the possibility that there was heterogeneity in the relationship conditional on procedural context, and the possibility of an alternative causal mechanism. We found no evidence that any of these issues confounded our statistical inferences. Thus, the conclusion we tentatively drew at the beginning of this chapter stands. We find systematic evidence that the Court is influenced by threats of noncompliance with its rulings. In the next chapter we consider what happens after the Court issues its ruling.

6

The Conditional Effectiveness Hypothesis

The European Court of Justice and economic integration

The theoretical model described in Chapter 2 generates a second prediction that identifies conditions under which rulings will have the desired impact on policy. This prediction, the Conditional Effectiveness Hypothesis, states that European Court of Justice (ECJ) rulings against governments are more likely to change government behavior (i.e., change policy) when the briefs filed by third-party governments are (net) against the government. That is, when the threats of noncompliance with ECJ rulings by national legislative and executive institutions are the least viable, we would expect rulings to manifest more pronounced changes in policy, and thus greater change in substantive outcomes, than when threats are the strongest.

Our argument about how and when international rulings have a substantive effect consistent with the treaty obligations addresses a fundamental issue regarding the performance of international agreements. As Martin (2013) argues, we can imagine national governments adhering to international agreements in very narrow terms and having very little effect on the substantive outcomes at issue in the agreement (e.g., trade liberalization).[1] Put differently, states might adhere to the letter, not the spirit, of the rules. So, to explain why international agreements matter substantively, we need a story about how and under what conditions the members would be compelled to change their behavior sufficiently to advance the goals of the international regime (e.g., cause increased trade). Our theoretical model provides such a story, describing how an international court can serve that role. Specifically, the Conditional Effectiveness Hypothesis identifies when we would expect to find a substantive

---

[1] Martin (2013) takes issue with the commonly ascribed equivalence between an agreement that is effective in substantive terms and one that gains government "compliance," where *compliance* is understood in narrow legal terms. Given that we defined *compliance* in broader terms (see Chapter 3), we refrain from using the term here so as to avoid confusion.

impact of rulings. Thus, this hypothesis addresses a key issue in how international institutions can influence the performance of international agreements.

In this chapter, we test this prediction by examining how ECJ rulings affect European Union (EU) interstate commerce. The liberalization of intra-EU trade is one of the core missions of the EU. It is enshrined in both the EU treaties and secondary legislation. But, consistent with our discussions in previous chapters, compliance with these laws ultimately lies in the hands of the member-state governments. Thus, perhaps the most important compliance issue involving the impact of EU law, historically, has been whether and to what extent national institutions abide by their obligations to market liberalization. Not surprisingly, the ECJ has played a prominent role in defining those obligations. Indeed, the first decades of ECJ rulings dealt largely with such questions. Consequently, the success of EU market liberalization has hinged in no small part on whether trade-liberalizing rulings by the ECJ meet with government compliance, leading to real change in government policies.

Based on the theoretical model in Chapter 2, we would expect rulings by the ECJ to vary in their effect on interstate trade as a function of whether pro-trade rulings involving governments enjoyed the support of briefs submitted by third-party governments. We empirically evaluate this claim in the present chapter.

The chapter is organized as follows. In the first part of the chapter, we set some context for our empirical analysis by discussing two related literatures. We first review the general empirical literature on the policy consequences of domestic court rulings. In the area of "judicial impact," scholars have for many years been interested in whether and to what extent domestic court rulings have an influence on policy, both in terms of the behavior of the parties in the case at hand and the broader policy issues raised by the legal issue in the case. Although much of this literature developed out of studies of civil rights and social policy, trade policy has received attention as well. We next discuss the empirical literature on the impact of international institutions, in particular dispute resolution mechanisms, on trade. This literature is focused primarily, though not solely, on studies of the World Trade Organization (WTO). The discussion in this section is not critical to setting up and testing the Conditional Effectiveness Hypothesis. However, it is helpful for seeing the connections between our study and related research in the domestic and international arenas. Readers primarily interested in the test of our prediction can move straight to Section II.

In Section II, we narrow our focus to the EU and studies done on the impact of ECJ rulings (which tend to focus on trade as we do). Because our study builds off the general research design of these past studies, we pay particular attention to the outstanding design issues we seek to address in our study. Section III presents the data and statistical methodology used in the analysis. Section IV presents and describes the results.

To preview the results, we find that, in general, rulings by the ECJ – whether one looks at preliminary rulings and infringement rulings independently or combined – have at best a small, temporary effect on intra-EU trade. That is the conclusion one would reach if one considers all rulings by the ECJ – that is, without consideration for our theoretical argument regarding compliance. This turns out to be a crucial consideration. Based on our theoretical model, trade-liberalizing rulings against governments should be most impactful when they enjoy the support of third-party government briefs and should be least effective when they do not enjoy that support. Once the rulings are distinguished in our analysis by this criterion, we find systematic and substantively important effects of ECJ rulings on intra-EU trade under the conditions that foster compliance. And, when those conditions do not obtain, ECJ rulings have no discernible effect on commerce. This more nuanced set of results provides evidence on key implications of our theoretical model presented in Chapter 2. It also has important implications for our understanding of the impact and role of the ECJ on economic integration in Europe.

I. JUDICIAL IMPACT

Before describing our test of the effects of rulings on intra-EU trade, we first consider the general issue of why court decisions may lack impact on the social, economic, and political environment they address. We discussed this briefly in motivating the theoretical model in Chapter 2. But because that issue is central to the argument and testing in this chapter, we provide a more detailed discussion here.

Perhaps the most compelling arguments for and evidence of the limited impact of many court rulings on the social and economic world they address come from national courts. This is not, of course, because national courts suffer from more or greater compliance problems than international courts do. Quite the contrary, we typically expect the opposite, and thus limits on judicial impact are likely more pronounced for international courts. But, largely because of the focus of judicial scholars, much greater attention has been paid to documenting, measuring, and explaining variation in judicial impact at the domestic level.[2] We therefore engage that literature, as well as related literature on international courts, here.

---

[2] As Martin (2013) discusses, the international politics literature has often focused exclusively on compliance, narrowly conceived, rather than impact, as used in the domestic context.

Discussing the literature on judicial impact also helps illustrate how our analysis, although focused at the international level, also speaks to issues of judicial impact at the domestic level. As we discuss later, courts are often asked to interpret and monitor adherence with rules governing market integration and commercial liberalization both in domestic and international settings. As a result, our empirical analysis has implications for a broad literature in judicial politics. This section provides relevant background to appreciate the contribution of our empirical evidence.

a. *Judicial impact and trade*

A long research tradition examining the impact of judicial rulings has asked the following question: "what happens after a court's decision is rendered?" (Canon 1991: 435). This includes specific questions involving compliance by lower courts with appellate rulings, compliance by parties to the case with the specific ruling, compliance by government institutions with the broader policy implications of the ruling (e.g., school desegregation), and whether a ruling actually achieves its stated (or desired) outcome.

The working assumption in much of this research is that government institutions do not necessarily comply and implement court rulings, which means we should not take for granted that rulings affect the relevant policy or socio-economic goals. There is a fairly obvious reason for this assumption. Courts typically lack an independent means of enforcing and implementing their decisions beyond the parties to the case; rather, they often rely on executive agencies for enforcement. And a vast body of research on the United States indicates that we should not assume that government agencies, or the bureaucrats who staff them, faithfully implement judicial rulings (e.g., Wood and Waterman 1991, 1993). Similar conclusions result from studies of judicial politics in domestic settings outside the United States (e.g., for reviews, see Staton and Moore 2011; Vanberg 2005). This is the general point made by Epp (1998) in his seminal work on "the rights revolution" in the United States, Canada, India, and the United Kingdom. Unless an interested party commands resources sufficient to mount similar cases across many domestic jurisdictions over an extended period of time, judicial impact is dictated by the voluntary compliance of legislative and executive actors.

The empirical literature on judicial impact has focused primarily on civil rights and social issues and has devoted comparatively little attention to the economic effects of rulings (Canon 1991: 449). However, the general concerns regarding judicial impact are relevant to rulings addressing the flow of goods. To have a substantive effect on policy outcomes (commerce), court rulings must overcome a general compliance problem involving the parties to the case and, more importantly, involving the government authorities responsible for execution of the relevant policy. And this compliance problem is not easily solved, even in a setting where the court enjoys legitimacy and where respect for the rule of law is widespread.

For a relevant example related to trade, consider the 2005 US Supreme Court ruling in *Granholm v. Heald*. The *Granholm* decision struck down discriminatory state statutes on the direct shipping of wine. The ruling, based on the Commerce Clause of the US Constitution, held out the promise of increasing interstate trade in wine across the United States. However, the consequences of this ruling for interstate trade are currently ambiguous. The states have varied dramatically in their statutory response to this ruling (Ohlhausen and Luib 2008). Several states did in fact eliminate restrictions on shipments from out-of-state wineries. Other states replaced restrictions on interstate shipping with new provisions that imposed similar (or stronger) burdens on wine imports. For example, Indiana adopted new on-site purchase requirements whereby the purchaser must travel to the winery to arrange for shipment back to the state. Indiana also restricted shipping (in-state and out-of-state) to wineries selling no more than 500,000 gallons per year (Ohlhausen and Luib 2008–9). This effectively restricted shipping from out of state, where the large exporting wineries are located. More generally, Ellig and Wiseman (2011a) demonstrate that where states erected new restrictions, the expected economic impact of the ruling was undermined. The basic point here is that the liberalizing effect of the *Granholm* ruling on interstate trade depends on whether and how the ruling is implemented by state legislative and executive institutions.

This point applies generally to the current and historical record of judicial efforts to liberalize US interstate commerce. Statutory and regulatory barriers to interstate trade persist in a number of areas where, ostensibly, the Commerce Clause prohibits restrictions on the free movement of goods (Craig and Sailors 1987; McAllister 1940; Ohlhausen and Luib 2008–9: 544–5). Moreover, this problem is not a new phenomenon (Lockhart 1940; McAllister 1940). For example, barriers to trade between states had reached such dramatic levels in the late 1930s that the state of affairs was referred to as the "Balkanization" of the United States (Green 1940). The economic depression of the 1930s had spawned efforts by state legislatures to protect state business and to tax interstate business (Lockhart 1940). Not surprisingly, businesses harmed by these measures sought relief in federal courts.

This led to visible divisions on the Supreme Court about the practical limits of judicial relief and the necessity of congressional action to liberalize interstate commerce (Lockhart 1940: 1254). For example, in a joint dissent in *McCarroll* v. *Dixie Greyhound Lines* in 1940, Justices Black, Frankfurter, and Douglas argued:

> Spasmodic and unrelated instances of litigation cannot afford an adequate basis for the creation of integrated national rules which alone can afford that full protection for inter-state commerce intended by the Constitution. We would, therefore, leave the question raised by the Arkansas tax for consideration of Congress in a nation-wide survey of the constantly increasing barriers to trade among the States. (309 U.S. 176, 189 [1940])

The problem of eliminating barriers to trade is typically a constant battle, because the local or state businesses with an economic interest in such barriers tend to remain in place even after a favorable regulation is struck down. Thus, the demand for protectionist policies can lead to new regulations or taxes with a comparable effect. Indeed, the same protectionist policies may be erected. Lockhart (1940: 1287n172), for example, noted that as of 1940 three states had instituted discriminatory taxes on interstate merchant–truckers that had clearly been deemed invalid by the federal courts for decades. Reflecting on US interstate trade barriers in 1940, Lockhart concluded:

> In the absence of revolutionary changes in human nature or our federal form of government, we shall always have some barriers to interstate trade. Judicial decisions or Congressional actions may condemn them, but they constantly recur and at least temporarily restrain those lacking financial ability or inclination to seek judicial relief. The first line of attack on these trade barriers is, therefore, in the state legislative and executive bodies.

In sum, scholars have long been concerned with the impact of domestic judicial rulings in the United States (and beyond). Further, the lesson from the US experience is that even in a domestic setting with a well-respected judiciary, we should not assume that court rulings with policy implications for trade translate into substantial general effects on trade. We could imagine rulings have anything from no effect to a strong persistent effect depending on whether the state-level political and economic climate supports compliance by the legislature and executive. We now turn to the empirical literature that has focused on estimating the actual effect of rulings on trade.

b. *Statistical evidence of judicial impact on trade*

What effect do court rulings have on commerce? The primary venue for the study of the impact of trade-liberalizing rulings is at the international level. The observed differences in the success of international trade regimes have raised the following question: does the variation in performance reflect institutional differences regarding dispute resolution? Kono (2007) finds this to be the case, with the success of preferential trade agreements in increasing trade positively associated with the presence of a third-party dispute settlement mechanism (DSM). But Kono (2007) does not examine the effect of individual rulings, only the existence of a dispute settlement mechanism. And, interestingly, Kono (2007) does not find that the impact of DSMs varies with their level of "legalization" – that is, whether the DSM issues third-party rulings that enjoy the force of domestic law. This suggests that the value of DSMs for trade liberalization may not be because of the legal effect of individual rulings, but may instead be because of how DSMs facilitate interstate cooperation (Kono 2007).

Studies that directly estimate the impact of rulings on trade also provide limited evidence that DSM rulings enhance trade. Specifically, Bown (2004a, 2004b) finds mixed evidence of whether a determination of guilt by the arbitrating body of the General Agreement on Tariffs and Trade/Word Trade Organization (GATT/WTO) affects trade.[3] Research on intra-EU trade (reviewed in the next section) also provides mixed evidence.

Moreover, none of these studies have investigated the key empirical questions for our Conditional Effectiveness Hypothesis. First, no work to date has distinguished among these rulings according to whether and to what extent they face a compliance problem. Thus, these mixed results may reflect heterogeneity in the compliance issues across cases heard by these tribunals. Second, with the exception of Gabel et al. (2012), none of the studies of the relationships among DSMs, rulings, and trade examines whether trade-liberalizing effects actually are lasting. For example, the studies by Gowa and Kim (2005), Goldstein, Rivers, and Tomz (2007), and Tomz, Goldstein, and Rivers (2007) all measure the impact of GATT membership by evaluating the effect of GATT membership (or for Goldstein et al., membership in particular GATT regimes) on trade levels with effectively a pre/post design. The statistical analyses do not typically distinguish short-run and long-run effects on trade.[4] The same is true of the studies of court decisions on trade by Bown and others.

---

[3] Bown (2004a) finds that a determination of guilt by the GATT/WTO arbitrating body does increase the defendant state's imports in the good affected by the decision. Although highly suggestive, this evidence is unavoidably limited – with only sixty-four observations – and the sample includes only cases with developing nations as plaintiffs. Further, Bown also finds no effect of a guilty determination in a separate study (Bown 2004b).
[4] Tomz, Goldstein, and Rivers (2007: 2014) discuss dynamic effects in a footnote. They report a long-run multiplier but do not discuss short- vs. long-run effects or estimate standard errors on the long-run effect.

Our analysis of the impact of ECJ rulings on trade liberalization addresses both of these shortcomings. Our theoretical model informs our differentiation between rulings when noncompliance is more or less likely to obstruct a judicial impact on trade. And our statistical analysis enables us to estimate both short- (temporary) and long-run effects of ECJ rulings on trade.

II. THE ECJ AND THE REGULATION OF TRADE

The European Union is an attractive setting in which to examine whether court rulings affect trade. For most of its history, the EU's primary policy objective has been the economic integration of the member states (i.e., completion of its common market). Starting with the Treaty of Rome, the member states committed to the elimination of quantitative restrictions on intra-EU imports and exports (Articles 30 and 34 of the EEC Treaty). The treaty stipulated that member states were prohibited from introducing new quantitative restrictions and from making existing quotas more restrictive. It also specified a transition period in which the member states were required to eliminate all quantitative restrictions. Once the transition concluded on December 31, 1969 (Article 32, EEC Treaty), all remaining treaty provisions went into effect (Oliver 1996: 71). At that point, the central concern was how to treat national measures that had the "equivalent effect" of a quantitative restriction. Both the Commission and the ECJ have defined *equivalent effect* broadly. For example, in 1970 the Commission defined *measures* to include both formal rules (e.g., laws, regulations, and administrative practices) and nonbinding acts (e.g., recommendations).[5] For its part, the ECJ in 1974 interpreted measures of equivalent effect on imports to include "All trading rules enacted by Member States, which are capable of hindering, directly or indirectly, actually or potentially, intra-Community trade ... "[6] Finally, it is important to note that Article 30 (EEC), which prohibits trade restrictions on imports, gained direct effect at the end of the transition period. These developments provided ample opportunity for legal challenges to national laws with implications for intra-EU trade, including national policies justified on noncommercial grounds – for example, environmental protection.

The ECJ's primary responsibility in its first three decades was to resolve cases involving the free movement of goods, broadly construed.[7] Consequently, ECJ

---

[5] Directive 50/70, *Official Journal of the European Communities* L13/29.
[6] *Procurer de Roi* v. *Dassonville* (Case 8/74).
[7] For example, excluding staff-related cases, through 1986 the vast majority of cases involved the free movement of goods, agriculture, tax, and competition (*Synopsis of the Work of the Court of Justice of the European Communities in 1986 and 1987*, pp. 20–1).

rulings are obviously relevant to understanding judicial impact on trade. And their impact on trade is also pertinent to evaluating our theoretical model from Chapter 2. Recall that our model had specific implications for which rulings are most likely to cause change in government behavior (i.e., enjoy government compliance) and thereby have judicial impact. Given the prevalence of trade-related cases before the Court, we therefore would expect the theoretical expectations to be particularly relevant to understanding the impact of ECJ rulings on intra-EU trade liberalization.

a. *The judicial impact of ECJ rulings on intra-EU trade*

Just as there are state-level compliance challenges to implementing rulings designed to liberalize interstate trade in the United States, international court rulings that strike barriers to trade are vulnerable to noncompliance by member governments. This is certainly the case with the rulings by the ECJ. We already discussed the general compliance problems faced by the ECJ in our detailed treatment in Chapter 3. But it is important to recall that the ECJ's compliance issue – and its implications for judicial impact – is not simply a function of the ECJ's position as an international tribunal. Even if we assume the ECJ enjoys the authority of a national court, we should not assume that rulings consistently or powerfully influence policy. As Conant (2001: 16) puts it:

> If supranational legal authority has become functionally equivalent to domestic legal authority, traditional limits on judicial power must be addressed in accounts of the ECJ. In particular, judicial policy impact cannot be assumed to accompany an operational legal system. Effective legal systems resolve disputes between particular parties. Compliance with the individual rulings that settle these disputes does not necessarily lead to any broader change in policy. Indeed, in the EU context, national governments frequently evade the policy implications embedded in ECJ case law by containing their compliance... What requires explanation, then, is how and why innovative legal interpretation exerts any general impact on policy outcomes.

Further, note that Conant (2002) questions the judicial impact of all ECJ rulings – including preliminary rulings – where government implementation is at issue. We could imagine that compliance problems are stronger for infringement rulings than for preliminary rulings. For example, Tallberg (2002a) concludes that the decentralized enforcement through the preliminary ruling system allows the ECJ rulings to enjoy the authority of domestic courts. In contrast, infringement rulings are generally perceived to have a weak enforcement mechanism (Dehousse 1998: 48) and often meet with noncompliance from litigant governments (Panke 2010: 851).[8] However, as Conant (2002) demonstrates, a resistant government can effectively contain the policy impact of preliminary rulings as well. Consequently, we should not generally assume that ECJ rulings have policy impact whatever the judicial procedure employed.

For the empirical evidence of judicial impact on trade, a variety of scholars have examined whether and to what extent ECJ rulings influence intra-EU commerce. The focus has been exclusively on preliminary rulings, perhaps because of the alleged greater potency of such rulings (Fligstein and Stone Sweet 2002; Pitarakis and Tridimas 2003; Stone Sweet 2004; Stone Sweet and Brunell 1998a, 1998b; Stone Sweet and Caporaso 1998; Wind, Sindbjerg Martinsen, and Pons Rotger 2009). The empirical tests generally examined whether annual change in total intra-EU trade (exports plus imports) covaries with annual changes in the total number of preliminary references.[9] The most specific tests are for the effect of preliminary references from a member state on that country's intra-EU trade. The results of those studies have been mixed, with some work finding a positive relationship between references and total trade (e.g., Stone Sweet and Brunell 1998a) and others not (e.g., Wind, Sindbjerg Martinsen, and Pons Rotger 2009).

Although suggestive, these studies do not speak directly to the question of whether the ECJ, through liberalizing rulings, has influenced intra-EU trade. First, these studies all examined total trade. However, ECJ trade cases are overwhelmingly over restrictions on imports.[10] To illustrate, in a sample of 189 preliminary ruling cases consisting of 325 legal issues, only 7 of the legal issues dealt with export restrictions.[11] Thus, in testing for an effect of preliminary rulings on trade for a member state, we would like to know whether preliminary rulings influenced intra-EU imports, not trade in general.

Second, these studies used total references as a proxy for total pro-liberalizing preliminary rulings. Yet, many references do not conclude in a preliminary

---

[8] Prior to the Maastricht Treaty, which is the relevant period for our analysis in this chapter, the Commission could only bring repeated infringement proceedings if a government refused to comply. Afterward, the Commission, after winning an infringement ruling, could subsequently return to the Court to seek financial penalties for noncompliance.

[9] Pitarakis and Tridimas (2003) exclusively analyze the temporal relationship between total references and total intra-EU trade/GDP for the EU as a whole, not country-year observations. In some studies, trade is normalized by GDP and total references are normalized by population.

[10] As with infringement rulings, the typical case addresses import restrictions that can, at least potentially, affect trade with multiple member states. As a result, it is often very difficult to discern the exact bilateral trade relationships that would be affected by a ruling.

[11] The sample consists of all preliminary rulings with government litigants between 1970 and 1993.

ruling. They may be withdrawn, settled with an order of the court, or joined with another preliminary reference. Further, although the ECJ is often thought of as a body that favors European economic and political integration, not every decision swings that way.[12] Thus, ideally we would like a measure of preliminary *rulings* – not *references* – that distinguishes rulings that are in favor of market liberalization from rulings that are not.

Third, the effect on intra-EU imports should be subsequent to the ruling. Yet these studies typically did not estimate an appropriately lagged effect, particularly if one wants to distinguish short-run from long-run effects. If we assume a two-year delay between references and rulings and another one- or two-year delay before the national court decides the original case, we would expect at least a three-year lag between references and national court rulings.[13] That is, a reference from France in 1980 should affect intra-EU imports to France no earlier than 1983. Only two studies have examined such a lag length, and none has considered a longer delay in impact (Pitarakis and Tridimas 2003; Wind, Sindbjerg Martinsen, and Pons Rotger 2009).

Fourth, these studies considered all preliminary references as relevant to trade. But Conant (2001: 114–15; 2002: 88) shows that the inclusion of all references, regardless of policy area, can undermine inferences about the effect of references on trade. In particular, she notes that cases involving social security, social policy, and free movement of workers have little, if any, connection to trade. According to Conant (2001: 114), the inclusion of such cases undermines statistical inference.

Fifth, these studies gave no consideration to infringement rulings. Recall that these rulings are directed at member states for incompatibility between EU obligations and national laws and administrative practices, and they often involve trade-related issues. These are exactly the sort of rulings that are designed to have a policy effect.[14]

The most recent study, Gabel et al. (2012), corrects for these five research design issues. That study estimated the separate effects of the number of a nation's preliminary rulings and infringement rulings on the level of that nation's intra-EU imports in subsequent years. The study also examined the robustness of the estimates to the exclusion of rulings in issue areas that Conant

---

[12] For example, again drawing on the same sample of cases from earlier, we find that the ECJ made a pro-integration decision for only 207 out of 325 legal issues.

[13] According to Alter (2001: 42), the delay between the reference and ruling is usually about two years.

[14] No study has examined other types of rulings either, perhaps because they typically do not have clear implications for trade and, when they do, it is difficult to assign trade effects to specific member states.

(2001) identified as unrelated to trade. Finally, Gabel et al. estimated short- and long-run effects of rulings. Their results show only a limited impact of ECJ rulings on intra-EU imports. Infringement rulings had no systematic effect on intra-EU imports. Preliminary rulings had a substantively modest positive impact on a nation's intra-EU imports two years after the rulings. The timing of this effect is consistent with expectations and therefore appears to provide some limited support for the impact of ECJ rulings on trade. However, this effect was short-lived, disappearing after one year.

These limited findings could simply indicate the Court has a modest and temporary effect on trade during the period of these studies. This interpretation is consistent with the traditional account of member states' trade policies and the process of European integration in the 1970s and 1980s. The single market initiative and the Single European Act (SEA) were, at least in part, a response to the persistent and growing nontariff barriers that national governments created to protect their markets from intra-EU imports during that period (Commission of the European Communities 1985a; Moravcsik 1998: 353–4). Thus, before the SEA, national political pressures may have been sufficiently powerful to dilute or outright thwart the policy effect of liberalizing ECJ rulings.

b. *Return to the Conditional Effectiveness Hypothesis*

However, an alternative interpretation is that these general results hide important heterogeneity in the impact of ECJ rulings on trade. This was Conant's (2002) point, quoted previously. We should not expect ECJ rulings to typically have a significant policy impact. Indeed, we need an explanation for "how and why innovative legal interpretation exerts any general impact on policy outcomes." Our theoretical model provides one such explanation. When the threats of noncompliance with ECJ rulings by executive and administrative institutions are the least viable, we would expect rulings to manifest more pronounced changes in policy than when threats are the strongest. Specifically, the Conditional Effectiveness Hypothesis stated that Court rulings are more likely to change government behavior (i.e., change policy) when the briefs filed by third-party governments are (net) against the government.

This prediction provides a plausible interpretation of the evidence in Gabel et al. (2012). Recall that the vast majority of infringement rulings receives no third-party government briefs. Thus, the Conditional Effectiveness Hypothesis would anticipate that the vast majority of infringement rulings would have little or no policy impact. This is basically what Gabel et al. (2012) find. Preliminary rulings attract more third-party government briefs than infringement rulings do, but still many preliminary rulings do not feature net government briefs against a government litigant. Thus, although we would expect a greater trade effect of preliminary rulings than of infringement rulings, the overall effect should still be modest.

Whether this theoretical account is valid, though, would require distinguishing among trade-liberalizing infringement and preliminary rulings according to whether third-party briefs were net against the government and then reestimating the statistical models in Gabel et al. (2012). That is the strategy we pursue in the next section.

III. EMPIRICAL ANALYSIS

a. *The baseline model*

We examine the hypothesis by adapting the empirical strategy employed by Gabel et al. (2012) to test for the trade impact of ECJ rulings. We therefore begin by reviewing their strategy and their results, which serve as a baseline for comparison with subsequent analyses. We deviate from their analysis in one important way: we consider the impact of total rulings (preliminary rulings + infringement rulings). Our theoretical expectation is that both types of rulings are relevant, and our theory does not give one priority over the other. But we recognize that past studies distinguish between the two, putting much greater emphasis on preliminary rulings as a source of trade liberalization. Consequently, we estimate both their combined effect and their separate effects on trade.

Data and measurement

The data consist of observations by nation-year for the original six EU member states (France, West Germany, Italy, Belgium, Luxembourg, and the Netherlands) from 1970 to 1993. Belgium and Luxembourg are combined because of the format of available trade data, leaving us with five national panels. The time period is restricted for substantive and practical reasons. As discussed earlier, the original treaties provided for a transition period ending on December 31, 1969 (Oliver 1996: 61). The prescribed elimination of explicit tariffs and quantitative restrictions led to a dramatic increase in intra-EU trade during the transition period (Eichengreen and Vazquez 2000: 107). During this period, the ECJ played a limited role, reflecting both the inexperience of national legal communities with EU law and the limited scope of EU law regarding interstate commerce. Starting in 1970, however, the full set of rules governing the free movement of goods gained direct effect, thereby providing a broad legal basis for preliminary references related to trade (Oliver 1996: 72). By focusing on the post-1970 period, we therefore avoid confounding our analysis with transition effects of membership that reflect national changes in trade policy and the slow engagement of the ECJ by national courts. We are also constrained to the post-1970 period by the availability of relevant economic data for constructing the dependent variable. At the other end, we truncate at 1993 because of missing data. After 1993, the Court no longer provides a comprehensive record of all Commission briefs, information we use to determine whether a ruling was trade liberalizing in nature.[15]

We restrict the analysis to the original six member states for estimation purposes. Our data set involves multiple panels, which raises a variety of methodological problems. In this setting, Beck (2001) recommends a balanced panel design with time series of at least sixteen years for the estimation of panel-corrected standard errors. This condition disqualifies later member states. Further, restricting our analysis to the original six members also ensures that all member states enter the data set having completed a common transition period. Finally, focusing on these countries facilitates controlling for common temporal shocks (e.g., enlargement).[16]

Our dependent variable is the level of intra-EU imports into each country (as a share of its GDP) in each year in our study. This multilateral focus is consistent with past studies of this issue and reflects the fact that ECJ rulings typically do not specify a bilateral relationship or imply an effect on trade that is exclusive to imports from any one country. The national laws and regulations in question involved products potentially imported from many countries. This is fairly typical of the national laws, regulations, and practices at issue in infringement and preliminary rulings. For example, in a sample of infringement and preliminary rulings involving trade, the majority did not specify a bilateral trade relationship.[17]

---

[15] See the discussion of measurement error in Chapter 5. The measurement problem is particularly worrisome in the present context because we need an accurate measure of over-time change in the count of rulings with Commission support. This sort of descriptive accuracy was not critical to our analyses in the previous chapters.

[16] We also considered including the members of the first and second enlargements (Denmark, the United Kingdom, Ireland, and Greece). There are obvious advantages to their inclusion (e.g., much greater variation in infringement rulings with third-party briefs). But their inclusion comes with serious liabilities. For one, we cannot estimate panel-corrected standard errors with panels of different lengths. Also, we would expect new members to experience transition effects in their judicial processes and their international trade. That said, we have estimated the models presented here with the inclusion of these countries, and the results are largely consistent with the conclusions reported here.

[17] We considered only rulings with explicit trade implications, in which one could plausibly expect an exporting country to be identified. The sample of preliminary rulings is drawn from all cases with a government litigant (189) and 70 randomly drawn cases without a government

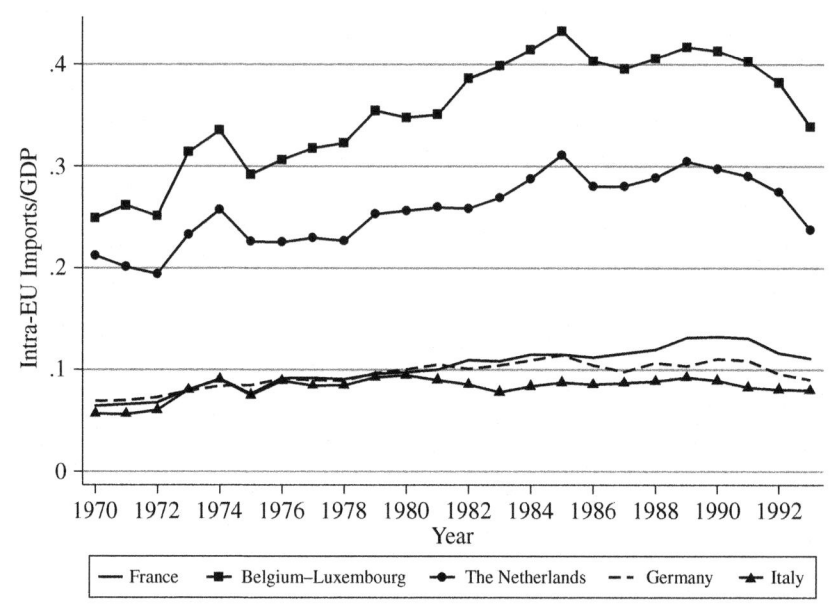

FIGURE 6.1 Trends in the ratio of intra-EU imports to GDP by country

We normalize imports by GDP for two reasons. First, GDP growth has had a very strong effect on the growth of intra-EU trade (Eichengreen and Vazquez 2000: 107). Second, larger economies typically feature larger changes in the value of imports over time and likely experience greater changes in imports in response to rulings than do smaller economies. This can cause heteroskedastic errors. Both intra-EU imports and GDP are measured in millions of current US dollars. All data come from the Organisation for Economic Co-operation and Development (OECD).[18] Based on the Levin-Lin-Chu test for unit roots in cross-sectional time-series data (Levin, Lin, and Chu 2002a), we find no evidence of nonstationarity in intra-EU imports/GDP.[19] Figure 6.1 summarizes

---

litigant. The sample of infringement rulings is based on a random draw from all such rulings in our data set.

[18] The data on trade in goods are available at the OECD website in the database "Total trade in value by partner country (1960–2008)."

[19] We estimated the test coefficient both with and without the cross-sectional trends demeaned. The lag length was selected by the Akaike Information Criteria. The p value on the coefficient was 0.01 (not demeaned) and 0.05 (demeaned).

Empirical analysis 171

the ratio of intra-EU imports to GDP for each of the five panels from 1970 to 1993.

Our key independent variable is the number of trade-liberalizing ECJ rulings related to a country in a year. As in Gabel et al. (2012), we measure the number of rulings (infringement rulings and preliminary rulings), not the number of references or infringement proceedings.[20] Recall from Chapter 3 that a case may have more than one ruling. For example, many preliminary references involve multiple legal issues, and each of these legal issues may apply to different questions of EU law and/or national law. Thus, for our purposes, a preliminary ruling refers to a preliminary ruling on a legal issue in a preliminary reference. Third, we distinguish rulings that favor market liberalization from those that do not. Consistent with Stone Sweet and Brunell (1998a), we rely on the Commission's position on each legal issue as an indicator of the market liberalizing position. We sum such rulings across all policy areas, which is consistent with the bulk of past studies on this question. However, we also construct a measure that excludes policy areas that Conant (2001: 114) identified as unlikely to influence trade: social policy, social security, and the free movement of workers.[21]

In our data, this distinction is of little significance. The correlation (within country) between the number of pro-Commission preliminary rulings with and without these policy areas is 0.90; the same correlation for pro-Commission infringement rulings is 0.99.[22] Not surprisingly, the results of our analysis are very similar whether we use the full set or a subset of the issue areas.

Figures 6.2 and 6.3 present the trends in the number of pro-Commission ECJ preliminary rulings and infringement rulings from 1970 to 1993 by country for the six original members. Cross-national patterns are quite different between preliminary rulings and infringement rulings in these figures. For example, Italy leads in infringement rulings, whereas Germany leads in preliminary rulings. However, note that the intranational trends in these two types of

---

[20] We do not include annulment or other rulings because we found it difficult, if not impossible, to identify trade-related effects of the rulings. For example, as described in Chapter 3, annulment rulings typically involve Commission decisions regarding Competition Policy and implementation of the Common Agricultural Policy. It is often difficult to discern an obvious trade effect from these decisions or to assign any such effect to a specific national economy.

[21] Policy areas were assigned based on the data set by Stone Sweet and Brunell (1999). This leaves the following issue areas: agriculture, free movement of goods, competition and dumping, external relations, freedom of establishment, taxation, commercial policy, environment, transportation, and approximation of laws.

[22] We controlled for nation in calculating the partial correlation.

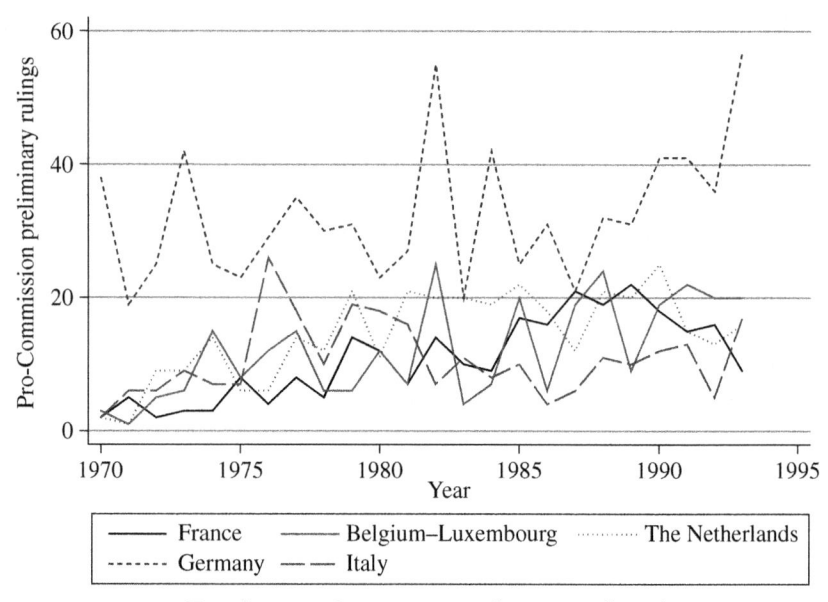

FIGURE 6.2 Trends in pro-Commission preliminary rulings by country

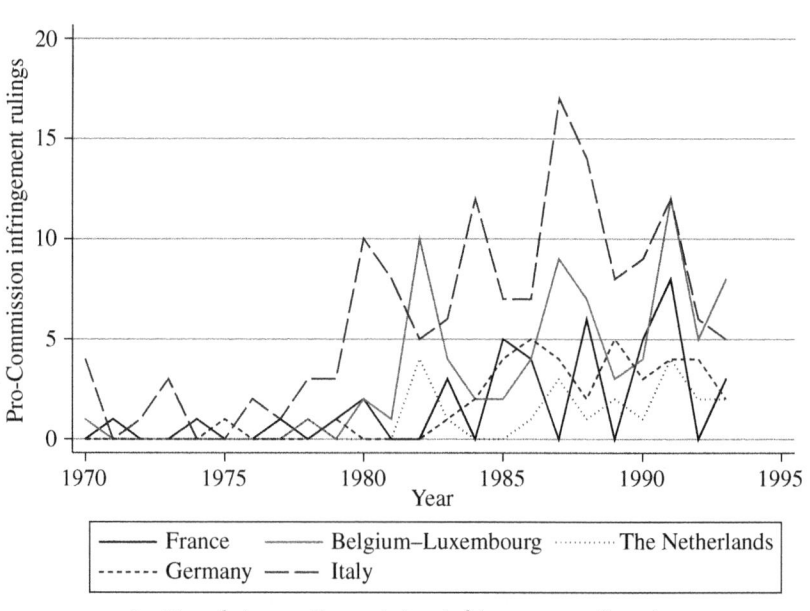

FIGURE 6.3 Trends in pro-Commission infringement rulings by country

TABLE 6.1 *Descriptive statistics, 1970–93, original six member states*

	Overall mean	Standard deviation	Min./Max.	Intranational standard deviation
Intra-EU Imports/GDP	18.0%	11.4%	5.6/43.3	2.9%
Pro-Commission Infringement Rulings				
All Policy Areas	2.7	3.5	0/17	3.0
Subset of Policy Areas	2.4	3.3	0/16	2.8
Pro-Commission Preliminary Rulings				
All Policy Areas	16.4	10.8	1/57	7.2
Subset of Policy Areas	11.9	9.3	0/50	6.3

rulings are positively correlated.[23] Table 6.1 provides descriptive statistics on the four key variables (preliminary and infringement rulings, with and without the excluded policy areas).

We include both country and year fixed effects in all models. We are concerned that unobserved national factors could cause cross-national variation in infringement or preliminary rulings and cause or be associated with cross-national variation in intra-EU trade patterns. This concern is illustrated in Figure 6.1. First, we see persistent national differences in intra-EU imports/GDP. These trade patterns could well be due to factors other than national differences in ECJ rulings but that correlate with the pattern of rulings. For example, Börzel et al. (2010) argue that national bureaucratic efficiency is negatively related to the number of infringement rulings, with Italy defined as low efficiency and the Netherlands defined as high efficiency. Italy also has systematically lower levels of intra-EU imports/GDP than the Netherlands does. Similarly, domestic sources of variation in rates of preliminary references to the ECJ could also confound our analysis to the extent they are correlated with cross-national trade patterns.[24]

We also want to control for common temporal shocks that would affect trade and, potentially, the rates of infringement rulings and preliminary rulings. The trends in Figure 6.1 suggest such shocks are an issue for our estimation. For example, we would expect the accession of new EU members to increase

[23] Controlling for country, the partial correlation between pro-Commission infringement rulings and pro-Commission preliminary rulings is 0.24 (p = 0.01) for all policy areas.
[24] See Wind, Sindbjerg Martinsen, and Pons Rotger (2009) for a summary of arguments about domestic factors.

intra-EU imports into the six original members. Figure 6.1 shows patterns generally consistent with this. But enlargement may also increase ECJ rulings because of the influx of novel legal issues. Thus, without temporal fixed effects we could find a spurious relationship between rulings and imports. Finally, EU-wide factors – such as the adoption of EU legislation – could affect intra-EU imports and be related to EU litigation.[25] We evaluate the necessity of country and year fixed effects in all models with an F-test for the joint significance. These tests always support the inclusion of fixed effects.

Note that because we are including a full slate of country and year fixed effects, there is no need to include other control variables that would only vary by country or year. For example, one might plausibly expect a nation's intra-EU imports to increase with the size of EU membership and with the number of EU laws (Fligstein and Stone Sweet 2002). Because these factors vary by year and are common to all members, they are captured by the year dummy variables in the model. One obvious factor that varies within a country and is not common across countries is the size of national GDP. As a country's GDP grows, it has more income to spend on intra-EU imports. But this is captured in our normalization of the dependent variable (intra-EU imports/ GDP).

Estimation strategy

Consistent with Gabel et al. (2012), we estimate the effect of rulings on intra-EU imports/GDP with an autoregressive distributed lag (ADL) model. The ADL is a general model that subsumes more constrained models that impose restrictions on the characters of the lag structure and the dynamic effects (see De Boef and Keele 2008). This generality fits our needs well. We expect that any effect of rulings should be in a future period (i.e., a lagged effect on trade), but we do not have clear guidance on the exact lag length to specify. Similarly, we want our model to distinguish between temporary and long-run impacts on trade. This is particularly true when we evaluate the predictions of the theory, which imply that some rulings have larger and longer-lasting effects than others do. An ADL model allows us to test these claims. Specifically, an ADL model allows us to test whether a static model (e.g., a Prais–Winsten model), which assumes an immediate and no long-run effect of rulings, or a lagged dependent variable model, which assumes the effect of rulings decays geometrically over time, accurately captures the dynamics of the effect of rulings on imports (De Boef and Keele 2008). Gabel et al. (2012) provides further description of the estimation strategy.

---

[25] For example, Fligstein and Stone Sweet (2002) show that the effect of references on trade becomes statistically insignificant in the presence of a control for EU legislative activity.

Our theoretical discussion provides some limited guidance in specifying the lag structure of the independent variables in the ADL model. For preliminary rulings, we would expect the earliest discernible effect of rulings on imports to be one or two years after the ECJ ruling. The delay allows for the national court to rule and the relevant economic agents to act.[26] We have a similar expectation regarding the lagged effect of infringement rulings, based on the Commission's estimates of delays in compliance with infringement rulings.[27] We therefore estimate an ADL model that includes one-, two-, and three-year lags of rulings.[28]

We employ panel-corrected standard errors to account for the standard set of violations of ordinary least squares (OLS) assumptions associated with time-series cross-sectional data (Beck and Katz 1995). Finally, based on the Lagrange Multiplier test, we verified that the time series in intra-EU imports/GDP follows an AR1 process and is successfully captured by a lagged dependent variable (Beck 2001: 279).

Results of the baseline model

Table 6.2 reports the results of the baseline analysis, which assumes compliance concerns do not influence the effect of rulings. The table includes the OLS regression coefficients and standard errors, the Long-Run Multiplier (LRM), and the Lagrange Multiplier (LM) test for autocorrelation. The null hypothesis of the LM test is the presence of autocorrelation (AR1). The LRM provides the total substantive influence (short-run plus long-run) on intra-EU imports of rulings at a one-year lag. The basic story from these results is that neither the combined ECJ rulings nor the infringement rulings have a systematic short-run or long-run impact on intra-EU trade. The results for preliminary rulings differ in one significant way. The coefficient on lagged rulings is positive and statistically significant at the second lag. But the third lag coefficient is negative and of comparable magnitude. Specifically, based on a Wald test, we cannot reject the null hypothesis that $\beta_{lag3} = -\mu\beta_{lag2}$.[29] Thus, the rulings have

---

[26] Note that litigants, and the government, can react to a preliminary ruling without waiting for the national court decision. For example, it is not uncommon for litigants to desist, accepting the ruling and settling out of court (Nykios 2003).

[27] Although no Commission report covers the period of our study, reports based on subsequent periods indicate that, on average, it took the member states in our study about 1.5 years to adjust national laws and practices in response to the rulings (*Internal Market Scoreboard*, No. 18, from European Communities 2009). Thus, we would not expect to see a change in a member state's trade as a result of infringement rulings for at least one to two years.

[28] We have also estimated models with a four-year lag, which has a coefficient that cannot be distinguished from zero.

[29] The χ^2 is 0.01 ($p > 0.92$) for the full set of policy areas and 0.82 ($p > 0.36$) for the subset of policy areas.

TABLE 6.2 *The effect of rulings on intra-EU imports/GDP, all rulings*

	Preliminary rulings		Infringement rulings		Combined rulings	
Set of issue areas	Full	Subset	Full	Subset	Full	Subset
Intra-EU Imports/ GDP $(t-1)$	0.813** (0.081)	0.817** (0.084)	0.806** (0.086)	0.799** (0.087)	0.819** (0.084)	0.818** (0.082)
Pro-Commission Rulings $(t-1)$	0.002 (0.014)	0.001 (0.015)	−0.032 (0.045)	−0.041 (0.048)	−0.005 (0.014)	−0.008 (0.014)
Pro-Commission Rulings $(t-2)$	0.024** (0.014)	0.018 (0.015)	−0.013 (0.048)	−0.009 (0.053)	0.018 (0.014)	0.010 (0.014)
Pro-Commission Rulings $(t-3)$	−0.024** (0.015)	−0.035** (0.015)	0.007 (0.048)	−0.017 (0.052)	−0.021* (0.015)	−0.036** (0.014)
Constant	3.93** (1.76)	3.91** (1.75)	4.03** (1.79)	4.17** (1.82)	3.87** (1.75)	3.92** (1.75)
Long-Run Multiplier $(t-1)$ (standard error)	0.010 (0.13)	−0.08 (0.13)	−0.19 (0.29)	−0.33 (0.27)	−0.05 (0.18)	−0.19 (0.17)
LM Test χ^2 (p value)	0.60 (0.44)	1.08 (0.30)	0.20 (0.66)	0.14 (0.71)	0.40 (0.53)	0.64 (0.42)
Mean number of rulings	16.41	11.86	2.72	2.39	19.1	14.3
Min./Max. number of rulings	1/57	0/50	0/17	0/16	1/59	0/52
N	115	115	115	115	115	115

Comment: All models include fixed effects for nations and years. Panel-corrected standard errors are in parentheses. The long-run multiplier and standard error were estimated via a Bewley (1979) transformation.
**$p < 0.05$, *$p < 0.10$, one-tailed test.

no long-run effect; the effect at $t-2$ is temporary. The results for preliminary and infringement rulings are exactly the same as those presented in Gabel et al. (2012).

Figure 6.4 provides a visual presentation of the key results. This figure presents the impulse response function (IRF), which plots the change in intra-EU imports/GDP associated with an increase of one ruling across a ten-year period. After one year, the effect is simply the coefficient on *Pro-Commission Rulings* $(t-1)$. As time progresses, the effect incorporates the coefficients on the subsequent lags, with appropriate adjustments for the temporal dependence

Empirical analysis 177

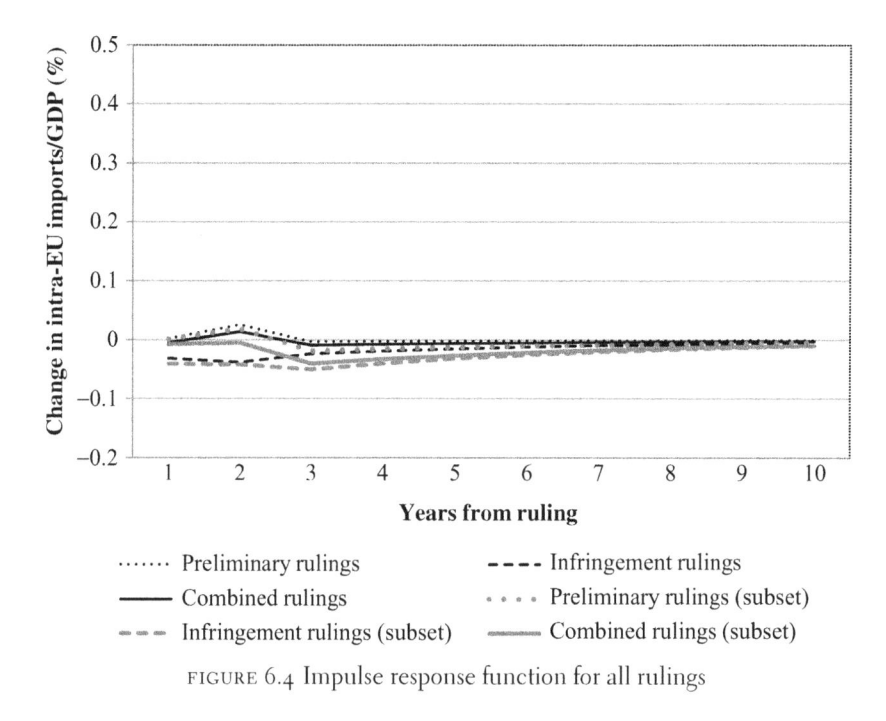

```
······· Preliminary rulings          ---- Infringement rulings
——— Combined rulings                 ···· Preliminary rulings (subset)
--- Infringement rulings (subset)    ━━━ Combined rulings (subset)
```

FIGURE 6.4 Impulse response function for all rulings

captured by the lagged dependent variable. As the figure shows, the impact of a ruling is close to zero over time and is often negative.

These results indicate what one would find if one ignored our theoretical concerns and assumed the effect of rulings on trade were not influenced by compliance concerns. Thus, these findings provide an interesting benchmark for comparison with the results (presented subsequently) from the theoretically justified subsets of rulings.

b. *Tests of the theoretical expectations*

The Conditional Effectiveness Hypothesis indicates that rulings should differ systematically depending on the likelihood the national government will implement a trade-liberalizing ruling. First, an increase in trade-liberalizing rulings by the ECJ that enjoy the (net) support of third-party government briefs should have a systematic and substantively important positive effect on intra-EU imports/GDP in the country to which the rulings are directed. Second, an increase in trade-liberalizing rulings by the ECJ that do not enjoy the (net) support of third-party governments should cause, at best, a weak increase in intra-EU imports/GDP in the country to which the rulings are directed.

In testing these claims, we measure the litigant supported by net third-party government briefs in the same way as described in Chapter 3.

We begin by testing the first claim. As with the analysis in Chapter 3, we operationalize this hypothesis in two ways. We first specify a test that maps onto the model and its predictions as closely and literally as possible. The theoretical model assumed a government as a defendant in the ruling. We therefore estimate the effect of trade-liberalizing rulings on a nation's intra-EU imports only for rulings in which that nation's government was the defendant and the pro-trade position enjoyed the (net) support of third-party government briefs.[30] The second set of tests generalizes to a wider set of conditions under which threats of noncompliance may be present. We consider the relationship between a nation's level of intra-EU imports and the number of rulings in which that national government was a litigant and for which the pro-trade position enjoyed the (net) support of third-party government briefs.

The main difference between the two settings is that the first is more restrictive regarding preliminary rulings, because they can involve a government litigant as a plaintiff. The second approach includes such rulings. We see that this distinction is not particularly important for the substantive findings.

Table 6.3 presents the results for models with rulings in which the government is the defendant and the pro-trade position has net support from third-party government briefs. Table 6.4 presents the results when the government is a litigant and the pro-trade position has net support from third-party government briefs. The results of both analyses differ substantially from those in Table 6.2. Focusing on all such rulings (the Combined column), we find all positive coefficients on lagged rulings with the most pronounced immediate effect felt after two years. Importantly, the coefficient on the third lag is positive, indicating rulings have a long-run effect on trade. This is summarized by the long-run multiplier, which is positive and substantively large compared to the results in Table 6.2. The long-run effect is also apparent from a comparison of the impulse response functions for these models (see Figures 6.5 and 6.6) with those in Figure 6.4. In sum, focusing on the combined results, we find that rulings have the expected delay in impact (roughly two years), and their impact is positive and significant, both in the short term and long term.[31] This

---

[30] For reasons of tractability, we make a simple distinction between trade-liberalizing rulings (1) with net support and (2) without net support from third-party briefs. The level of net support does vary across rulings in category 1.

[31] The substantive effect of a ruling after a two-year lag is plausible, given the value of imports from the EU into the countries in our study. For example, consider the average impact after two years estimated for the combined rulings in Table 6.4 (0.10 percent of GDP). It is difficult if not impossible to match the goods or services specified in a ruling to a specific category

TABLE 6.3 *The effect on intra-EU imports/GDP of rulings when government is defendant and with net support from third-party government briefs*

	Preliminary rulings		Infringement rulings	Combined rulings	
Set of issue areas	Full	Subset	Full	Full	Subset
Intra-EU Imports/ GDP $(t-1)$	0.813** (0.082)	0.806** (0.083)	0.823** (0.085)	0.822** (0.082)	0.814** (0.082)
Pro-Commission Rulings $(t-1)$	0.117 (0.108)	0.104 (0.110)	0.415 (0.344)	0.148* (0.107)	0.142* (0.110)
Pro-Commission Rulings $(t-2)$	0.185** (0.106)	0.167* (0.108)	−0.045 (0.379)	0.189** (0.105)	0.176** (0.108)
Pro-Commission Rulings $(t-3)$	0.075 (0.108)	0.102 (0.109)	0.069 (0.404)	0.088 (0.107)	0.118 (0.110)
Constant	3.94** (1.72)	4.05** (1.74)	3.72** (1.78)	3.76** (1.72)	3.89** (1.73)
Long-Run Multiplier $(t-1)$ (standard error)	2.01** (0.93)	1.93** (0.99)	2.48 (3.85)	2.38** (1.08)	2.35** (1.14)
LM Test χ^2 (p value)	0.04 (0.84)	0.04 (0.84)	0.24 (0.63)	0.02 (0.89)	0.02 (0.89)
Mean number of rulings	0.37	0.26	0.07	0.44	0.33
Min./Max. number of rulings	0/7	0/7	0/1	0/7	0/7
N	115	115	115	115	115

Comment: All models include fixed effects for nations and years. Panel-corrected standard errors are in parentheses. The long-run multiplier and standard error were estimated via a Bewley (1979) transformation. The subset of issue areas for infringement rulings is the same as the full set.
**$p < 0.05$, *$p < 0.10$, one-tailed test.

provided in trade statistics. But, by looking at trade sectors, we can evaluate whether import markets were large enough to support our estimated effect both in terms of the value in a year and in terms of the variation from year to year in the value of the import markets. For instance, consider French imports from the EU in the 1990–4 period (OECD statistics, STAN Bilateral Trade Index). On average, 0.10 percent of French GDP in those years was about $1.1 billion (current prices). In 1993, imports in transport equipment and mining and quarrying were much larger than that ($21 billion and $2 billion, respectively), and imports in wood and wood/cork products were a bit less than that (approximately $800 million). During that 1990–4 period, several sectors saw change in the value of imports comparable to or greater than 0.10 percent of GDP. For example, average annual variation in EU imports in both the machinery

TABLE 6.4 *The effect on intra-EU imports/GDP of rulings with government litigant with net support from third-party government briefs*

Set of issue areas	Preliminary rulings Full	Preliminary rulings Subset	Infringement rulings Full	Combined rulings Full	Combined rulings Subset
Intra-EU Imports/ GDP $(t-1)$	0.803** (0.084)	0.798** (0.084)	0.823** (0.085)	0.804** (0.084)	0.800** (0.084)
Pro-Commission Rulings $(t-1)$	0.003 (0.071)	0.013 (0.075)	0.415 (0.344)	0.018 (0.071)	0.031 (0.074)
Pro-Commission Rulings $(t-2)$	0.097* (0.073)	0.104* (0.078)	−0.045 (0.379)	0.098* (0.073)	0.104* (0.077)
Pro-Commission Rulings $(t-3)$	0.037 (0.071)	0.066 (0.071)	0.069 (0.404)	0.042 (0.073)	0.072 (0.072)
Constant	4.09** (1.77)	4.17** (1.76)	3.72** (1.78)	4.05** (1.77)	4.12** (1.76)
Long-Run Multiplier $(t-1)$ (standard error)	0.69 (0.61)	0.90 (0.72)	2.48 (3.85)	0.81* (0.63)	1.03* (0.75)
LM Test χ^2 (p value)	0.09 (0.77)	0.00 (0.99)	0.24 (0.63)	0.08 (0.78)	0.00 (0.99)
Mean number of rulings	0.83	0.64	0.07	0.90	0.70
Min./Max. number of rulings	0/7	0/7	0/1	0/7	0/7
N	115	115	115	115	115

Comment: All models include fixed effects for nations and years. Panel-corrected standard errors are in parentheses. The long-run multiplier and standard error were estimated via a Bewley (1979) transformation. The subset of policy areas for infringement rulings is the same as the full set.
**$p < 0.05$, *$p < 0.10$, one-tailed test.

conclusion holds regardless of whether we consider rulings in all issue areas or only the subset.[32]

The table also shows that preliminary rulings and infringement rulings do not contribute equally to this judicial impact. Although the general pattern of lagged effects is fairly similar (see Figures 6.5 and 6.6), the estimates for the infringement rulings are much less precise than those for the preliminary

and equipment sector and the chemical, rubber, plastics, and fuel products was approximately $2 billion.

[32] The issue areas for infringement rulings were all in the subset of policy areas, and thus we report only one set of results.

Empirical analysis 181

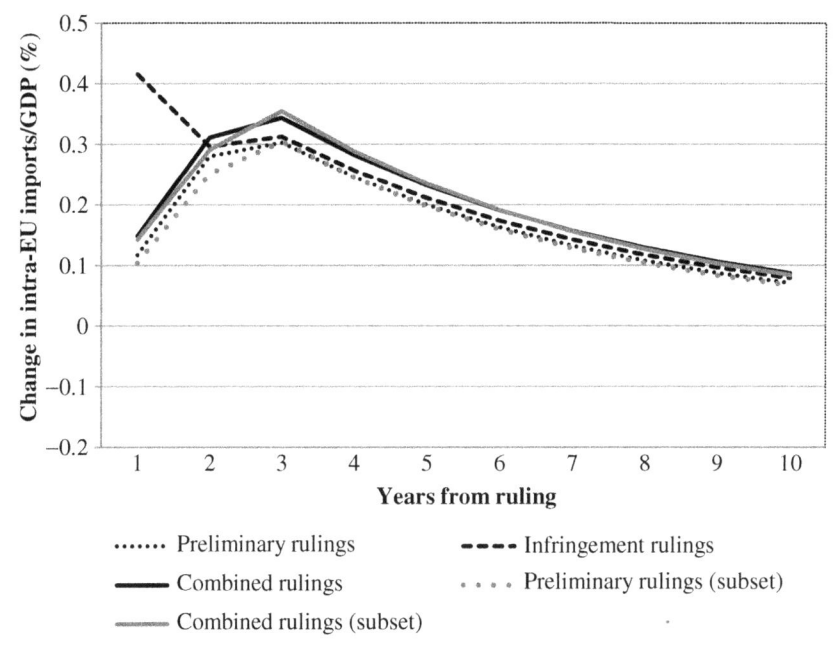

FIGURE 6.5 Impulse response function with a government defendant and net support from third-party government briefs

rulings. Given the very small variation in the number of infringement rulings, this is not surprising. The maximum number of such rulings in a year was 1 and the mean was 0.07.

The results presented in Tables 6.3 and 6.4 indicate that ECJ rulings with third-party government support have a substantively important effect on intra-EU trade. The long-run multiplier (LRM) provides a summary of this, indicating the total effect over time of a ruling. In Table 6.4, this LRM for combined rulings indicates that an increase of one trade-liberalizing ruling causes a 0.81 percent total (short- and long-run) increase in the share of GDP represented by intra-EU imports. To put this into context, recall from Table 6.1 that intra-EU imports/GDP has a mean of 18 percent, and the within-country variation (one standard deviation) is 2.6 percent. Thus, the 0.81 percent figure represents about 40 percent of a standard deviation change in intra-EU imports/GDP. It is also important to note that, on average, we saw slightly less than one such ruling per year in a country in our data set.

Finally, note that the substantive impact of the Court's rulings is similar across results in Tables 6.3 and 6.4, after we consider the observed variation in the number of lagged rulings in the two contexts. Although the coefficients

182   *The Conditional Effectiveness Hypothesis*

⋯⋯⋯ Preliminary rulings   ▬ ▬ ▬ Infringement rulings
▬▬▬ Combined rulings   • • • • Preliminary rulings (subset)
▬▬▬ Combined rulings (subset)

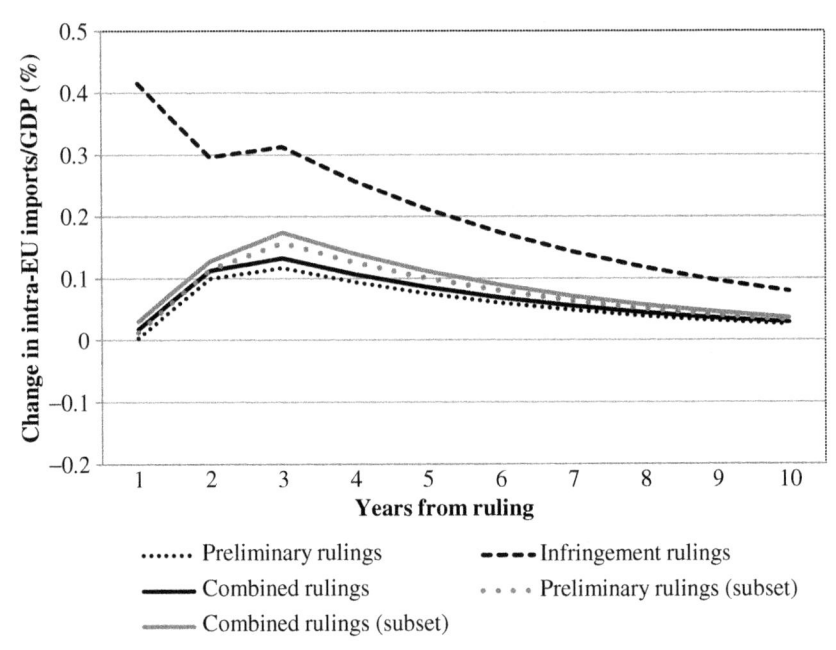

FIGURE 6.6 Impulse response function with a government litigant and net support from third-party government briefs

on the lagged rulings decrease by about half when we move to Table 6.4, the average number of rulings roughly doubles.

That said, the results in Tables 6.3 and 6.4 are not identical. In particular, the first lag has a stronger effect in the models in Table 6.3 than in the models in Table 6.4, and this contributes to a larger LRM in that model. One can also see this by comparing the impulse response function in Figure 6.5 with that of Figure 6.6. But overall the results of the two analyses tell the same story, with a much stronger effect of trade-liberalizing ECJ rulings on intra-EU imports than found when all rulings were considered in the baseline model in Table 6.3. This is consistent with the Conditional Effectiveness Hypothesis.

We now turn to the second claim: that trade-liberalizing ECJ rulings that lack the (net) support of third-party government briefs will have, at best, a weak positive effect on intra-EU imports. As we did with the first claim, we test this in two ways. First, we consider only trade-liberalizing rulings against a member-state defendant when the ruling does not have net support from third-party government briefs. Those results are presented in Table 6.5. We then broaden the criteria for inclusion of rulings to accept preliminary rulings in which the government is a plaintiff or defendant and the trade-liberalizing

Empirical analysis 183

TABLE 6.5 *The effect on intra-EU imports/GDP of rulings with a government defendant and without net support from third-party government briefs*

Set of issue areas	Preliminary rulings Full	Preliminary rulings Subset	Infringement rulings Full	Infringement rulings Subset	Combined rulings Full	Combined rulings Subset
Intra-EU Imports/ GDP $(t-1)$	0.823** (0.083)	0.822** (0.083)	0.807** (0.085)	0.800** (0.087)	0.810** (0.083)	0.802** (0.085)
Pro-Commission Rulings $(t-1)$	−0.150* (0.105)	−0.143* (0.105)	−0.037 (0.045)	−0.047 (0.048)	−0.059* (0.040)	−0.065* (0.040)
Pro-Commission Rulings $(t-2)$	0.052 (0.105)	−0.000 (0.106)	−0.009 (0.048)	−0.005 (0.053)	0.012 (0.042)	0.004 (0.043)
Pro-Commission Rulings $(t-3)$	−0.034 (0.113)	−0.049 (0.113)	0.005 (0.047)	−0.019 (0.051)	−0.005 (0.042)	−0.024 (0.043)
Constant	3.67** (1.76)	3.70** (1.75)	4.02** (1.78)	4.15** (1.81)	3.93** (1.75)	4.08** (1.77)
Long-Run Multiplier $(t-1)$ (standard error)	−0.75 (1.17)	−1.07 (1.20)	−0.21 (0.28)	−0.35* (0.26)	−0.27 (0.29)	−0.43** (0.26)
LM Test χ^2 (p value)	0.12 (0.73)	0.07 (0.79)	0.18 (0.67)	0.14 (0.70)	0.13 (0.72)	0.09 (0.76)
Mean number of rulings	0.59	0.50	2.65	2.32	3.23	2.83
Min./Max. number of rulings	0/6	0/6	0/17	0/16	0/17	0/16
N	115	115	115	115	115	115

Comment: All models include fixed effects for nations and years. Panel-corrected standard errors are in parentheses. The long-run multiplier and standard error were estimated via a Bewley (1979) transformation.
**$p < 0.05$, *$p < 0.10$, one-tailed test.

position does not enjoy net support from third-party government briefs.[33] Table 6.6 presents those results.

The results in both tables paint the same, very clear, picture. Lagged rulings typically do not have a positive effect on intra-EU imports. In the results for all rulings (the Combined column), the short-run and long-run effects are

---

[33] Note that these categories are not the complement of the categories used in analyses presented in Tables 6.3 and 6.4. Cases without a government litigant do arise in preliminary references and are excluded from this analysis.

TABLE 6.6 *The effect on intra-EU imports/GDP of rulings with a government litigant and without net support from third-party government briefs*

	Preliminary rulings		Infringement rulings		Combined rulings	
Set of issue areas	Full	Subset	Full	Subset	Full	Subset
Intra-EU Imports/ GDP $(t-1)$	0.812** (0.083)	0.811** (0.084)	0.807** (0.085)	0.800** (0.087)	0.809** (0.084)	0.800** (0.085)
Pro-Commission Rulings $(t-1)$	−0.046 (0.059)	−0.053 (0.071)	−0.037 (0.045)	−0.047 (0.048)	−0.036 (0.032)	−0.044* (0.035)
Pro-Commission Rulings $(t-2)$	0.035 (0.062)	0.007 (0.073)	−0.009 (0.048)	−0.005 (0.053)	0.006 (0.034)	−0.002 (0.038)
Pro-Commission Rulings $(t-3)$	0.019 (0.071)	0.004 (0.092)	0.005 (0.047)	−0.019 (0.051)	0.004 (0.036)	−0.015 (0.040)
Constant	3.93** (1.76)	3.95** (1.76)	4.02** (1.78)	4.15** (1.81)	3.98** (1.76)	4.14** (1.79)
Long-Run Multiplier $(t-1)$ (standard error)	0.04 (0.50)	−0.22 (0.67)	−0.21 (0.28)	−0.35* (0.26)	−0.13 (0.25)	−0.30* (0.23)
LM Test χ^2 (p value)	0.16 (0.69)	0.16 (0.69)	0.18 (0.67)	0.14 (0.70)	0.16 (0.69)	0.14 (0.70)
Mean number of rulings	1.35	1.17	2.65	2.32	4.00	3.49
Min./Max. number of rulings	0/10	0/7	0/17	0/16	0/19	0/19
N	115	115	115	115	115	115

Comment: All models include fixed effects for nations and years. Panel-corrected standard errors are in parentheses. The long-run multiplier and standard error were estimated via a Bewley (1979) transformation.
**$p < 0.05$, *$p < 0.10$, one-tailed test.

generally associated with *decreasing* intra-EU imports, although the substantive effect of rulings is basically zero. This is apparent from the impulse response functions (Figures 6.7 and 6.8) and the LRMs. The independent results for preliminary rulings and infringement rulings show these same patterns. And these conclusions are robust to including rulings over all issue areas or only the subset of issue areas. In sum, these results are also consistent with the Conditional Effectiveness Hypothesis.

Figure 6.9 provides a summary comparison of the results. This figure represents the impulse response functions for the combined rulings from the

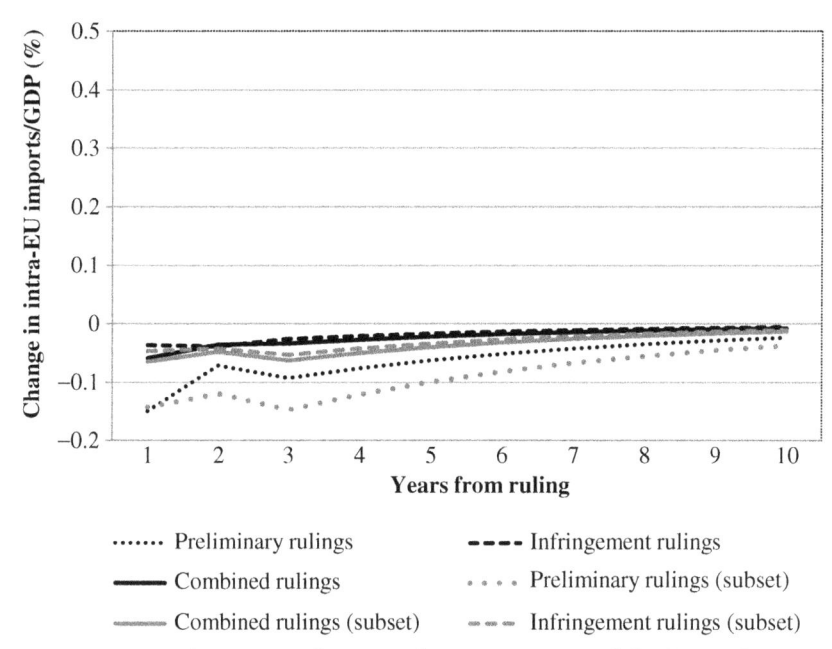

FIGURE 6.7 Impulse response function when government is defendant without net support from third-party government briefs

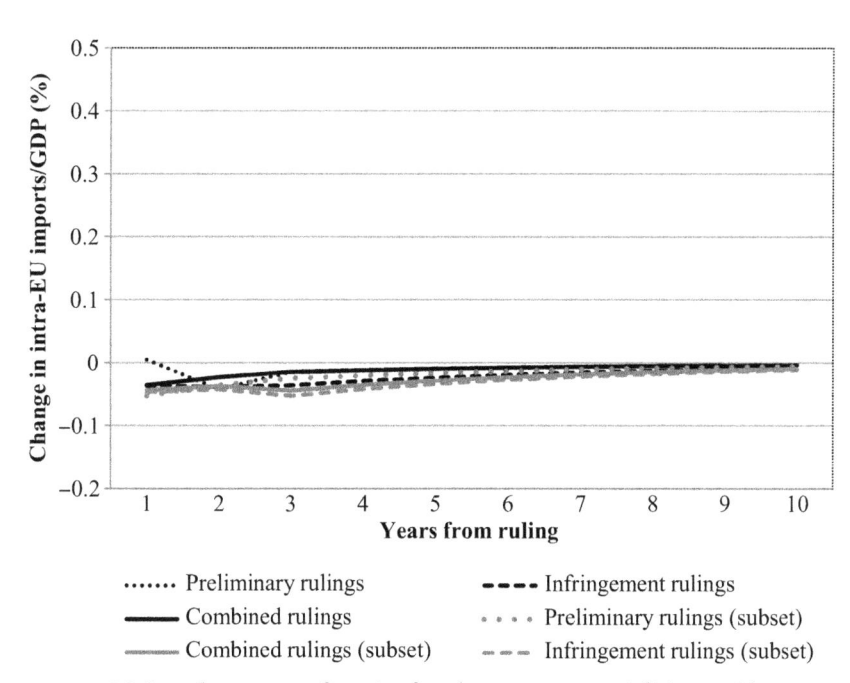

FIGURE 6.8 Impulse response function for when government is litigant without net support from third-party government briefs

186   The Conditional Effectiveness Hypothesis

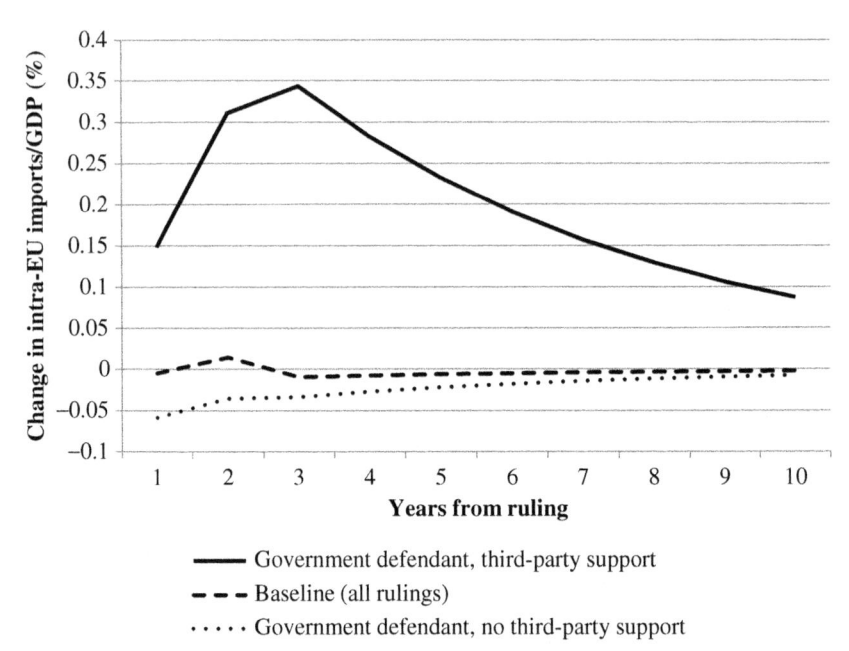

FIGURE 6.9 Impulse response function for combined rulings (all issue areas)

baseline model, the model with government defendant and third-party support, and the model with government defendant and no third-party support. Rulings in the baseline model have little to no effect on trade. But this general finding hides important heterogeneity in the impact of rulings on trade. On the one hand, pro-trade rulings with the support of third-party government briefs are associated with increased intra-EU trade. On the other hand, trade-liberalizing rulings lacking third-party government support have a slightly negative effect on trade. The theoretical guidance from our model in Chapter 3 is therefore critical to isolating and estimating the trade-liberalizing impact of rulings. Ignoring this distinction and estimating the baseline model would lead one to conclude from these data that rulings have little or no effect on trade.

c. Considering alternative explanations

Before concluding, two further points are warranted. First, it is important to note that these tests were not designed to identify and evaluate all possible theoretical arguments about the conditions that determine the judicial impact of ECJ rulings. For example, Conant (2002) argues that policy change in response to an ECJ ruling depends on whether the conditions obtain for domestic legal and political mobilization supporting the ECJ's legal interpretation. For Panke (2010: 46), compliance depends on whether the ruling itself can change the legal discourse to complement a dominant political frame in the domestic arena. We do not test these claims in our analysis because they make no clear predictions regarding the relationship between the presence of third-party government briefs and the impact of rulings on trade. That is, they do not present a possible confound for our hypotheses.

Second, one alternative explanation deserves further discussion because it could plausibly account for the results reported here.[34] Our measure of third-party government support for the liberalizing position is indicated by whether the net third-party government briefs favored the trade-liberalizing position. But perhaps this indicator is actually measuring something more straightforward: the economic importance of the case. If so, then one can construct an alternative explanation for our results.

The argument goes as follows. Assume that third-party governments are more likely to submit briefs on cases with substantial potential economic impact than on cases with minimal impact. In addition, assume that litigant governments generally comply with ECJ rulings. We would then expect to find differential trade effects of rulings as a function of the presence of third-party government briefs. Rulings that attract third-party briefs would be associated with much larger changes in trade than would rulings without third-party government briefs. Consequently, we would expect to find differential trade effects of rulings in the absence of the compliance concerns at the heart of our theoretical model.

Could this alternative story account for our statistical results? First, note that our distinction between rulings with and without net third-party government support does not simply distinguish between rulings with and without any third-party briefs. In particular, a ruling that attracted net third-party briefs against the liberalizing position was counted the same as a ruling with no third-party briefs. These were the rulings without support used in the analyses presented in Tables 6.5 and 6.6. Thus, at best, our results provide a crude test of this alternative story. And, if this story is correct, we should see much stronger effects of rulings if we replace our measure of rulings that enjoy third-party

---

[34] One could raise potential endogeneity concerns regarding the relationship between a nation's number of preliminary rulings and intra-EU trade. See Gabel et al. (2012) for a description of the concern and an argument for why it is implausible in an empirical setting such as the analyses conducted here.

government support with one that simply indicates the number of rulings that attracted any third-party briefs.

We checked that directly with one further analysis using the number of liberalizing rulings that attracted *any* third-party government briefs in the statistical models presented in Tables 6.3 and 6.4. The results do not support the alternative explanation for our findings. This is best summarized by comparing the long-run multipliers (LRMs) for the number of rulings. In all models, the LRMs are smaller when we use the alternative measure of liberalizing rulings than what we found originally. For example, for combined rulings with a defendant government, the LRM decreases by 50 percent. This is inconsistent with the alternative explanation because we should have found an increased effect of rulings with a better measure of the specific hypothesis regarding economic import. Consequently, we are confident our results are consistent with our compliance argument and do not simply capture differences in the economic importance of the rulings.[35]

IV. DISCUSSION

The analysis in this chapter provides tests of two implications of the second prediction from our theoretical model. The general empirical question was whether trade-liberalizing rulings by the ECJ affect the level of intra-EU commerce. Our theoretical model generated a clear empirical implication in this context: that trade-liberalizing rulings that attract the net support of third-party government briefs should be more likely to enjoy government compliance and thereby have a policy impact than would trade-liberalizing rulings that lack such third-party support. We found exactly that in our analysis. Pro-trade rulings with the support of third-party government briefs are associated with increased and sustained intra-EU trade. Trade-liberalizing rulings lacking third-party government support do not have such an effect. Indeed, if anything, these rulings have a slightly negative effect on trade.

Beyond providing evidence as to the empirical relevance of our theoretical model, this evidence is also important for our understanding of the role of the ECJ in European integration. Most obviously, the theoretical guidance

---

[35] A related alternative explanation is that the presence of briefs against the government simply indicates a greater impact of compliance on imports than does the absence of such briefs. Consequently, assuming governments always comply, trade-liberalizing rulings with support of third-party briefs should be associated with a greater impact on trade (which we find). However, according to this explanation, we should still find a systematic positive, but smaller, effect for rulings that lack third-party support. We find no such effect.

from our model in Chapter 2 is critical to isolating and estimating the trade-liberalizing impact of rulings. Ignoring this distinction and estimating the effect of rulings in general would lead one to conclude from these data that rulings have little or no effect on trade.

In addition, the results speak to longstanding claims about the relative importance of infringement and preliminary rulings for the liberalization of the EU market. Recall that the previous empirical literature on rulings and trade has focused exclusively on preliminary rulings. One reason for that focus is the assumption that infringement rulings, because they are not articulated through national court rulings, are not as influential on policy outcomes as are preliminary rulings. Our findings confirm part of the conventional wisdom: the impact of ECJ rulings on trade is primarily through preliminary references. However, the reason for this is different from the conventional account. The result holds because the bulk of trade-liberalizing rulings receiving the support of government briefs is generated through preliminary references. It is not because of the legal procedure itself.

That said, when trade-liberalizing infringement rulings are supported by third-party government briefs, these rulings also have, on average, a positive effect on trade. Indeed, as the results shown in Figures 6.5 and 6.6 suggest, the magnitude of the effect is similar to that of preliminary rulings. Granted, the impact is less robust for the infringement rulings, because the standard errors are large on some of the lagged coefficients. But we think it would be misleading to construe our results as indicating that infringement rulings have no effect. The major difference between the two types of rulings is one of quantity; we see many more impactful preliminary rulings than infringement rulings.

The evidence presented in this chapter contributes to our understanding of why and how international institutions, and particularly international courts, can have a significant impact on the substantive (e.g., social and economic) domains of their rulings. Our argument identified specific conditions under which we expect governments to honor the spirit, not just the letter, of international agreements. Our evidence from this chapter shows that these conditions provide a clear demarcation between rulings that change the relevant substantive outcomes (e.g., trade) and rulings that do not. Consequently, this evidence adds to our understanding of how and why international institutions can advance the goals of the international agreement. These findings show that international court rulings can have an important impact but that this effect is far from a general effect. Rulings can also have little or no substantive effect when the theoretical conditions supporting compliance are weak or absent.

Finally, the evidence in this chapter contributes to our specific understanding of the effect of international court rulings on trade liberalization. Past empirical work on the effect of rulings on trade has found ambiguous results. Although we suspect many scholars and observers have low expectations about the impact of rulings by international courts, our assessment provides a novel and nuanced record about that impact. Trade is important. As we noted earlier, the literature on the impact of rulings on trade that has examined GATT/WTO rulings and ECJ rulings has found mixed evidence. The recent EU literature, in particular, has found at best only limited, short-run trade effects of rulings (Gabel et al. 2012; Wind, Sindbjerg Martinsen, and Pons Rotger 2009). But these studies did not distinguish among rulings according to the conditions identified by our theory. The analysis in this chapter shows this distinction is critical: we can find large, substantively important effects when the conditions obtain. Thus, the general effects estimated in past studies hid an important heterogeneity in the impact of rulings that is theoretically meaningful and substantively important.

7

Conclusion

In this book, we proposed and tested a theory of international court adjudication that seeks to help us understand to what extent international courts can develop and enforce an international rule of law. To conclude, we put this analysis in broader context. In the first part of the chapter, we briefly summarize our argument and findings. Then we discuss the implications of our analysis for alternative explanations. To what extent are our argument and findings in tension with and complementary to other arguments put forward for international court influence? Next we describe the implications for our understanding of the European Union, the European Court of Justice, and the process of adjudication in the EU. After that, we discuss broader implications for our understanding of international courts and international law in general. Finally, we consider what our study implies about the relationship between domestic and international rule of law.

I. SUMMARY OF THE THEORETICAL ARGUMENT AND EMPIRICAL FINDINGS

Our theory of international court adjudication is predicated on the canonical first principle that common regulatory regimes are created to overcome collective action problems among the member states (i.e., the member states would benefit from mutual adherence with some set of policies, but they each have individual incentives to shirk their policy obligations). We depart from the canonical view by adopting a more realistic depiction of the trade-offs faced by member states. Specifically, we allow the costs of compliance with the regime's rules to vary over time and to be private information of the government experiencing the costs. When this cost is sufficiently large cooperation is no longer net beneficial (and the game is no longer a prisoners' dilemma).[1]

This characterization of costs makes the politics of common regulatory regimes more complex in two ways; it both creates conditions under which governments might not want to sustain cooperation with the regulatory regime and makes sustaining cooperation harder. In theory, governments willing to invest the necessary resources and coordinate behavior can sustain net beneficial cooperation despite these challenges. However, doing so becomes prohibitively cumbersome as the number of participant states increases and the breadth of policy domains expands. An international court offers an efficient institutional solution to these challenges by serving as a fire alarm and information clearinghouse for the member states.[2]

Our model demonstrates that, in this context, international courts can facilitate compliance with international law, but only within limits. Although the court is free to rule against any government defendant it wishes, the court will only get compliance when other governments are willing to back up the court and punish the defendant for evading an adverse court ruling. As a result, the court's ability to facilitate targeted punishment defines the extent, and limits, of its ability to promote international rule of law. The court in our model can and does promote government compliance with international rule of law. However, it does so only to the extent that international law codifies restrictions on state behavior that the member states agree serve their purposes (i.e., that governments consider net beneficial). If and when the court tries to enforce international laws in a way that the governments do not see as enhancing their welfare, the court will be ineffectual.

Note that this answer is complementary to arguments in the "rational design" tradition. For example, Rosendorff (2005) demonstrates how the use of retaliatory penalties through the World Trade Organization (WTO) dispute resolution mechanism helps compliance be sustainable for a wider range of costs. However, Rosendorff's argument does not make the agreement stable to any cost. Similarly, Koremenos (2005) proposes that limited-duration agreements help states stabilize agreements in the face of changing trends in costs (i.e., costs might become permanently higher in the future than they are today).

[1] That is, the game is no longer a prisoners' dilemma in any given period.
[2] None of this is to say that governments, when designing international agreements, will always choose to create a court and implement targeted punishment. There are trade-offs. A court system does not ensure that net beneficial compliance will be sustained. Whether governments are better off with or without a court depends on a variety of factors, including the likely costs of compliance. See Carrubba (2005) for an analysis of this trade-off using a simpler version of the model presented here.

That solution does not address how the agreement can be stable to short-run shocks to the costs of compliance. And as a final example, Helfer (2013) discusses how allowing derogations can make agreements stable to short-run shocks. That argument is consistent with what we formalize, present, and test here.

Two substantive predictions arise from our analysis. First, the Political Sensitivity Hypothesis states that court decisions will cue off of third-party government involvement; the more opposition the defendant government receives and the less it is supported, the more likely the court will rule against the government. Second, the Conditional Effectiveness Hypothesis states that the likelihood of compliance with an adverse court decision depends on third-party government involvement in the case; the more opposition the defendant government receives and the less it is supported, the less likely the court's ruling will be evaded and thus the greater chance the ruling will lead to a change in the relevant substantive outcomes (e.g., trade). It is worth emphasizing that, because we explicitly model the information transmission component of the court's role, the ability of governments (both litigants and not) to communicate the costs and benefits of an instance of compliance is central to our theory. And, far from being in an informationally privileged position, the court can cue off of only the information it can learn through the litigation process. This strategic dynamic is what makes third-party governments so important to what happens.

To test our argument, we collected and coded forty years worth of cases decided by the European Court of Justice (ECJ). We used these data to test the two predictions described previously. First, consistent with the Political Sensitivity Hypothesis, we found the Court was less likely to interpret EU law to accommodate the litigant member-state government as the net opposition to that government increased among third-party governments. This relationship held even when we controlled for a variety of possible confounds and alternative explanations. Perhaps most importantly, we showed that this empirical relationship did not simply capture the merits of the case or the influence of the European Commission on ECJ rulings. We also accounted for the possibility that threats of legislative or treaty revision override were driving the relationship, as well as other possible confounds.

For the second prediction, the Conditional Effectiveness Hypothesis, we found evidence that the impact of ECJ rulings is greater when those rulings enjoy the net support of third-party government briefs. Our substantive focus was on intra-EU commerce. The most recent study indicates that ECJ rulings associated with particular member states have only a small effect on subsequent imports into those countries (Gabel et al. 2012). But this study did not distinguish between rulings that enjoyed the net support of government briefs from those that did not, which is a critical component of the Conditional Effectiveness Hypothesis. Once that distinction is made, we discover a striking and nuanced relationship between rulings and trade. First, intra-EU imports into an EU member state grew substantially, and enduringly, as that member state received increasing numbers of pro-trade ECJ rulings that enjoyed the support of third-party government briefs. Second, this positive effect of rulings on intra-EU imports into a member state was completely absent when we considered rulings that did not enjoy net third-party government support. Indeed, if anything, the relationship was negative in that setting. Combined, these two findings provide nuanced and strong support for the Conditional Effectiveness Hypothesis. Furthermore, the combined evidence increases our confidence that our theoretical model, and not another explanation, generates the regularities identified in these two distinct empirical settings.

Finally, the evidence demonstrates an important point about the effectiveness of international institutions. It suggests that we need to move past asking whether international institutions are effective at changing government behavior to asking under what conditions international institutions are effective. That is, the effectiveness of international institutions is not simply a product (or not) of the institution existing. It is an equilibrium outcome of behavior that may arise only under certain conditions given the existence of the institutions.

II. ALTERNATIVE EXPLANATIONS

What do our argument and evidence imply for other theories of international courts? For some arguments, our evidence is problematic. Simply put, arguments that dismiss the possibility that threats of noncompliance are credible, influence court decisions, and influence implementation of those court decisions are inconsistent with our findings. To be fair, few people today would make such an extreme claim. However, there is some disagreement over the relative extent and importance of these threats. Ours is the strongest evidence to date,[3] and it suggests a substantively meaningful effect on both court decisions and the impact of those decisions. It is worth highlighting this most obvious, but also quite important, implication.

Our study is also inconsistent with more nuanced versions of this argument that focus on procedural differences across rulings by the ECJ. First, some scholars have argued the ECJ's engagement with national courts obviates

---

[3] The only other systematic study we are aware of is our previous work, Carrubba, Gabel, and Hankla (2008).

the influence of government threats of noncompliance. If true, we would have expected to find that the ECJ was insensitive to third-party briefs in its preliminary rulings. And we would expect the balance of third-party briefs to have no systematic effect on the impact of preliminary rulings. Our evidence is inconsistent with both of these expectations.[4] Second, others have argued that the imposition of financial sanctions for noncompliance can eliminate (or at least reduce) the effectiveness of threats of noncompliance. Again, we tested for but found no evidence consistent with this claim.

For other arguments, our study is complementary. As mentioned in Chapter 3, Alter and Vargas (2001a), Slepcevic (2009a), Conant (2001), and Panke (2010) all share our assumptions that international courts cannot expect voluntary compliance by member-state governments and that compliance will vary with conditions surrounding the ruling. They differ from us in terms of the character of those conditions – for example, Conant (2001) focuses on the distribution and resources of organized domestic political interests. Nothing in our analysis suggests that these other mechanisms do not hold as well. In fact, these and other alternative arguments could map into our argument quite cleanly in one of two ways.

First, a variety of exogenous factors might shift government calculations about compliance. For example, consider the argument that a "norm of compliance" exists once an agreement is signed. As long as violating the norm is merely costly, not impossible, our argument would still hold. All it would do is create an exogenous cost to a government evading decisions. Governments would still experience variable costs of compliance, they would sometimes defect, they would sometimes be brought to court, and they would sometimes be ruled against. Third-party governments would also still be a primary source of enforcement of rulings. The only difference would be that sometimes governments would comply with an adverse ruling when doing so is net costly. How often this would happen would depend on the costliness of violating the norm of compliance. However, even with this extra cost of evasion, when the cost of compliance is sufficiently high, the home government still evades. The government is willing to eat the political cost of evading a decision for the sake of avoiding the political consequences of following the ruling.[5]

---

[4] Specifically, trade-liberalizing preliminary rulings lacking third-party government support were not associated with greater trade. In fact, the relationship was negative and statistically significant for the first lag (see Table 6.5 in Chapter 6). The total effect, captured by the long-run multiplier, was negative but far from statistically significant.

[5] To be precise, the cost of evading a ruling will only change government behavior in our model if compliance would be net costly and the cost of evading the domestic court ruling is larger than the litigating government's cost of compliance. If compliance would be net beneficial,

Second, some of these arguments provide microfoundations to aspects of our theory that are formally black-boxed. For example, Conant (2001) argues that the distribution and resources of organized domestic political interests affect the likelihood of government compliance. In our model, we just assert that there are domestic costs and benefits to compliance. Conant describes part of what helps determine how costly (or beneficial) compliance would be. The more powerful the domestic political interests opposed to compliance, the higher the government's costs. The higher the government's costs, the more likely it will want to try to evade (and that it will be successful).

Finally, it is worth separately highlighting how our argument and evidence relate to a prominent Neofunctionalist account of the role of the Court proposed by Stone Sweet and Brunell (1998a, 2012a) and Stone Sweet (2004). According to Stone Sweet and Brunell, the ECJ is a strongly independent court that can, and does, promote European integration. ECJ rulings help create an environment within which pro-integration forces are empowered, and, together, they push integration forward mostly independently of the member states. In their account, the preferences of member states should not have a major impact on ECJ rulings.[6]

We also believe the ECJ promotes European integration. Our difference with Neofunctionalists is in the microfoundations of the "how" and "why." As discussed previously, in our model, the ECJ's rulings matter and help facilitate integration *because of* government preferences, not in spite of them. The Court is influential because it facilitates mutually beneficial compliance. If the Court attempts to do more, it cannot anticipate compliance. Government willingness to comply critically determines the boundaries of the application of the agreement. And, when those boundaries are encountered, the Court should tend to be deferential.

Stone Sweet and Brunell also contend that the ECJ's rulings have cultivated and empowered domestic forces that have used the international system to further their integrative agendas. We see no obvious conflict between our argument and this consequence of rulings. Our only difference would be that we would expect this to occur because those domestic forces, through the electoral constraint, induce their governments to internalize the benefits for further integration. Thus, by influencing (indirectly) how the governments

---

the government would comply anyway, and if the cost of evading a domestic court is less than the cost of compliance, the litigating government's calculation is unaffected by the added cost.

[6] "If we are right, another proposition follows: State preferences will not have a significant effect on judicial outcomes" (Stone Sweet and Brunell 1998a: 75).

define their interests regarding further integration, the Court can promote further integration.

Finally, Stone Sweet and Brunell argue that the ECJ has contributed to the liberalization of the EU market through its preliminary rulings (e.g., Stone Sweet and Brunell 1998a: 72). Specifically, domestic interests challenge national barriers to trade in domestic courts, the domestic courts then request preliminary rulings from the ECJ, the ECJ rules the national barriers in violation of EU law, the national courts then rule against these barriers, and trade is liberalized in those national markets. Furthermore, this contributes to a feedback loop in which liberalizing rulings and the related expansion of trade encourage more domestic litigation challenging trade barriers.

Our theoretical model is distinct from this argument in that we do not expect preliminary rulings to automatically cause a change in government behavior. We do not anticipate government compliance with rulings unless the rulings enjoy the support of third-party governments. As a result, we do not expect all trade-liberalizing rulings by the ECJ to cause an observable change in interstate commerce. Our empirical results support this expectation. In Chapter 6, we showed that the number of trade-liberalizing preliminary rulings issued to a nation's courts is associated with significantly greater intra-EU imports only when those rulings enjoy net support from third-party governments.

This finding does not support the general feedback loop by which the market liberalization process is self-propelled through the dynamic between trade and liberalizing rulings. It may still be true that greater trade liberalization generates more preliminary rulings (Carrubba and Murrah 2005; but see Wind, Sindbjerg Martinsen, and Pons Rotger 2009). But we find no general and enduring influence of preliminary rulings on interstate commerce.[7] That said, in our theoretical model and our empirical evidence, the Court serves a critical role in ensuring the member-state governments overcome collective action problems to secure the benefits of market liberalization. And, specifically, we find ECJ rulings can and do enhance trade. But the impact of those rulings is conditional, not automatic.

In sum, we believe our argument is fundamentally complementary to a variety of arguments in the literature. Only if scholars argued that one or more exogenous factors obviate the relevance of our argument would there be a direct conflict. Furthermore, short of that claim, our evidence does not generally speak directly to the empirical veracity of these arguments. That was not the intent of our empirical tests. Several ancillary tests in Chapter 5 evaluate

---

[7] Consistent with Gabel et al. (2012), we find only a temporary influence of preliminary rulings on intra-EU imports.

alternative claims, but those tests were performed to ensure that our argument held across a variety of institutional settings. Consequently, it is perfectly possible that additional factors exogenous to our model influence government decisions to comply with rulings and that the particular microfoundations articulated by other scholars are also correct. We hope this exercise is seen as the basis on which to extend arguments that can complement the first principles promoted in this study.

III. ADDITIONAL IMPLICATIONS FOR THE JUDICIAL SYSTEM OF THE EU

To this point, we have focused on discussing the implications of our work for international courts in general and the ECJ in particular. Although not the driving motivation for this book, our work also has implications for three secondary, related, topics: the nature of an "important case," and the motivations and actions of two additional, and important, actors in the European Union: the Advocate General and the European Commission. We start by discussing the Advocate General and the Commission.

a. The Advocate General

Our study presents the first theoretical and empirical examination of the independence of the Advocate General (AG) from the appointing government. We found that the extent of political influence was quite limited. As previously reported, the institutional rules of assignment of AGs to cases broadly insulate AGs from the appearance and possibility of obvious conflicts of interest involving their appointing government (Tridimas 1997: 1356). That said, conflicts could arise when, on rare occasions, a national government submits an amicus brief in a case to which an AG from that nation is assigned. When in this setting, AGs appear to be sensitive to the interests of the home government, provided the home government is likely to affect the AG's career advancement.

These findings were important for validating the AG's position on a legal issue as a proxy for the litigant favored by the legal merits in the case. But they also provide novel and important evidence for our understanding of the role and impact of the AG in the ECJ litigation process. First, we confirm the conventional wisdom that AG opinions and ECJ rulings are strongly correlated, and that this is consistent with a shared valuation of the legal merits of the case. We also provide the most comprehensive estimate of the correspondence in positions because past estimates were based on subsets of the rulings considered here (Carrubba, Gabel, and Hankla 2008; Dashwood 1982;

Tridimas 1997). Second, our findings regarding political influence on the AG opinion call into question the common characterization of the AG as completely apolitical. We find political conflicts, although rare, appear to systematically influence AG opinions. And, interestingly, the ECJ ruling is less likely to agree with the AG's position in this context.

b. *The Commission's impact on ECJ rulings*

Our analysis in Chapter 5 involved the estimation of the relationship between the Commission's position on a legal issue and the ECJ's ruling on that issue. Past research indicates that the Commission is influential on the Court for at least four reasons. First, the Commission is an important repeat player, and the Court may be deferential to the Commission because of its dependence on the Commission for supplying cases. Second, the Commission's briefs may articulate a persuasive pro-integration agenda that is shared by the Court. Third, the Commission's briefs may convey the legal merits of the case. Finally, the Commission's position may shape Court rulings because it serves as a bellwether for the Court regarding member-state government preferences on the ruling.

Our empirical analysis sheds light on these explanations. First, we found evidence that the legal merits of the case support the Commission's position. When we control for the merits (with the position of the Advocate General), the substantive impact of the Commission's position declines dramatically. However, the presence of a control for the legal merits does not eliminate completely the impact of the Commission. Thus, an outstanding research question for the study of the ECJ is to explain this modest but systematic Commission effect.

Which of the remaining explanations accounts for this effect? We suspect it is not the "bellwether" argument. In our analysis, we included a measure of net-weighted government briefs. This is likely correlated with the balance of member-state preferences.[8] Consequently, the systematic effect of the Commission's position presented in Table 5.2 is likely due to either the "deference" argument or the "pro-integration" argument. Future research could seek to understand which of these arguments is right.

---

[8] We also have evidence that the Commission's position serves as the hypothesized bellwether. We find that the substantive impact of the Commission position, although not presented in Chapter 5, is reduced by the inclusion of the variable for government briefs. This is consistent with a depiction of the Commission position as a bellwether for the position of the member-state governments on the ruling.

c. *Implications for understanding important cases*

Scholars and public commentators interested in courts often focus on important cases. This is particularly true in the EU, in which a great deal of scholarship and legal analysis has focused on analyzing key or important ECJ rulings. For the most part, these rulings are deemed noteworthy because they are constitutional cases that ended in rulings that expanded the scope of EU authority and the role of the court in shaping EU law. For example, Stein (1981) reviewed eleven significant cases that, through 1980, had advanced the legal integration of the European Community. Such cases are notable because they pushed the boundaries of EU law, expanding the reach of EU authority relative to national authority in ways that were not explicitly foreseen or promoted by the member-state governments.

The theoretical model developed in Chapter 2 provides a different perspective on how ECJ rulings can be important to the EU. In the model, noncompliance by a member-state government could indicate that the government faces high political costs and should be given an exception, or it could reflect a government that is attempting to skirt its obligations and that would be willing to comply if ruled against. The adjudication process in our model plays a critical role in distinguishing between the two scenarios and thereby facilitates cooperation among the member states when the conditions warrant. In so doing, the Court improves the performance of the organization, providing flexibility that enhances the value of the agreement to its members. From this perspective, one of the key roles of rulings is to define the limits on members' obligations to the EU. That is, rulings that determine what line EU law does not cross – where EU law makes exceptions for a nation's interests – are also important to the performance of the EU. These are the rulings that keep a deep agreement such as the EU treaties from going off the rails.

What characterizes such rulings? From the model, we would expect the ECJ to be increasingly tolerant of apparent violations of treaty obligations as the number of third-party government briefs in support (opposition) of the member-state government litigant rises (falls). As these third-party government briefs increase in support of the litigant government, the likelihood grows that the action by the national government in question is due to high domestic costs and should be allowed. In turn, as those third-party government briefs increase, we would expect the Court to be more likely to rule that the national action in question is valid under EU law.

To help illustrate this, consider the following example. In June 2003, the ECJ ruled in *Schmidberger* v. *Republic of Austria* (Case 112/00), a preliminary reference from an Austrian court. In the national court, Eugen Schmidberger,

Internationale Transporte und Planzüge, a German trucking company, sought compensation from the Austrian government for loss of revenue due to the closure of the Brenner motorway (the Brenner Pass) in Austria, which was a key route for Schmidberger. The Austrian government had authorized the closure, granting an environmental protection advocacy group, Transitforum Austria Tirol, permission to hold a demonstration on part of the Brenner motorway that stopped traffic for 30 hours.

Schmidberger's claim relied on EU law.[9] According to Schmidberger, the Austrian authorities had an obligation under EU law to ensure the free movement of goods and thereby were liable for loss of earnings due to the closure of the motorway. The Austrian court (the Oberlandesgericht Innsbruck) sought guidance from the ECJ through the preliminary reference system. The Austrian court asked the ECJ whether the treaty obligations regarding the free movement of goods require member-state governments to keep all major intracommunity transit routes clear, and if so, whether this required the national authorities to deny permission to public protests that could obstruct such routes. In posing its questions, the Austrian court explicitly raised the issue of whether national constitutional commitments to freedom of assembly and political demonstration could limit or override the government's EU obligations to ensure the free movement of goods.

Schmidberger's argument relied heavily on the ECJ's 1997 ruling in *Commission v. France* (Case 265/95). In that case, the Court found that France had failed to fulfill its obligations to ensure the free movement of goods because the government did not prevent actions by private individuals that impeded intracommunity transport of goods. The ECJ's conclusion was based on its recognition of the centrality of the free movement of goods to Community law and its interpretation of Article 30 EC Treaty, which prohibits all restrictions on imports, and Article 5 EC Treaty, which requires that member states take all appropriate measures to ensure fulfillment of the treaty.

In *Schmidberger*, the Court again engaged Articles 5 and 30 EC Treaty and noted that Austria had an obligation to ensure the free movement of goods. On that score, the Court concluded that the failure of a member-state government to ban a demonstration that completely closed a major transit route constituted a measure restricting intracommunity trade.[10] Thus, the Court stated that, in principle, this action by the Austrian government was incompatible with its

---

[9] Technically, the question was one of European Community (EC) law at the time. To avoid confusion given our discussion of the EU, we use EU law and understand it to comprise EC law.
[10] See para. 64 of the ruling, *Schmidberger v. Republic of Austria*.

treaty obligations. However, the Court allowed that such a restriction on trade could be acceptable under Community law if the failure to ban the protest could be justified on other grounds. The Court ruled that a justification was present under the circumstances of *Schmidberger*, and this distinguished it from *Commission v. France*. Specifically, the Court recognized that freedom of expression and freedom of assembly, protected under the Austrian constitution and the European Convention on Human Rights, were relevant considerations in the case.[11] The ECJ observed that such fundamental rights are integral parts of EU law and can, in principle, justify actions that violate other obligations of Community law. Thus, a member-state government could, in protecting these fundamental rights, justify a restriction on intracommunity transport. The Court found that actions such as those by the Austrian government were reasonable and proportionate in balancing the free movement and human rights concerns.

The ruling in *Schmidberger*, and its comparison with the ruling in *Commission v. France*, has attracted considerable attention among legal scholars.[12] Perhaps most importantly, *Schmidberger* is distinguished because it is the first ruling in which the ECJ identified human rights considerations as a valid justification for apparent violations of treaty obligations by a member-state government (e.g. Hartley 2007: 145). France offered no such human rights claim in *Commission v. France*. The case is also significant because the Court described a set of criteria for balancing human rights and economic obligations in determining whether a member-state government has infringed EU law. The Court highlighted that, unlike the French government's actions that precipitated *Commission v. France*, the Austrian government had demonstrated care in ensuring that the costs to transport were minimized while providing the demonstrators with sufficient, but limited, opportunity to exercise their right to assemble and protest.

Revisiting *Schmidberger*

The conventional account of the *Schmidberger* ruling highlights significant aspects of the case in terms of the development of human rights considerations in EU jurisprudence. However, from the perspective of our theoretical model, we find a ruling like this important to the EU for different reasons. The *Schmidberger* and *Commission v. France* rulings are interesting because they

---

[11] In para. 72 of the ruling, the Court also makes reference to the preamble of the Single European Act and the Treaty on European Union.
[12] See Morijn (2006: 16n7) for review of scholarship on this ruling.

illustrate how court rulings help distinguish the limits of member-state government obligations concerning a central tenet of the EU Treaty obligations: the free movement of goods between the member states. To substantiate this point, we revisit these two cases and consider them through the lens of our theoretical argument.

According to our model, the Court can facilitate mutually beneficial cooperation among the member states because the litigation process helps the member states distinguish between instances of noncompliance that reflect serious domestic costs from those when the costs are more modest. The underlying concern is that, without some means to filter valid from invalid claims for exceptions, governments will be tempted to abuse any flexibility in the treaties. In the model, we expect third-party amicus briefs and the effort by the litigant government to help elucidate whether the violations in question are indeed valid exceptions to the treaty obligations.

Returning to the two cases, our theoretical expectation is that the rulings reflected differences in the nature of the exception to the treaty obligation and the political costs associated with it and that third-party amicus briefs facilitated distinguishing the cases from one another. Indeed, this is what we find. In *Commission v. France*, the governments of Spain and the United Kingdom intervened on behalf of the Commission against France. No member-state government filed a brief on behalf of France. In *Schmidberger*, in contrast, the defendant government, Austria, received supporting amicus briefs from the governments of Greece, Italy, and the Netherlands. No amicus brief was filed against the Austrian government. Based simply on the balance of third-party government briefs, our theoretical expectation would have been that the Court would be more likely to rule in favor of Austria in *Schmidberger* than in favor of France in *Commission v. France*. The Court rulings comported with these expectations.

The substance of these rulings and of these amicus briefs is also consistent with the litigation process characterized in our model.[13] In particular, the rulings engaged the basic question of whether the domestic political and economic costs warranted the alleged infringement of community law. This proceeded in two general steps. First, the rulings, with the support of the amicus briefs, distinguished between the cases in terms of whether the failure to ensure the free movement of goods was excessive, regardless of the justification offered by the defendant government. That is, the rulings were based, in part, on

---

[13] Recall that government amicus briefs are not published or made public. Thus, we rely on the depiction of the content of these briefs in the published court materials: the summary of the case, the opinion of the Advocate General, and the ECJ's ruling.

whether the government in question abused the potential flexibility in EU law regarding the free movement of goods. The Court recognizes some flexibility in the obligations of the member states, and particularly when the required actions by the authorities would provoke serious domestic problems.[14] But that flexibility does not allow for persistent or general failure to fulfill treaty obligations. Exceptions can be made only for "specific incidents" that are of a limited duration and scope.[15] Thus, one of the key questions in the two cases was whether the alleged infringements fit this criterion.

In *Commission v. France*, France was accused of persistent failure to ensure free movement of goods, going back over ten years. Imports of fruits and vegetables from Spain had been directly targeted by protests, and the protests had impeded intra-EU transport in general. The defense by the French government was that, in response to the original Commission complaints, it had implemented police and prosecutorial reforms that had significantly improved the situation. But, the French defense continued, given the evasive tactics of the protesters and the practical constraints on enforcement and prevention, one could not expect perfect compliance.[16] In short, France contended the problem had been contained and its response was reasonable. The briefs from Spain and the United Kingdom argued and provided evidence to the contrary. The UK and Spanish governments documented that the violent disturbances had continued for more than ten years, that they followed a predictable seasonal pattern, and that several incidents were reported just before the briefs were filed.[17] The Spanish government even provided video evidence that France overstated the difficulty of identifying and prosecuting protesters.[18] The ruling reviewed these arguments from the French government and the third-party briefs and sided with Spain and the United Kingdom. The Court concluded that "the preventive and penal measures to which the French Government refers in defence are in practice neither adequate nor proportionate for the purposes of deterring the perpetrators of such offenses."[19] In support of this conclusion, the Court highlighted exactly the arguments advanced by the third-party briefs.[20]

In *Schmidberger*, the amicus briefs from Greece, the Netherlands, and Italy also evaluated the extent of the breach of the obligation to ensure the free movement of goods. The amicus briefs explicitly distinguished the facts in the

---

[14] For example, see *Commission v. France*, para. 58; Opinion of Advocate General Lenz, para. 62.
[15] *Commission v. France*, para. 58.   [16] Opinion of Advocate General Lenz, para. 52.
[17] Opinion of Advocate General Lenz, para. 58.
[18] Opinion of Advocate General Lenz, para. 74.   [19] *Commission v. France*, para. 18.
[20] *Commission v. France*, para. 18, 45.

Austrian case from those in *Commission v. France*.[21] They noted that although the protest by Transitforum blocked a major transit route, the obstruction was limited to a single route, for a limited amount of time, and on a single occasion.[22] These briefs appear to have been persuasive because the Court's ruling repeated these arguments in explaining why it distinguished the Austrian context from the ruling in *Commission v. France*.[23] Thus, in the Court's judgment, the Austrian government had not abused its discretion, whereas the French government had.

The second part of the flexibility issue is whether the government in question had reasonable grounds for failing to fulfill its treaty obligations. In other words, regardless of whether the government abused its discretion in enforcing the treaties, was any derogation justified? The Court considered several justifications. One important rationale was that compliance would cause a breakdown of public order that would generally undermine the benefits of the treaty. Put in the terms of our theoretical model, this is similar to asking whether the noncompliance in question was due to a high domestic cost of compliance.

Both defendant governments claimed that they would have faced serious domestic backlash had they complied with their treaty obligations to ensure the free movement of goods in their respective contexts. In *Commission v. France*, the French government considered the discretion exercised by the police as necessary for this reason (Chalmers, Davies, and Monti 2010: 903). Specifically, France claimed that such restraint in enforcement was justified because more aggressive intervention "would entail even greater or more serious risks to those protected legal interests."[24] In *Schmidberger*, the Austrian government submitted that "all the alternative solutions which could be countenanced would have risked reactions which would have been difficult to control and would have been liable to cause much more serious disruption to intra-Community trade."[25]

The Court evaluated these claims and reached different conclusions in each case. In *Commission v. France*, the Court rejected the French government's defense.[26] This conclusion was consistent with the amicus briefs submitted by the United Kingdom and Spain, which argued and provided evidence for the general passivity of the French authorities rather than any judicious use of restraint when faced with a threat to public order. In

---

[21] Opinion of Advocate General Jacobs, para. 78.
[22] Opinion of Advocate General Jacobs, para. 78.
[23] *Schmidberger*, para. 84–8.   [24] Opinion of Advocate General Lenz, para. 54.
[25] *Schmidberger*, para. 92.   [26] *Schmidberger*, para. 56–7.

contrast, the Court was sympathetic to the claim of the Austrian government in *Schmidberger*.[27]

In neither case did the Court provide extensive analysis supporting the conclusions on this point. But a general appreciation for the political salience of the compliance issues in the two contexts supports the different conclusions drawn by the Court about the risks of domestic fallout. In both cases, the domestic government faced political opposition to compliance. In *Commission v. France*, the compliance required of the French government would engender organized political opposition, particularly from the group Coordination Rurale, which was formed in opposition to reforms of the EU agricultural policies in the early 1990s. And, given the tolerance of French citizens to protests that disrupt public order, the French government could have faced broader political costs from intervening to prevent or prosecute protesters (Keeler and Hall 2001). However, there is little evidence that the French government depended critically on the support of these interest groups or that the level of public antipathy for the EU was such that greater government efforts to ensure intra-EU transport would have provoked a crisis at that time.

The Austrian context was significantly different, with the intracommunity transport issue and the related costs of EU membership of high political salience nationally. First, the Austrian public was skeptical of EU membership at the time of the litigation. The standard public opinion surveys consistently placed Austrians among the weakest supporters of the EU.[28] Furthermore, it is worth noting that public antipathy toward the EU has been particularly high in Tyrol, the Austrian state containing the Brenner motorway and the location of the environmental demonstration at issue in *Schmidberger*. That region has consistently expressed the greatest opposition to EU membership. Indeed, in the national referendum on EU membership, its voters recorded the lowest support in the country.[29] Finally, it is important to note that the late 1990s saw the dramatic ascent of the Freedom Party, which attracted protest voters based on its strong Euroscepticism (Bieler 2000: 99–100). That party won its highest

---

[27] *Schmidberger*, para. 92.
[28] For example, in 2000, the year of the protest in question on the Brenner motorway, 34 percent of Austrians considered Austria's membership a "good thing," which ranked third from last; that was only five points higher than the last place United Kingdom. In contrast, 53 percent of French respondents indicated EC membership was a good thing in 1995, the year the Commission brought France to court in *Commission v. France* (sources: Standard Eurobarometer reports, various years, http://ec.europa.eu/public_opinion/archives/eb_arch_en.htm; Directorate-Generale X, Brussels).
[29] In the referendum on Austrian accession to the EU, Tyrol had the lowest level of support (57 percent), a full ten percentage points lower than the overall national average.

vote share (27 percent) in a national election in 1999, just a year before the protest at the Brenner Pass at issue in the preliminary ruling.

Second, transport, particularly by heavy trucks, between Italy and Germany was (and remains) a hot-button issue in Austrian domestic politics and its international commercial relations. In Austria, the primary concern with intracommunity commerce has been with limiting the environmental damage associated with increased traffic in this scenic region of the country. For example, regulating pollution and traffic from the Brenner motorway figured prominently in Austria's negotiations to join the European Economic Area in 1992 and the EU in 1995. Thus, the Austrian government faced the threat of serious political blowback from meeting its obligations to ensure transport of intracommunity goods without exception. The Court's ruling in *Schmidberger* acknowledges this fact.[30]

In sum, the difference in the rulings is largely consistent with the model. First, the rulings reflect the position favored by the balance of the third-party government briefs. Second, often reflecting the specific arguments and evidence offered in these briefs, the rulings evaluated whether the defendant governments could justify their failure to ensure the free movement of goods based on their domestic costs of compliance. Third, the Court reviewed whether the member-state governments in question had abused the potential flexibility in the application of EU law by inflicting disproportionate harm on intracommunity transport. These considerations are central to the role of the adjudication process in our model: to identify valid reasons to renege on treaty obligations.

Recall that, if the adjudication process serves the purpose identified in our theoretical model, it enhances the value of the treaty to its members. Specifically, this requires the Court to identify when a member state is not obliged to comply with a treaty obligation (i.e., ensure free movement of goods). Thus, the ruling in *Schmidberger* is important because it does exactly that: it draws a line beyond which a member-state government is not required to adhere to the treaty.

In highlighting this aspect of the case, we are not denying that the ruling is interesting for other reasons, such as the treatment of fundamental human rights. The purpose of the discussion was to illustrate how our theoretical model identifies a sometimes overlooked feature of EU jurisprudence that helps explain both the decisions of the Court and the relevance of the case to the performance of the EU as an international regulatory regime.

---

[30] *Schmidberger*, para. 92–3.

IV. IMPLICATIONS FOR THE DESIGN OF INTERNATIONAL COURTS

Returning focus to our primary subject, our study suggests international courts actually can influence compliance with international regulatory regimes. At the same time, it also suggests real limits on that influence. A natural question, therefore, is what makes some international courts more influential than others? Or, more saliently, could a better institutional design improve an international court's ability to institute a rule of law over sovereign governments? The answer, based on the lessons from our theoretical model, is "it depends."

We can think about three types of design issues: those that affect the appointment and removal of judges, those that affect how cases come to court, and those that affect the procedure by which the court adjudicates the case. Tinkering with the appointment and removal processes of international judges can have only a limited impact on the compliance concerns raised in this book. When scholars talk about the appointment and removal process, they are focused on designing a process that insulates judges from political pressure; one that helps ensure that judges are not beholden to those they are supposed to be regulating. The concern is that if judges are politically beholden, they will be unwilling to rule against member governments when they should. This is one of the reasons Helfer and Slaughter (1997a, 2005) argue that judicial independence is a critical element for the efficacy of international courts.

Obviously, if courts are unwilling to rule against the member governments, the court could not fulfill the function described in this book. And anything that makes courts more reticent to do so will be problematic. At the same time, the central concern here is not whether the court rules against the governments, but rather how the court gains compliance with its ruling. The courts we are studying are ones designed by governments to help them overcome a collective action problem. The issue is that those judges will be ignored or evaded, not that they do not want to rule against the governments. Thus, depoliticizing the appointment process, increasing judicial tenure, and making it harder to remove judges from office for political reasons will not affect the ability of those judges to constrain sovereign government behavior. This implication is consistent with Posner and Yoo's (2005) argument that judicial independence is not sufficient to ensure judicial efficacy.[31] It just reduces the risk of judges not ruling against governments when they should.

The case generation process *is* a promising option. Recall that, in our model, governments want to maximize mutually beneficial cooperation and minimize mutually costly cooperation. Further, also recall that one of the downsides of

---

[31] Posner and Yoo argue that independence is actually a problem. Governments are more likely to rely on politically dependent courts because politically dependent courts are ones more likely to prioritize helping states solve the kinds of collective action problems identified in this

a court system is that it lets some mutually beneficial cooperation leak out of the system because not all government violations will be brought to court. By implication, anything that helps make litigation easier can tremendously improve the situation. The broader the standing, the easier and cheaper it is to bring a case to court, and the more aware those potentially hurt by a government violation are of their rights, the more mutually beneficial compliance can be sustained.

Recall that one of the biggest innovations in the history of the ECJ was the introduction of the direct effect and supremacy doctrines. These doctrines helped solidify the preliminary ruling process as a tool for EU citizens to protect their rights under EU law. Specifically, it lets them challenge noncompliance with EU law in national courts. Thus, broadening standing under the preliminary ruling system helps decrease the amount of leakage from the system. Accordingly, if governments wanted to increase the effectiveness of other international legal regimes, such as the WTO/GATT, broadening standing would be one excellent method for doing so.[32]

Finally, we turn to innovations in the procedural rules of adjudication. The most promising option here, given our theoretical model, is to explicitly provide an international court with politically relevant information. To see why this would help, recall from the model that some mutually beneficial cooperation goes unrealized because the court does not rule against the litigant government when cooperation would have been mutually beneficial. This oversight happens because the court is less informed about the actual costs and benefits of compliance than are the governments involved in the case. Although the court observes what the governments do in court (file briefs, make cases defending their actions, and so on), it does not observe any communication going on outside of the courtroom. In our model, this could be corrected by allowing governments to introduce politically grounded arguments into the cases they make in the courtroom. Although this would not make the court fully informed, it would at least allow the court to consider all of the information governments consider relevant to their cost–benefit calculations. A variety of permutations on this theme are possible; the one previously

---

book (Posner and Yoo 2005: 7). This argument is consistent with ours to the extent that a court with a particular focus on helping solve collective action problems is going to be particularly efficacious. However, the arguments are different to the extent that we do not need the court to be politically dependent for it to be efficacious. Posner and Yoo also make a point about the need for the court to be impartial, meaning that the court is a neutral provider of legally relevant information (Posner and Yoo 2005: 14). In our argument, the court provides no information; it is simply a venue in which information is exchanged. Thus, for us impartiality as Posner and Yoo define it is not necessary.

[32] This observation is consonant with the legalization literature that examines how legalization of international agreements affects their impact (e.g., Kono 2007; Smith 2000).

provided is just an example.[33] That said, this sort of innovation is unlikely to be implemented because it violates the standard normative view that proper adjudication should focus exclusively on the law and the quality of the legal arguments. It certainly goes against the trend of legalization, in which international tribunals are considered more legalized, or mature, if they explicitly disallow such arguments to be made.

Another potential innovation would be to mandate compliance with court rulings. Such a mandate could work if a court can issue an automatic, unavoidable sanction for noncompliance with its decisions. This, of course, is far from trivial to design. One could imagine requiring defendant states to surrender a significant financial deposit with the court that would be returned only if the government were found innocent or the government complied with an adverse ruling. However, it is difficult to imagine a set of governments willing to implement such a reform. Governments do not want to sustain mutually costly compliance, and this innovation empowers courts to do exactly that. Perhaps this is why the sanctioning mechanism for noncompliance with ECJ infringement rulings is limited to voluntary payment of the penalty. A second problem is that it is unclear whether one would want the innovation in the first place. At first blush, we might suppose the answer is an unequivocal yes. After all, what is wrong with more consistent rule of law? By reducing a government's ability to ignore a court ruling, we ensure that the common regulatory regime is going to be more consistently and even-handedly applied. Governments are no longer going to be able to argue that their particularistic political interests should justify an exemption. Domestic interests are going to be able to depend on a more predictable legal environment. Lots of generally accepted goods arise. The problem is one of trade-offs.

As has already been noted in important previous work (Gilligan, Johns, and Rosendorff 2010; Helfer 2013; Koremenos 2005), a less flexible legal regime can lead to shallower agreements. To illustrate, suppose the governments were deciding on what sort of common regulatory regime to design. The more flexible the agreement – that is, the easier noncompliance – the deeper they can make the agreement. That is, governments will make more regulatory commitments entailing higher average costs of compliance if they know they can derogate when necessary. Thus, instituting mechanisms that limit the

---

[33] Note that some courts do not have a codified process for third-party government interventions. Although it is not strictly necessary for third parties to signal their opinions on a case, this signaling certainly facilitates governments indicating to courts how they think. Because third-party government preferences are an important component in determining whether cooperation is mutually beneficial, systems without formal tools for intervention would benefit from them based on the logic described.

ability to derogate is not costless; it will likely limit the depth of the regulatory agreements as well.

In sum, institutional innovations in the international legal system will be most effective when they work in tandem with what governments are seeking to get out of the international agreements overall. When these innovations help promote net beneficial cooperation, all parties gain and a more consistent international rule of law is sustainable at no real cost. Innovations meant to constrain governments are difficult to institute and, even if feasible, can come at a cost.

V. TOWARD A GENERAL THEORY OF COURTS

The previous section focused on the design of judicial institutions at the international level. In this section we consider how our study helps inform a more general theory of courts, writ large. Obviously, much of this discussion must be theoretical and speculative. However, we believe our study, in conjunction with other recent work on judicial politics, starts to paint a compelling picture of how judicial systems come to be, what powers they have when first created, how those powers can evolve over time, and how to think very concretely about the relationship between international and domestic courts.

We structure this discussion in four steps. The first step is to investigate more fully the role of the law in our theory. Defining our conception of law is critical to understanding how our theory fits with the wider judicial influence literature. The second step is to consider what our theory implies about how international law works. The third step is to move the conversation to the domestic level. And the last step is to attempt to link the two arenas together.

a. What is the law?

In our model, we assume some set of regulatory rules that governments are expected to follow. Each period they choose to follow them or to derogate. If a government derogates, it may be brought to court, and, if brought, the court may declare the government's actions invalid. The government is never erroneously brought to court, and therefore the only two options are that the court correctly rules against the government or that it fails to do so.[34]

---

[34] Incidentally, if one stuck with this interpretation, one could allow litigants to incorrectly observe a violation of the regime's rules. As a result, governments would sometimes be taken to court when they did follow the rules. The court would have no incentive to rule against the government, and nothing in our theory or its predictions would change.

Superficially, our model appears to assume an always-knowable objective truth to the law. The regulatory rules clearly parse legally acceptable and unacceptable behavior, and governments can be held to account for violating that objective truth. Although a reasonable reading of our model, we believe a very different reading is more appropriate.

Start from the first principle that all laws are incomplete contracts. Thus, the regulatory regime's rules spell out what governments are supposed to do in some, but not all, circumstances. For example, a rule requiring no tariff barriers on particular goods is a relatively clear and objectively verifiable rule. But a rule eliminating all policies that have an equivalent effect to a tariff is much less so (e.g., should some particular environmental law be considered?). Thus, the rule is incomplete in that it does not provide a clear answer in all possible contexts in which it could be applied.[35]

Assuming all laws are incomplete contracts, how can we understand the law in our model? First, a violation – or defection, in our model's parlance – is an instance in which following an inclusive conception of the regulatory regime's rules would be costly to the government. The potential plaintiff would benefit from that interpretation. Third-party governments might or might not benefit from that interpretation. The combination of filing briefs and the defendant government exerting effort in its defense helps identify whether it is an interpretation the governments would like to see enforced today and into the future. And finally, the court makes a ruling, declaring that interpretation either valid or not. Thus, there is no underlying objective truth about what "law" is in our model. When litigated, de jure law becomes what the court says it is. And, whether litigated or not, de facto law is how the rules are implemented on the ground (e.g., if governments obey the law or not). Or, stated slightly differently, our model is built on the implicit assumption that the law in abstract consists of written instructions with the expectation of flexibility in the application of those instructions. This abstraction is filled out in practice through the articulation of further general principles (perhaps in part through precedent) and the resolution of how to apply those general principles within the context of specific conditions (importantly including political concerns).

b. *Implications for how international law works*

Based on this conception of the law, what are the implications for the execution of international law? Within the confines of the model (i.e., assuming the

---

[35] Note that ambiguity also can be created even when individual rules are quite clear. The reason is that different legal rules sometimes conflict, and the job of the court is to determine how to balance across those conflicting rules.

regime was designed to resolve collective action problems), we observe very "law-like" behavior. By that term we mean that governments are taken to court for potential violations of the law, courts hear facts, and courts interpret and apply the law. The law is some combination of the written rules of the regulatory regime and the interpretation of those rules by the court.[36] The only non-law-like aspect is that governments will, sometimes, evade court rulings.

Importantly, how often this non-law-like behavior will occur depends on how good the governments are at sculpting the regulatory regime's rules in the first place. The better governments are at anticipating the likely costs of complying with a particular interpretation of the regime's rules, and the better they are at writing the law so that those conditions are clearly identified as not being required by the law, the less frequently governments will evade court interpretation of the law. Because governments do not gain anything from going to court when compliance with an adverse court decision would be net costly, the governments have every incentive to try to write the regime's rules carefully. Thus, there is no reason to expect to observe rampant evasion of international court decisions, even though the threat is always present. But, of course, because no law can be written to anticipate every possible contingency (i.e., they are incomplete contracts), some noncompliance is likely.[37]

In sum, our study suggests that a great deal of de jure and de facto international law, as depicted in our model, should strongly resemble how we traditionally think the law is supposed to work. Most of the time, rules are written down, courts interpret the rules, and governments follow the rules as written and interpreted. However, underneath this characterization lies a critical driver: everything happens conditionally on implicit government acquiescence. This seeming paradox, a traditional conception of how the law is supposed to work arising in a setting in which everything that happens is driven by political forces, has some strong parallels in the domestic legal world.

---

[36] Strictly speaking, this version of law is a common law understanding.
[37] The preceding discussion assumes international law is designed to help resolve collective action problems. If it is not, these specific implications do not apply. That said, our study does have an implication for these other types of regimes. In particular, our study suggests that we should observe adherence to international law, and international courts in particular, only when governments do gain from compliance. One alternative mechanism by which governments might gain from compliance is through side payments. For example, suppose the United States wanted a smaller, poorer state to abide by some agreement that was not in the interests of the other state's government. The United States might provide side payments by way of international aid in exchange. Other scenarios in which compliance is beneficial could be imagined as well. The key is simply that some microfoundation of this sort must hold for an international court not built to help overcome a collective action problem to be effectual.

c. Comparing international law to domestic law

Initially, it might seem like our study can have little relevance to how domestic law works. As Staton and Moore (2011) aptly note, scholars generally believe that domestic legal systems are characterized by "hierarchy," meaning "under government there is someone to enforce contracts and property rights" (Wagner 2007a: 123). That is, the government solves the compliance problem for the court. In contrast, international law is typically "anarchic," lacking an enforcement mechanism. Our entire study is predicated on this characterization of the international context of a treaty. Given this fundamental difference between domestic and international legal contexts, how can our study be relevant to understanding domestic courts and their impact on domestic law?

Although it is certainly true that hierarchy characterizes a domestic court's role in enforcing "*individual-to-individual* contracts in domestic politics" (Staton and Moore 2011: 560; emphasis added), it does not characterize domestic judicial review of government actions. In this context, domestic courts face a very similar challenge to what international courts face. According to Staton and Moore (2011: 561), "In the domestic context the state does not contract under the shadow of anything. For this reason, theorists that wrestle with the domestic problems often associated with the enforceability of state obligations find themselves on precisely the same conceptual footing as theorists who tackle problems that emerge out of anarchy in the international system." Simply put, states cannot credibly commit to be bound by the rules they put in place. Staton and Moore (2011: 561) conclude by noting that domestic courts cannot be the solution to this problem:

> But here the 78th Federalist injects another theoretical challenge. Lacking financial and violent means of coercion, judiciaries are uncommonly weak institutions that depend on outside political actors to implement their decisions.[38] This is a fundamental problem of judicial policy-making. When the actor whose behavior is under review is the same actor responsible for implementation (i.e., the government), the problem is most acute. For this reason, it is not clear how courts come to constrain governments or even if they ever really do.

Thus, domestic courts attempting to constrain national government behavior face very much the same challenge that international courts do.

Scholars have proposed a number of explanations for how domestic courts overcome this most fundamental of challenges. The most recent, and most

---

[38] Hamilton, Madison, and Jay (2009a).

widely tested, work has highlighted how the domestic public can act as an indirect enforcement mechanism for a national court. Specifically, if the public is sufficiently aware of the case, if the case is sufficiently transparent (i.e., not too legally complex) such that the public can tell whether the government complies with the court ruling, and if the public agrees with the court's preferred outcome, then the public can act as an indirect enforcement mechanism by sanctioning its government for evasion of a court ruling. This line of argument was developed first by Georg Vanberg (2005) in the context of the German Constitutional Court. Later, it was applied to the Mexican High Court by Jeff Staton (2006, 2010) and to the Supreme Court of the United States by Carrubba and Zorn (2010).[39]

Thus, in these literatures domestic courts face the same underlying challenge that international courts do. Both courts can declare actions of a national government invalid, but neither has a direct means to ensure governments obey the ruling. The difference is that domestic courts are allowed to rely on domestic publics to help constrain national governments, whereas international courts are not. Specifically, domestically, governments are constrained when the public supports the court; internationally, governments are constrained when other national governments support the court.

This similarity is interesting in its own right. If these literatures are correct, we should be studying domestic and international courts as of a kind, as Staton and Moore (2011) argue. However, the difference between the domestic and international literatures raises a perhaps more interesting question. Why the difference in emphasis? Cannot an international court rely on a national government's domestic audience for indirect enforcement of its decisions? Are we (and similarly grounded work) implicitly assuming domestic and international courts are still somehow fundamentally different? Connecting these dots can provide some insights into the conditions under which courts in general can constrain national government behavior.

d. *Connecting the dots: the role of the public in international courts*

Stepping back for a moment, we can see that domestic publics can care about two things: the specific decisions a court renders and the role of the court in the political system. Both can help a domestic court constrain a national

---

[39] These arguments do not rely on notions of diffuse support for the court. However, if the public supported the court's rulings against the government simply because of high levels of diffuse support, irrespective of the public's opinion of the decision, the rest of their arguments still would follow.

government. If the domestic public likes the decisions the court renders, it may sanction its government for evading the desired court decision. If the domestic court has high "diffuse" support (i.e., the public believes the court has the right to arbitrate what a national government can and cannot do), the same is true.[40] Thus, domestic courts can rely on domestic publics to support their decisions either when the public likes the specific decision or when the public believes that the national government should obey the court's ruling.

The former mechanism has started to be explored in the international setting. In an important study, Dai (2007) argues exactly that domestic interests can prevent national governments from evading particular applications of international law that the domestic interests desire. Thus, this dot has already been connected. However, in some ways it is less interesting than the second mechanism: the court constraining the government because it enjoys public support independent of whether the public prefers the particular outcome of the ruling. To see why, return to our model. In our theory, governments make decisions about whether to comply with the regime's rules based on the cost of compliance. When the cost is lower, they are more likely to comply; when it is higher, they are less likely to comply. All the domestic audience does in this setting is shift the cost of compliance. A domestic public's preference for application of international law simply is one of the components of domestic politics that determines the government's politically induced preferences for compliance; it does not change the underlying strategic tensions of the model or its implications. Thus, the argument that domestic publics act as indirect enforcement mechanisms for courts because they have preferences for the outcomes of specific cases is consistent with, and in fact already implicitly integrated into, rationalist arguments (including ours) for how international law works.[41]

The more interesting mechanism is how diffuse legitimacy can lead a public to support a court over its government even when the public does not necessarily agree with the ruling. To recap, the public has a preference for how the political system as a whole should run; if the court has high diffuse

---

[40] For a discussion of these concepts and the related argument, see Gibson, Caldeira, and Baird (1998).

[41] Simmons (2009) makes a similar argument. In her argument, Simmons describes how the act of signing a treaty can change which policies a domestic audience will mobilize around. Thus, the act of signing the treaty can affect the incentives for a government to comply with an agreement because it changes the types of actions on which a domestic public will put domestic pressure. Like Dai's (2007), this argument also complements ours in that it describes the ways domestic politics affect the costs and benefits of compliance for the government. It does not change the underlying tension unless one argues that the public impact is so substantial that it obviates the collective action dilemma by making compliance always unilaterally desirable.

legitimacy, governments should respect court decisions when the court rules actions invalid. The trick is that the court must have high diffuse legitimacy for the mechanism to work. When an international court is first created, a domestic public has good reason not to favor the court or grant it any legitimacy. The court is an international body, created by an agreement among a number of political actors, most of whom do not represent that public. Further, the public would have to be predisposed to back that court over its duly elected government. It seems implausible that a significant share of any domestic public would make this choice. Instead, we expect that the public's support would have to be earned by the international court.

If granted this point, the interesting question then becomes, how does an international court earn diffuse legitimacy? Carrubba (2009) offers a formal model that provides an answer to this very question. In brief, suppose a set of governments creates a common regulatory regime as in the model in Chapter 2. However, in addition to what is described in our model, a domestic public is also associated with each national government and that public is, however imperfectly, watching how the governments and court interact. It periodically notices when governments are taken to court, what the resolution of the case is, and whether the government tries to evade the court decision. The public does not directly care about any of this. What the public cares about is how the regulatory regime affects its interests. And it is savvy enough to know that the impact of that regulatory regime is going to depend on not just what international laws are agreed to but how those laws are actually applied. Further, the public also knows that its duly elected government has similar preferences to its own, but that the government is not a perfect agent of its interests and sometimes will want the laws applied (or not) in ways at variance with the public's preferences. Similarly, the public knows the court has its own preferences. Finally, the public does not necessarily know how any given application of the international regulatory regime's rules will affect its interests. It will experience the consequences only after the application of the law is implemented for some period of time.

The task for the public, then, is to evaluate whether it wants to sanction its government for evading a court ruling, as in Vanberg's and others' work. However, it must make this decision based on whether it thinks the political system as a whole better serves its interests if its domestic government follows adverse court decisions whenever the court rules against it or only if its government chooses to voluntarily acquiesce. Thus, this model examines how diffuse legitimacy can endogenously develop. Carrubba (2009) demonstrates that high levels of diffuse legitimacy can endogenously arise under the assumptions of this model.

The key point is that international courts, within the rationalist model proposed in this book, can acquire diffuse legitimacy. Thus, domestic publics can act as indirect enforcement mechanisms for international courts in exactly the same ways as they can for domestic courts. International courts simply may not start with the same public awareness and public support that domestic courts do.

In sum, many of the traditional distinctions between the challenges faced by domestic courts and by international courts when trying to constrain national governments disappear on close inspection. But one possible distinction remains; we have not considered whether the collective action dilemmas, and the government-oriented enforcement mechanism underpinning our model (and related models), apply in the domestic setting. If they do, a plausible general theory of judicial influence comes into focus.

Connecting the dots: are domestic courts simply successful international courts?

As stated previously, our model applies to international agreements designed to help resolve collective action problems. The value of this model to understanding domestic courts depends on the extent to which these same types of problems characterize politics in the domestic setting.

As it turns out, we find similar collective action problems in many domestic settings. Consider any federal system. The constituent states of that system typically encounter collective action problems similar to those faced by countries in the international system. For example, federal systems generally commit to maintaining a common market (free trade), establishing national environmental standards, maintaining free flow of cross-border labor, sustaining a variety of social policies, and so forth. Courts can contribute to resolving these collective action problems.

Consider the United States, federal system. Carrubba and Rogers (2003) demonstrate that the construction of the Dormant Commerce Clause doctrine is consistent with a simpler version of this book's model. In the early 1800s the Supreme Court of the United States had to construct a doctrine for how it would enforce free trade among the states. During this period, the federal government had few levers with which to strong-arm states. There was no expectation of military intervention in response to state violations of federal law, and the federal government did not have the monetary resources to provide financial sticks and carrots to induce compliance. Thus, the justices could rule however they wished, but they ultimately had to rely on the voluntary compliance of the states (which could be induced through retaliatory barriers by other states). Although there is evidence that the justices supported an unconditional doctrine (that is, states were never allowed to burden interstate trade), the justices ultimately agreed on a doctrine in which burdening trade was allowed under certain conditions. Those conditions are the ones described by our model; that is, states can burden trade whenever the costs of compliance are sufficiently high. Thus, the development of the Dormant Commerce Clause for regulating interstate trade is consistent with arguments for how cross-national trade is regulated. Similarly, Carrubba (2010) demonstrates that the US Supreme Court was most efficacious when it ruled in policy areas characterized by collective action problems among the US states; it struggled with compliance problems whenever it tried to issue rulings for which it could not count on other interested states supporting its decisions.

Putting all of this information together, we see a picture very similar to the one described for international courts. An early domestic court in a federal system was tasked with helping enforce regulatory agreements among the constituent states. When those regulatory agreements required the states to overcome collective action problems, the court was efficacious, but only within the bounds as described by our theory.

References

Achen, Christopher. 2006. "Evaluating Political Decision-Making Models." In *The European Union Decides*, edited by Robert Thomson, Frans Stokman, Christopher Achen, and Thomas König, 264–98. New York: Cambridge University Press.

Aksoy, Deniz. 2012. "Institutional Arrangements and Logrolling: Evidence from the European Union." *American Journal of Political Science* 56 (3): 538–52.

Alter, Karen. 1996. "The European Court's Political Power." *Western European Politics* 19 (July): 458–87.

Alter, Karen. 1998. "Who Are the 'Masters of the Treaty'?: European Governments and the European Court of Justice." *International Organization* 52 (Winter): 121–47.

Alter, Karen. 2000. "The European Union's Legal System and Domestic Policy: Spillover or Backlash?" *International Organization*, Summer, 489–518.

Alter, Karen J. 2001. *Establishing the Supremacy of European Law: The Making of an International Rule of Law in Europe*. Oxford, England: Oxford University Press.

Alter, Karen. 2008. "Agents or Trustees? International Courts in Their Political Context." *European Journal of International Relations* 14 (Spring): 33–63.

Alter, Karen, and Sophie Meunier-Aitsahalia. 1994. "Judicial Politics in the European Community." *Comparative Political Studies* 26 (4): 535–61.

Alter, Karen, and Jeannette Vargas. 2000. "Explaining Variation in the Use of European Litigation Strategies: European Community Law and British Gender Equality Policy." *Comparative Political Studies* 33 (4): 452–82.

Angrist, Joshua, and Joern-Steffen Pischke. 2009. *Mostly Harmless Econometrics*. Princeton, NJ: Princeton University Press.

Aron, R. 1981. *Peace and War: A Theory of International Relations*. Malabar, FL: Robert E. Krieger.

Badinger, Harald, and Fritz Breuss. 2004. "What Has Determined the Rapid Post-War Growth in Intra-EU Trade?" *Review of World Economics* 140 (1): 31–51.

Bailey, Michael, Brian Kamoie, and Forrest Maltzman. 2005. "Signals from the Tenth Justice: The Political Role of the Solicitor General in Supreme Court Decision Making." *American Journal of Political Science* 49 (1): 72–85.

Bailey, Michael, and Forrest Maltzman. 2011. *The Constrained Court: Law, Politics, and the Decisions Justices Make*. Princeton, NJ: Princeton University Press.

Bauer, Michael, and Miriam Hartlapp. 2010. "Much Ado About Money and How to Spend It! Analysis of 40 Years of Annulment Cases against the European Union Commission." *European Journal of Political Research* 49: 202–222.
BBC News. 2003. "France Warned on 'Illegal' Alstom Aid." August 5. http://news.bbc.co.uk/2/hi/business/3126357.stm.
Beach, Derek. 2005. "Why Governments Comply: An Integrative Compliance Model That Bridges the Gap between Instrumental and Normative Models." *Journal of European Public Policy* 12 (1): 113–42.
Beck, Nathaniel. 2001. "Time-Series-Cross-Section Data: What Have We Learned in the Past Few Years?" *Annual Review of Political Science* 4: 271–93.
Beck, Nathaniel, and Jonathan Katz. 1995. "What to Do (and Not to Do) with Time-Series Cross-Section Data." *American Political Science Review* 89: 634–47.
Beck, Nathaniel, and Jonathan Katz. 2009. "Modeling Dynamics in Time-Series-Cross-Section Political Economic Data." Social Science Working Paper 1304. California Institute of Technology.
Benoit, Kenneth, and Michael Laver. 2006. *Party Policy in Modern Democracies.* London: Routledge.
Bernhard, William, and David Leblang. 2006. *Democratic Processes and Financial Markets.* New York: Cambridge University Press.
Bernhard, William, and Brian Sala. 2006. "The Remaking of an American Senate: The 17th Amendment and Ideological Responsiveness." *American Journal of Political Science* 68 (2): 345–57.
Bewley, R. A. 1979. "The Direct Estimation of the Equilibrium Response in a Linear Dynamic Model." *Economic Letters* 3: 357–61.
Bieler, Andreas. 2000. *Globalisation and Enlargement of the European Union.* London: Routledge.
Bilder, R. B. 1989. "International Third Party Dispute Settlement." *Denver Journal of International Law Policy* 17 (3): 471–503.
Bork, R. H. 1989–90. "The Limits of 'International Law.'" *National Interest* 18: 3–10.
Börzel, Tanja, Tobias Hofmann, Diana Panke, and Carina Sprungk. 2010. "Obstinate and Inefficient: Why Member States Do Not Comply with European Law." *Comparative Political Studies.* doi:10.1177/0010414010376910.
Bown, Chad P. 2004a. "Developing Countries as Plaintiffs and Defendants in GATT/WTO Trade Disputes." *Canadian Journal of Economics* 37 (3): 678–720.
Bown, Chad P. 2004b. "On the Economic Success of GATT/WTO Dispute Settlement." *Review of Economics and Statistics* 86 (3): 811–23.
Box-Steffensmeier, Janet, and Bradford S. Jones. 2007. *Event History Modeling.* New York: Cambridge University Press.
Boyle, F. A. 1980. "The Irrelevance of International Law." *California Western International Law Journal* 10: 193.
Brambor, Thomas, William Roberts Clark, and Matt Golder. 2006. "Understanding Interaction Models: Improving Empirical Analyses." *Political Analysis* 14 (1): 63–82.
Brown, L. Neville, and Tom Kennedy. 2000. *The Court of Justice of the European Communities.* 5th ed. London: Sweet and Maxwell.
Bulterman M. K., and M. Kuijer. 1996. *Compliance with Judgments of International Courts.* The Hague: Martinus Nijhoff.

Burley, Anne-Marie, and Walter Mattli. 1993. "Europe Before the Court: A Political Theory of Legal Integration." *International Organization* 47 (Winter): 41–76.

Burrows, Noreen, and Rosa Greaves. 2007. *The Advocate General and EC Law.* Oxford, England: Oxford University Press.

Busch, Marc L., Rafal Raciborski, and Eric Reinhardt. 2009. "Does the Rule of Law Matter? The WTO and US Antidumping Investigations." Typescript. Emory University.

Busch, Marc L., and Eric Reinhardt. 2006. "Three's a Crowd: Third Parties and WTO Dispute Settlement." *World Politics* 58 (3): 446–77.

Busch, Marc L., Eric Reinhardt, and Gregory Shaffer. 2007. "Does Legal Capacity Matter? Explaining Dispute Initiation and Antidumping Actions in the WTO." Typescript. Emory University.

Byers, Michael. 1999. *Custom, Power, and the Power of Rules: International Relations and Customary International Law.* New York: Cambridge University Press.

Canon, Bradley. 1991. "Courts and Policy: Compliance, Implementation, and Impact." In *The American Courts: A Critical Assessment,* edited by John Gates and Charles Johnson, 435–66. Washington, DC: Congressional Quarterly Press.

Carrubba, Clifford. 2005. "Courts and Compliance in International Regulatory Regimes." *Journal of Politics* 67 (August): 669–89.

Carrubba, Clifford. 2009. "A Model of the Endogenous Development of Judicial Institutions in Federal and International Systems." *Journal of Politics* 71 (1): 55–69.

Carrubba, Clifford J. 2010. "Federalism, Public Opinion, and Judicial Authority in Comparative Perspective." *Michigan State Law Review,* Fall, 697–712.

Carrubba, Clifford J., and Matthew Gabel. 2011. "European Court of Justice Data." Emory University Department of Political Science. http://polisci.emory.edu/home/people/carrubba_ecjd/index.html.

Carrubba, Clifford, Matthew Gabel, and Charles Hankla. 2008. "Judicial Behavior Under Political Constraints." *American Political Science Review* 102 (40): 435–52.

Carrubba, Clifford J., Matthew Gabel, and Charles Hankla. 2012. "Understanding the Role of the European Court of Justice in European Integration." *American Political Science Review* 106 (1): 214–23.

Carrubba, Clifford, and Lacey Murrah. 2005. "Legal Integration and Use of the Preliminary Ruling Process in the European Union." *International Organization* 59 (2): 399–418.

Carrubba, Clifford J., and James Rogers. 2003. "National Judicial Power and the Dormant Commerce Clause." *Journal of Law, Economics, and Organization* 19 (2): 543–70.

Carrubba, Clifford J., and Christopher Zorn. 2010. "Executive Discretion, Judicial Decision Making, and Separation of Powers in the United States." *Journal of Politics* 72 (3): 812–24.

Chalmers, Damian. 2005. "Judicial Authority and the Constitutional Treaty." *International Journal of Constitutional Law* 2: 448–72.

Chalmers, Damian, Gareth Davies, and Giorgio Monit. 2010. *European Union Law.* Cambridge: Cambridge University Press.

Chang, Kelly. 2003. *Appointing Central Bankers.* New York: Cambridge University Press.

Chayes, Abram, and Antonio Handler Chayes. 1993. "On Compliance." *International Organization* 47 (2): 175–205.
Chayes, Abram, and Antonia Handler Chayes. 1995. *The New Sovereignty: Compliance with International Regulatory Agreements.* Cambridge, MA: Harvard University Press.
Choi, In. 2001. "Unit Root Tests for Panel Data." *Journal of International Money and Finance* 20: 249–72.
Cichowski, Rachel. 2004. "Sex Equality." In *The Judicial Construction of Europe*, edited by Alec Stone Sweet, 147–97. Oxford, England: Oxford University Press.
Cichowski, Rachel A. 2007. *The European Court and Civil Society: Litigation, Mobilization and Governance.* New York: Cambridge University Press.
Cohen, Antonin. 2008. "Scarlet Robes, Dark Suits: The Social Recruitment of the European Court of Justice." EUI Working Papers RSCAS 2008/35. http://cadmus.eui.eu/bitstream/handle/1814/10029/EUI_RSCAS_2008_35.pdf?sequence=1.
Commission of the European Communities. 1985. *Completing the Internal Market.* White Paper from the Commission to the European Council Brussels. COM (85) 310.
Conant, Lisa. 2001. "Europeanization and the Courts: Various Patterns of Adaptation among National Judiciaries." In *Transforming Europe*, edited by Maria Green Cowles, James Caporaso, and Thomas Risse, 97–115. Ithaca, NY: Cornell University Press.
Conant, Lisa. 2002. *Justice Contained.* Ithaca, NY: Cornell University Press.
Craig, Paul, and Grianne de Burca. 2003. *EU Law.* Oxford, England: Oxford University Press.
Craig, Steven, and Joel Sailors. 1987. "Interstate Trade Barriers and the Constitution." *Cato Journal* 6 (3): 819–35.
Dai, Xinyuan. 2007. *International Institutions and National Policies.* Cambridge: Cambridge University Press.
Damgaard, Erik. 2008. "Cabinet Termination." In *Cabinets and Coalition Bargaining*, edited by Kaare Strom, Wolfgang Mueller, and Torbjorn Bergman, pp. 301–26. New York: Oxford University Press.
Dashwood, A. A. 1982. "The Advocate General in the Court of Justice of the European Communities." *Legal Studies* 2 (2): 202–16.
Dashwood, Alan, and Robin White. 1989. "Enforcement Actions under Articles 169 and 170 EEC." *European Law Review* 14: 388–413.
De Boef, Suzanna, and Luke Keele. 2008. "Taking Time Seriously." *American Journal of Political Science* 52 (1): 184–200.
Dehousse, Renaud. 1998. *The European Court of Justice: The Politics of Judicial Integration.* London: Palgrave Macmillan.
Diehl, P. F. 1996. "The United Nations and Peacekeeping." In *Coping with Conflict After the Cold War*, edited by E. Kolodziej and R. Kanet, 147–65. Baltimore: Johns Hopkins University Press.
Dixon, W. J. 1993. "Democracy and the Management of International Conflict." *Journal of Conflict Resolution* 37 (1): 42–68.
Downs, George, David Rocke, and Peter Barsoom. 1996. "Is the Good News about Compliance Good News about Cooperation?" *International Organization* 50 (3): 379–406.

Drache, Daniel, Amy Arnott, and Yunxiang Guan. 2000. *WTO Dispute Settlement Report Card* 83. Toronto, Canada: Robarts Centre for Canadian Studies. www.yorku.ca/drache/academic/papers/wto_dispute_report.pdf.

Economist. 2003. "All for One and One for Alstom." www.economist.com/node/1973533?story_id=1973533.

Edward, David. 1995. "How the Court of Justice Works." *European Law Review* 20: 539–58.

Edward, David. 1996. "The European Court of Justice – Friend or Foe?" *European-Atlantic Journal*, pp. 60–76. http://www.law.du.edu/documents/judge-david-edward-oral-history/1996-the-european-court-of-justice.pdf.

Edward, Mansfield, Helen Milner, and Peter Rosendorff. 2002. "Why Democracies Cooperate More: Electoral Control and International Trade Agreements." *International Organization* 56 (3): 477–513.

Eichengreen, Barry, and Pablo Vazquez. 2000. "Institutions and Economic Growth in Postwar Europe: Evidence and Conjectures." In *Productivity, Technology and Economic Growth*, edited by Bart van Ark, Simon K. Kuipers, and Gerard H. Kuper, 91–130. Dordrecht, the Netherlands: Kluwer.

Ellig, Jerry, and Allen E. Wiseman. 2007. "The Politics of Wine: Trade Barriers, Interest Groups and the Commerce Clause." *Journal of Politics* 69 (3): 859–75.

Epp, Charles R. 1998. *The Rights Revolution: Lawyers, Activists, and Supreme Courts in Comparative Perspective*. Chicago: University of Chicago Press.

Everling, Ulrich. 1984. "The Member States of the European Communities Before Their Court of Justice." *European Law Review* 9: 215–41.

Falkner, Gerda, Oliver Treib, Miriam Hartlapp, and Simone Leiber. 2005. *Complying with Europe: EU Harmonisation and Soft Law in the Member States*. Cambridge: Cambridge University Press.

Feld, Werner. 1963. "The Judges of the Court of Justice of the European Communities." *Villanova Law Review* 9: 37–58.

Ferejohn, John A., and Barry R. Weingast. 1992. "A Positive Theory of Statutory Interpretation." *International Review of Law and Economics* 12 (2): 263–79.

Fischer, D. D. 1981. *Improving Compliance with International Law*. Charlottesville: University of Virginia Press.

Fischer, D. D. 1982. "Decisions to Use the International Court of Justice: Four Recent Cases." *International Studies Quarterly* 26 (2): 251–77.

Fligstein, Neil, and Alec Stone Sweet. 2002. "Constructing Polities and Markets: An Institutional Account of European Integration." *American Journal of Sociology* 107 (5): 1206–43.

Franchino, Fabio. 2007. *The Powers of Union*. Cambridge: Cambridge University Press.

Gabel, Matthew, Clifford J. Carrubba, Caitlin Ainsely, and Donald Beaudette. 2012. "Of Courts and Commerce." *Journal of Politics* 74 (4): 1125–37.

Garrett, Geoffrey. 1992. "International Cooperation and Institutional Choice: The European Community's Internal Market." *International Organization* 46 (2): 533–60.

Garrett, Geoffrey. 1995. "The Politics of Legal Integration in the European Union." *International Organization* 49 (Winter): 171–81.

Garrett, Geoffrey, Daniel R. Kelemen, and Heiner Schulz. 1998. "The European Court of Justice, National Governments, and Legal Integration in the European Union." *International Organization* 52 (Winter): 149–176.
Garrett, Geoffrey, and Barry R. Weingast. 1993. "Ideas, Interests, and Institutions: Constructing the EC's Internal Market." In *Ideas and Foreign Policy*, edited by Judith Goldstein and Robert Keohane, 173–206. Ithaca, NY: Cornell University Press.
Gelman, Andrew, and Jennifer Hill. 2007. *Data Analysis Using Regression and Multilevel/Hierarchical Models*. New York: Cambridge University Press.
George, Tracy E., and Lee Epstein. 1992. "On the Nature of Supreme Court Decision Making." *American Political Science Review* 86 (2): 323–37.
Gibson, James, Gregory Caldeira, and Vanessa Baird. 1998. "On the Legitimacy of National High Courts." *American Political Science Review* 92 (2): 344–58.
Gilligan, Michael, Leslie Johns, and B. Peter Rosendorff. 2010. "Strengthening International Courts and the Early Settlement of Disputes." *Journal of Conflict Resolution* 54 (1): 5–38.
Goldstein, Judith L., Douglas Rivers, and Michael Tomz. 2007. "Institutions in International Relations: Understanding the Effects of the GATT and the WTO on World Trade." *International Organization* 61 (1): 37–67.
Gowa, Joanne, and Soo Yeon Kim. 2005. "An Exclusive Country Club: The Effects of the GATT on Trade, 1950–94." *World Politics* 57 (3): 453–78.
Granger, Marie-Pierre. 2005. "When Governments Go to Luxembourg: The Influence of Governments on the Court of Justice." *European Law Review* 29 (1): 3–31.
Gray, Julia. 2012. "Life, Death, or Zombies? The Endurance of Inefficient Regional Economic Organizations." Paper presented at Political Economy of International Organizations conference, Princeton University, Princeton, NJ, January 25.
Gray, Julia, and Jonathan Slapin. 2012. "How Effective Are Preferential Trade Agreements? Ask the Experts." *Review of International Organizations* 7: 309–33.
Green, Thomas. 1940. "Government." *Public Opinion Quarterly* 4 (1): 162–70.
Grieco, Joseph M., Christopher F. Gelpi, and T. Camber Warren. 2009. "When Preferences and Commitments Collide: The Effect of Relative Partisan Shifts on International Treaty Compliance." *International Organization* 63 (2): 342–55.
Guzman, Andrew. 2002a. "A Compliance-Based Theory of International Law." *California Law Review* 90: 1826–87.
Guzman, Andrew. 2002b. "The Cost of Credibility: Explaining Resistance to Interstate Dispute Resolution Mechanisms." *Journal of Legal Studies* 31 (2): 303–26.
Guzman, Andrew. 2008. "International Tribunals: A Rational Choice Analysis." *University of Pennsylvania Law Review* 157 (1): 175–235.
Hamilton, Alexander, James Madison, and John Jay. 2009. *The Federalist Papers*, edited by Ian Shapiro. New Haven, CT: Yale University Press.
Hartley, Trevor. 1988. *The Foundations of European Community Law*. 2nd ed. Oxford, England: Clarendon Press.
Hartley, Trevor. 2007. *The Foundations of European Community Law*. New York: Oxford University Press.
Heckscher, Eli. 1955. *Mercantilism*. Vol. 1. London: George Allen and Unwin.

Helfer, Laurence. 2013. "Flexibility in International Agreements." In *Interdisciplinary Perspectives on International Law and International Relations*, edited by J. Dunoff and M. Pollack, 175–96. New York: Cambridge University Press.

Helfer, Laurence, and Anne-Marie Slaughter. 1997. "Toward a Theory of Effective Supranational Adjudication." *Yale Law Review* 107 (2): 273–391.

Helfer, Laurence, and Anne-Marie Slaughter. 2005. "Why States Create International Tribunals: A Response to Professors Posner and Yoo." *California Law Review* 93: 899–956.

Helmke, Gretchen. 2002. "The Logic of Strategic Defection: Court-Executive Relations in Argentina under Dictatorship and Democracy." *American Political Science Review* 96 (2): 291–303.

Helmke, Gretchen. 2005. *Courts under Constraints*. Cambridge: Cambridge University Press.

Hirschl, Ran. 2008. "The Judicialization of Mega-Politics and the Rise of Political Courts." *Annual Review of Political Science* 11: 93–118.

Hitchcock, William. 2002. *The Struggle for Europe*. New York: Doubleday.

Hix, Simon. 2008. "Towards a Partisan Theory of EU Politics." *Journal of European Public Policy* 15 (8): 1254–65.

Hix, Simon, and Bjorn Hoyland. 2011. *The Political System of the European Union*. 3rd ed. London: Palgrave.

Hoffmann S. 1956. "The Role of International Organization: Limits and Possibilities." *International Organization* 10 (3): 357–72.

Honec, J., P. Honec, P. Petyovský, S. Valach, and J. Brambor. 2001. "Transparent Materials Optical Inspection Methods." Paper presented at the 13th International Conference on Process Control, Štrbské Pleso, Slovakia, June 11–14.

Hooghe, Liesbet. 2001. *The European Commission and the Integration of Europe: Images of Governance*. Cambridge: Cambridge University Press.

Huber, Peter J. 1996. *Robust Statistical Procedures*. Philadelphia: Society for Industrial and Applied Mathematics.

European Communities. 2009. *Internal Market Scoreboard*. No. 18. Luxembourg: Office for Official Publications of the European Communities.

International Monetary Fund. 2003. *Direction of Trade Statistics*. Washington, DC: IMF.

Jackson, John H. 2004. "International Law Status of WTO Dispute Settlement Reports: Obligation to Comply or Option to 'Buy Out'?" *American Journal of International Law* 98: 109–25.

Jacobs, Francis. 2000. "Advocates General and Judges in the European Court of Justice: Some Personal Reflections." In *Judicial Review in European Union Law*, edited by David O'Keeffe and Antonio Bavasso, 17–28. London: Kluwer.

Jestaedt, Thomas, Jacques Derenne, and Tom Ottervanger (coordinators). 2006. *Study on the Enforcement of State Aid Law at National Level*. Luxembourg: Office for Official Publications of the European Communities.

Johns, Leslie. 2012. "Courts as Coordinators: Endogenous Enforcement and Jurisdiction in International Adjudication." *Journal of Conflict Resolution* 56 (2): 257–89.

Johns, Leslie. Forthcoming. *Strengthening International Courts: The Hidden Costs of Legalization*. Ann Arbor: University of Michigan Press.

Judson, Katherine, and Anne Owen. 1999. "Estimating Dynamic Panel Data Models: A Guide for Macroeconomists." *Economics Letters* 65: 9–15.
Jupille, Joseph, and Duncan Snidal. 2005. "The Choice of International Institutions: Cooperation, Alternatives, and Strategies." University of Colorado, Boulder. Typescript.
Jupille, Joseph. 2004. *Procedural Politics*. New York: Cambridge University Press.
Kakutani, Shizou. 1941. "A Generalization of Brouwer's Fixed Point Theorem." *Duke Mathematical Journal* 8 (3): 457–59.
Keele, Luke, and Nathan Kelly. 2005. "Dynamic Models for Dynamic Theories: The Ins and Outs of Lagged Dependent Variables." *Political Analysis* 14: 186–205.
Keeler, John, and Peter Hall. 2001. "Interest Representation and the Politics of Protest." In *Developments in French Politics*, edited by A. Guyomarch and H. Machin, 50–65. London: Palgrave.
Kenney, Sally J. 1998. "The Members of the Court of Justice of the European Communities." *Columbia Journal of European Law* 5: 101.
Keohane, Robert. 1984. *After Hegemony: Cooperation and Discord in the World Political Economy*. Princeton, NJ: Princeton University Press.
Keohane, Robert, and Lisa Martin. 1995. "The Promise of Institutionalist Theory." *International Security* 20 (1): 39–51.
Keohane, Robert, Andrew Moravscik, and Anne-Marie Slaughter. 2000. "Legalized Dispute Resolution: Interstate and Transnational." *International Organization* 54 (3): 457–88.
Kilroy, Bernadette. 1999. "Integration Through Law: ECJ and Governments in the EU." PhD diss., University of California–Los Angeles. http://search.proquest.com/docview/304497001.
King, Gary, Robert Keohane, and Sidney Verba. 1994. *Designing Social Inquiry*. Princeton, NJ: Princeton University Press.
King, Gary, Robert O. Keohane, and Sidney Verba. 2001. *Designing Social Inquiry: Scientific Inference in Qualitative Research*. Princeton, NJ: Princeton University Press.
Kiviet, Jan. 1995. "On Bias, Inconsistency, and Efficiency of Various Estimators in Dynamic Panel Models." *Journal of Econometrics* 68: 53–87.
Koh, Harold H. 1996. "Transnational Legal Process." *Nebraska Law Review* 75: 181.
Kono, Daniel Y. 2006. "Optimal Obfuscation: Democracy and Trade Policy Transparency." *American Political Science Review* 100 (3): 369–84.
Kono, Daniel Y. 2007. "Making Anarchy Work: International Legal Institutions and Trade Cooperation." *Journal of Politics* 69 (3): 746–59.
Koremenos, Barbara. 2005. "Contracting Around International Uncertainty." *American Political Science Review* 99 (4): 549–65.
Koremenos, Barbara. 2007. "If Only Half of International Agreements Have Dispute Resolution Provisions, Which Half Needs Explaining?" *Journal of Legal Studies* 36:189.
Koremenos, Barbara, Charles Lipson, and Duncan Snidal. 2001. "The Rational Design of International Institutions." *International Organization* 55: 761–99.
Kreps, David M. 1990. *A Course in Microeconomic Theory*. Vol. 41. Princeton, NJ: Princeton University Press.

Krislov, Samuel, Claus-Dieter Ehlermann, and Joseph Weiler. 1986. "The Political Organs and the Decision-Making Process in the United States and the European Community." In *Integration Through Law, Methods, Tools, and Institutions*, edited by M. Cappelltti, M. Seccombe, and J. Weiler, 3–112. Berlin: Gruyter.

Krugman, Paul, and Maurice Obstfeld. 1994. *International Economics*. 3rd ed. New York: HarperCollins.

Lasser, Mitchel. 2009. *Judicial Deliberations*. New York: Oxford University Press.

Laver, Michael. 2003. "Government Termination." *Annual Review of Political Science* 6 (1): 23–40.

Lax, Jeffrey R. 2011. "The New Judicial Politics of Legal Doctrine." *Annual Review of Political Science* 14: 131–57.

Levin, Andrew, Chien-Fu Lin, and Chia-Shang James Chu. 2002. "Unit Root Tests in Panel Data: Asymptotic and Finite-Sample Properties." *Journal of Econometrics* 108: 1–24.

Lockhart, William B. 1940. "State Tax Barriers to Interstate Trade." *Harvard Law Review* 53 (8): 1253–88.

Lupia, Arthur, and Kaare Strom. 2008. "Bargaining, Transaction Costs, and Coalition Governance." In *Cabinets and Coalition Bargaining*, edited by Kaare Strom, Wolfgang Mueller, and Torbjorn Bergman. New York: Oxford University Press.

Maduro, Miguel Poiatres. 1999. *We the Court: The European Court of Justice and the European Economic Constitution*. Oxford, England: Hart Publishing.

Maggi, Giovanni. 1999. "The Role of Multilateral Institutions in International Trade Cooperation." *American Economic Review* 89 (1): 190–214.

Mancini, Federico G. 1991. "The Making of a Constitution for Europe." In *The New European Community: Decision-Making and Institutional Change*, edited by Robert Keohane and Stanley Hoffman, 177–94. Boulder, CO: Westview Press.

Martin, Lisa. 2013. "Against Compliance." In *Interdisciplinary Perspectives on International Law and International Relations: The State of the Art*, edited by Jeffrey L. Dunoff and Mark A. Pollack, 591–610. Cambridge: Cambridge University Press.

Martin, Lisa, and Beth Simmons. 1998. "Theories and Empirical Studies of International Institutions." *International Organization* 52 (4): 729–757.

Mattli, Walter. 1999. *The Logic of Regional Integration*. New York: Cambridge University Press.

Mattli, Walter, and Anne-Marie Slaughter. 1995. "Law and Politics in the European Union: A Reply to Garrett." *International Organization* 49 (Winter): 183–90.

Mattli, Walter, and Anne-Marie Slaughter. 1998. "Revisiting the European Court of Justice." *International Organization* 52 (Winter): 177–209.

McAllister, Breck P. 1940. "Court, Congress, and Trade Barriers." *Indiana Law Review* 16: 144–68.

McElroy, Gail, and Kenneth Benoit. 2010. "Party Policy and Group Affiliation in the European Parliament." *British Journal of Political Science* 40 (2): 377–98.

McGown, Margaret. 2004. "The Free Movement of Goods." In *The Judicial Construction of Europe*, edited by Alec Stone Sweet, 109–46. Oxford, England: Oxford University Press.

Molle, Willem. 2006. *The Economics of European Integration*. 5th ed. Aldershot, England: Ashgate.

Moravcsik, Andrew. 1998. *The Choice for Europe*. Ithaca, NY: Cornell University Press.

Morgenthau, H. J. 1985. *Politics Among Nations: The Struggle for Power and Peace*. 6th ed. New York: Knopf.
Morijn, John. 2006. "Balancing Fundamental Rights and Common Market Freedoms in Union Law: Schmidberger and Omega in Light of the European Constitution." *European Law Journal* 12 (1): 15–40.
Mortelmans, K. 1979. "Observations in Cases Governed by the Article 177 of the EEC Treaty." *Common Market Law Review* 16: 557–90.
Nicol, Danny. 2001. *EC Membership and the Judicialization of British Politics*. New York: Oxford University Press.
Nykios, Stacy. 2003. "The Preliminary Reference Process: National Court Implementation, Changing Opportunity Structures and Litigant Dessistment." *European Union Politics* 4: 397–419.
Obermaier, Andreas. 2009. *The End of Territoriality?* Burlington, VT: Ashgate.
Pollack, Mark. 1997. "Delegation, Agency, and Agenda-Setting in the European Community." *International Organization* 51 (Winter): 99–134.
Ohlhausen, Maureen K., and Gregory P. Luib. 2008–9. "Moving Sideways: Post-Granholm Developments in Wine Direct Shipping and Their Implications for Competition." *Antitrust Law Journal* 75: 505–47.
Oliver, Peter. 1996. *Free Movement of Goods in the European Community*. 3rd ed. London: Sweet and Maxwell.
Panke, Diana. 2007. "The European Court of Justice as an Agent of Europeanization? Restoring Compliance with EU Law." *Journal of European Public Policy* 14 (6): 847–866.
Panke, Diana. 2010. *The Effectiveness of the European Court of Justice*. Manchester, England: Manchester University Press.
Pitarakis, Jean-Yves, and George Tridimas. 2003. "Joint Dynamics of Legal and Economic Integration in the European Union." *European Journal of Law and Economics* 16: 357–68.
Pollack, Mark. 2003. *The Engines of European Integration*. New York: Oxford University Press.
Posner, Eric, and John Yoo. 2005. "Judicial Independence in International Tribunals." *California Law Review* 93 (1): 1–74.
Powell, G. Bingham, and Georg Vanberg. 2000. "Election Laws, Disproportionality, and Median Correspondence: Implications for Two Visions of Democracy." *British Journal of Political Science* 30: 383–411.
Rasmussen, Hjalte. 1986. *On Law and Policy in the European Court of Justice: A Comparative Study in Judicial Policymaking*. Boston: Martinus Nijhoff.
Rasmussen, Hjalte. 1998. *European Court of Justice*. Aarhus, Denmark: Gadjura.
Ray, Leonard. 1999. "Measuring Party Orientations towards European Integration: Results from an Expert Survey." *European Journal of Political Research* 36 (2): 283–306.
Ritter, Cyril. 2005. "A New Look at the Role and Impact of the Advocate General – Collectively and Individually." *Columbia Journal of European Law* 12: 751.
Ritter, Emily Hencken, and Scott Wolford. 2012. "Bargaining and the Effectiveness of International Criminal Regimes." *Journal of Theoretical Politics* 24 (2): 149–71.
Rose, Andrew K. 2004. "Do We Really Know That the WTO Increases Trade?" *American Economic Review* 94 (1): 98–114.

Rosendorff, B. Peter. 2005. "Stability and Rigidity: Politics and Design of the WTO's Dispute Settlement Procedure." *American Political Science Review* 99 (3): 389.

Rosendorff, B. Peter, and Helen V. Milner. 2001. "The Optimal Design of International Trade Institutions: Uncertainty and Escape." *International Organization* 55 (4): 829–57.

Rubin, Donald. 1974. "Estimating Causal Effects of Treatments in Randomized and Nonrandomized Studies." *Journal of Educational Psychology* 66 (5): 688–701.

Schachter, O. 1991. *International Law in Theory and Practice*. Dordrecht, the Netherlands: Martinus Nijhoff.

Scheingold, Stuart. 1965. *The Rule of Law in European Integration*. New Haven, CT: Yale University Press.

Schofield, Norman. 1993. "Political Competition and Multiparty Coalition Government." *European Journal of Political Research* 23 (1): 1–33.

Schepel, Harm, and Erhard Blankenburg. 2001. "Mobilizing the European Court of Justice." In *The European Court of Justice*, edited by Grainne de Búrca and Joseph Weiler, 9–42. Oxford, England: Oxford University Press.

Schwartz, Warren F., and Alan O. Sykes. 2002. "The Economic Structure of Renegotiation and Dispute Resolution in the World Trade Organization." *Journal of Legal Studies* 31: S179–S204.

Segal, Jeffrey A., and Harold J. Spaeth. 1993. *The Supreme Court and the Attitudinal Model*. New York: Cambridge University Press.

Segal, Jeffrey A., and Harold J. Spaeth. 1996. "The Influence of Stare Decisis on the Votes of the United States Supreme Court Justices." *American Journal of Political Science* 40 (4): 971–1003.

Segal, Jeffrey A., and Harold J. Spaeth. 2002. *The Supreme Court and the Attitudinal Model Revisited*. New York: Cambridge University Press.

Setear, John K. 1996. "An Iterative Perspective on Treaties: A Synthesis of International Relations Theory and International Law." *Harvard International Law Journal* 37: 139.

Setear, John K. 1997. "Responses to Breach of a Treaty and Rationalist International Relations Theory: The Rules of Release and Remediation in the Law of Treaties and the Law of State Responsibility." *Virginia Law Review* 83: 1.

Simmons, Beth A. 1998. "Compliance with International Agreements." *Annual Review of Political Science* 1: 75–93.

Simmons, Beth A. 2009. *Mobilizing for Human Rights: International Law in Domestic Politics*. Cambridge: Cambridge University Press.

Simmons, Beth A. 2010. "Treaty Compliance and Violation." *Annual Review of Political Science* 13 (May): 273–96.

Slepcevic, Reinhard. 2009. "The Judicial Enforcement of EU Law through National Courts: Possibilities and Limits." *Journal of European Public Policy* 16 (3): 378–94.

Smith, Edwin M. 1991. "Understanding Dynamic Obligations: Arms Control Agreements. *Southern California Law Review* 64: 1549–75.

Smith, James McCall. 2000. "The Politics of Dispute Settlement Design: Explaining Legalism in Regional Trade Pacts." *International Organization* 54 (1): 137–80.

Smith, James McCall. 2003. "WTO Dispute Settlement: The Politics of Procedure in Appellate Body Rulings." *World Trade Review* 2 (1): 65–100.

Smith, Michael. 1986. "State Discriminations against Interstate Commerce." *California Law Review* 4: 1203–57.

Solanke, Iyiola. 2008-9. "Diversity and Independence in the European Court of Justice." *Columbia Journal of European Law* 89: 89–121.
Spaeth, Harold J., and Jeffery A. Segal. 1999. *Majority Rule or Minority Will: Adherence to Precedent on the US Supreme Court.* New York: Cambridge University Press.
Staton, Jeffrey K. 2006. "Constitutional Review and the Selective Promotion of Case Results." *American Journal of Political Science* 50 (1): 98–112.
Staton, Jeffrey K. 2010. *Constitutional Review and the Selective Promotion of Case Results.* New York: Cambridge University Press.
Staton, Jeffrey, and William Moore. 2011. "Judicial Power in Domestic and International Politics." *International Organization* 6: 553–87.
Stein, Eric. 1981. "Lawyers, Judges, and the Making of a Transnational Constitution." *American Journal of International Law* 1: 1–27.
Steiner, Josephine. 1993. "From Direct Effect to Francovich." *European Law Review* 18: 3–22.
Stone Sweet, Alec. 2004. *The Judicial Construction of Europe.* Oxford, England: Oxford University Press.
Stone Sweet, Alec, and Thomas L. Brunell. 1998a. "Constructing a Supranational Constitution: Dispute Resolution and Governance in the European Community." *American Political Science Review* 92 (January): 63–81.
Stone Sweet, Alec, and Thomas L. Brunell. 1998b. "The European Court and the National Courts: A Statistical Analysis of Preliminary References, 1961–95." *Journal of European Public Policy* 5 (March): 66–97.
Stone Sweet, Alec, and Thomas Brunell. 1999. The Alec Stone Sweet and Thomas Brunell Data Set on Preliminary References in EC Law, Robert Schuman Centre, European University Institute.
Stone Sweet, Alec, and Thomas L. Brunell. 2012. "The European Court of Justice, State Non-Compliance, and the Politics of Override." *American Political Science Review* 106 (1): 204–13.
Stone Sweet, Alec, and James Caporaso. 1998. "From Free Trade to Supranational Polity: The European Court and Integration." In *European Integration and Supranational Governance*, edited by Wayne Sandholtz and Alec Stone Sweet, 92–133. New York: Oxford University Press.
Strom, Kaare, Wolfgang Mueller, and Torbjorn Bergman. 2008. *Cabinets and Coalition Bargaining.* New York: Oxford University Press.
Taipei Times. 2004. "France, EU Agree on the Fate of Alstom." May 27. www.taipeitimes.com/News/worldbiz/archives/2004/05/27/2003157.
Tallberg, Jonas. 2002. "Paths to Compliance: Enforcement, Management, and the European Union." *International Organization* 56 (3): 609–43.
Tomz, Michael. 2007. "Domestic Audience Costs in International Relations: An Experimental Approach." *International Organization* 61 (4): 821–40.
Tomz, Michael, Judith L. Goldstein, and Douglas Rivers. 2007. "Do We Really Know That the WTO Increases Trade? Comment." *American Economic Review* 97 (5): 2005–18.
Tomz, Michael, Jason Wittenberg, and Gary King. (2003). *Clarify: Software for Interpreting and Presenting Statistical Results.* Version 2.0 Cambridge, MA: Harvard University, June 1. www.stanford.edu/~tomz/software/clarify.pdf.

Tridimas, George, and Takis Tridimas. 2004. "National Courts and the European Court of Justice: A Public Choice Analysis of the Preliminary Reference Procedure." *International Review of Law and Economics* 24: 125–45.

Tridimas, Takis. 1997. "The Role of the Advocate General in the Development of Community Law: Some Reflections." *Common Market Law Review* 34 (6): 1349–87.

Tsebelis, George, and Garrett, Geoffrey. 2001. "The Institutional Foundations of Intergovernmentalism and Supranationalism in the European Union." *International Organization* 55 (Spring): 357–90.

Vanberg, Georg. 2001. "Legislative-Judicial Relations: A Game-Theoretic Approach to Constitutional Review." *American Journal of Political Science* 45 (2): 346–61.

Vanberg, Georg. 2005. *The Politics of Constitutional Review in Germany*. New York: Cambridge University Press.

Wagner, Harrison. 2007. *War and the State: The Theory of International Politics*. Ann Arbor: University of Michigan Press.

Warntjen, Andreas, Simon Hix, and Christophe Crombez. 2008. "The Party Political Make-Up of EU Legislative Bodies." *Journal of European Public Policy* 15 (8): 1243–53.

Warwick, Paul. 1994. *Government Survival in Parliamentary Democracies*. New York: Cambridge University Press.

Wasserfallen, Fabio. 2010. "The Judiciary as Legislator? How the European Court of Justice Shapes Policy-Making in the European Union." *Journal of European Public Policy* 17 (8): 1128–46.

Weiler, Joseph. 1991. "The Transformation of Europe." *Yale Law Journal* 100 (8): 2403–83.

Westerland, Chad, Jeffrey Segal, Lee Epstein, Charles Cameron, and Scott Comparato. 2010. "Strategic Defiance and Compliance in the US Courts of Appeals." *American Journal of Political Science* 54 (4): 891–905.

Williams, Rhiannon. 1994. "The European Commission and the Enforcement of Environmental Law: An Invidious Position." *Yearbook of Euroupean Law* 14 (1): 351–99.

Wilson, Bruce. 2007. "Compliance by WTO Members with Adverse WTO Dispute Settlement Rulings: The Record to Date." *Journal of International Economic Law* 10 (2): 397–403.

Wind, Marlene, Dorte Sindbjerg Martinsen, and Gabriel Pons Rotger. 2009. "The Uneven Legal Push for Europe." *European Union Politics* 10 (1): 63–88.

Wiseman, Alan E., and Jerry Ellig. 2007. "The Politics of Wine: Trade Barriers, Interest Groups, and the Commerce Clause." *Journal of Politics* 69 (3): 859–75.

Wonka, Arndt. 2007. "Technocratic and Independent? The Appointment of European Commissioners and Its Policy Implications." *Journal of European Public Policy* 14 (2): 169–89.

Wood, B. Dan, and Richard W. Waterman. 1991. "The Dynamics of Political Control of the Bureaucracy." *American Political Science Review:* 85 (3): 801–28.

Wood, B. Dan, and Richard W. Waterman. 1993. "The Dynamics of Political-Bureaucratic Adaptation." *American Journal of Political Science* 37 (2): 497–528.

Index

adjudication process, factors influencing
  EC's position on legal issue, 133–7
  legal merits of case, 131–3
  measurement errors, 142–4
  substantive significance, 144–6
  threats of override, 146–50
  variation in judicial procedures, 137–41
adjudication process, innovations in, 209–10
adverse rulings, probability of being obeyed
  briefs against defendant and, link between, 43, 46–7
  defendant's effort and, link between, 43–4
  observational equivalence problem and, 45
Advocate General (AG)
  appointment process, 91, 93
  as legal advocate, 93–5
  as proxy for legal merits, 89, 114–15, 130, 198
  case assignment rules, 100–1
  controls for position of, 132
  legal opinions
    see AG's opinion
  professional responsibility, 93–4
  role at ECJ, 90–1
  served from 1960 to 1999, 91–3
  terms, 91
AG's opinion, 94
  control for legal merits, 118–19
  ECJ rulings and, comparison between, 94
  on legal issues answered by ECJ, 101–2
  supporting plaintiff, probit analysis of, 110, 116, 123
  usage in court proceedings, 94
AG's opinion, political influences on, 97, 118, 120, 199
  descriptive literature on, 96–7
  home member-state government, 96
  post-AG career goals, 96
  theoretical models for, 97, 102
    empirical evidence, 100–1
    home government's interests, 98–100
    home government briefs, 102, 109–14
    hypothesis testing, 102–3
    hypothesized relationships analysis, 108, 119
    necessary conditions for, 97–8, 100–1
    political survival forecasting model, 103–8
    unconditional hypotheses, 98–100
AG's opinion and ECJ rulings, agreement between, 95, 198
  home government briefs and, 115, 118
  probit analysis, 110–11, 123–4
  suspect AG opinions, 115–18
  systematic patterns of, 114
air quality, stringent requirements for, 28
Alstom, bailout of, 23
annulment actions, 62, 82
  against European Council, 80
  EU institution, 78
  France, 77
  litigant identity for, 71–2
  member-state as plaintiff, 83

annulment actions (*cont.*)
  member-state government compliance, 77–8, 149
  noncompliance with, 79–80
  private parties, 78
  threats of override, 149
assumptions of formal model
  out of scope for model, 17
  plausibility, 16–17
Autoregressive Distributed Lag (ADL), 174–5

briefs against defendant
  and probability of adverse ruling being obeyed, link between, 43, 46–7
  court ruling against governments, 56, 58
  ECJ and, 62–3
  filing of, 34, 42
  legal merits of case and, 86–7

cabinet survival, forecasting model for, 104–8
  bargaining environment, 106
  basic measure, 121–2
  causal arguments, 104–5, 107
  Cox proportional hazard model, 122–3
  determinants of, 105, 106, 122
  electoral system types, 106
  home government briefs and AG opinions, 109–14
  hypothesized relationships analysis, 108, 119
  life table, 121–2
  macroeconomic conditions, 106
  sophisticated measure, 122–3
  stable coalition, 106
  survival analysis statistical models, 105–6, 107–8
Cassis de Dijon, German restriction on sale of, 22
coalitions
  cabinet survival and, 106
  threats of override and, 148
collective action, need for, 27–30
collective action challenges, 7, 60–1
  costs of compliance, 11, 14
  ECJ and, 65
  environmental standards, raising, 28–9
  in domestic courts, 218–19
  international agreements for, 7

social policies, 29
trade barriers, lowering, 27–8
common regulatory regimes, 191
  compliance challenges for, 30
  domestic political contexts, 30–1
  expanding membership, 30
  policy goals, 30
  policy jurisdiction, 30
  variable costs of deeper agreements, 31, 32–3
dispute generation process model
  see dispute generation process, model of
dispute resolution process model
  see dispute resolution process, model of
enforcement of
  court's role in, 32–3, 44: *see also* international courts
  courts as fire alarm, 32
  courts as information clearinghouse, 32
enforcement strategies for, 39
  components of, 40
  factors influencing, 41
  punishment conditioning on litigation process, 40–1
  punishment for defection, 40
  punishment for *t* periods, 41
European Union
  see European Union (EU)
governments' choices and, 45
incomplete contracts and, 45
international, multilateral, 2–3
international court and state behavior
  see international court influence on state behavior, formal model of
motivation for creating
  need for collective action, 27–30
  resolving strategic dilemma, 29–30
  vested interest, 25
non-tariff barriers to trade, 45
obligations of, 44
policy goals of, 26–7
  environmental standards, raising, 28–9
  social policies, 29
  trade barriers, lowering, 27–8
politics of, 192
punishment strategies, 31
wider/narrower application of, 38

Index 235

common regulatory regimes, defecting
  from, 41
 bringing challenge against, 36–7
 incentives for, 7, 12, 30–1, 32–3, 46
 punishment for, 40–1
 rules allowing exceptions for, 31
Comparative Parliamentary Data Archive,
  121–2
competitiveness
 and environmental standards, 28–9
 and social policies, 29
 and trade barriers, 27–8
complete theory of court influence, 24–6
compliance dilemma, 34
compliance problem faced by courts, 130
Conditional Effectiveness Hypothesis, 19,
  58, 83, 193
 court ruling, 47
 statement, 156, 167
Conditional Effectiveness Hypothesis
  testing, 20, 167–8
 ADL model, 174–5
 baseline analysis, 175–6
 baseline model, 168
 data and measurement, 168–74
 descriptive statistics, 173
 during transition period, 168
 impact of total rulings, 168
 LRM and LM test, 175, 188
 panel-corrected standard errors, 169, 175
 theoretical model, 177–86, 188–9
 time-series analysis, 175
consent based arrangements, 6
coordination problems, 27, 60
Coordination Rurale, 206
cost of compliance, 33–4, 52, 191–2, 193
 domestic interests and, 216
 formal model, 52
 N government version, 35–6, 48
 two-state version, 34–5
courts
 definition of, 31
 domestic
  see domestic courts
 international
  see international courts
Cox proportional hazard model, 122

death penalty cases, legal characteristics of,
  87
deductive argument, 16

deeper agreements
 cooperation in, 8
 international courts and
  see international courts
 variable costs of, 31
defendant state, response to challenge, 32
democracies, 6
democratic political systems, appointing
  officials in, 120
derogations, 193
diffuse legitimacy, 216–18
direct actions, 62, 74, 77, 149
 annulment
  see annulment actions
 conflicts of interest in, 101
 enforcement actions
  see enforcement actions
 infringement rulings
  see infringement rulings
 noncompliance threat in, 138, 149, 150
 third-party government briefs in, 62–3,
  139, 140, 151
dispute generation process, model of, 44
 assumptions, 33
 cost of compliance, N government
  version, 35–6, 41, 48
 cost of compliance, two-state version,
  33–5
 cost of filing challenge, 36–7, 42
 filing challenge, 36
 government's decision, 34
 third party government's payoff, 34,
  42
dispute resolution, legalization of, 25
dispute resolution mechanism (DSM)
 for trade liberalization, 162
 preferential trade agreements, 57–8
dispute resolution process, model of, 26,
  44
 assumptions, 33
 bringing case, 36, 42, 55
 cost of compliance, 33–4, 52
 defendant's effort, 37, 42–3, 54
 divergence of court's preferences, 38
 filing briefs, 37, 42, 54
 government compliance with rulings,
  38–9, 52–3, 55
 legitimacy cost, 39
 payoff structure, 38–9
 ruling and judgment, 37, 43, 54, 56
 wider/narrower application of law, 38

domestic court rulings
  factors influencing, 15–16
  influence on government policy, 10
  judicial impact of
    effect on policy outcomes, 159–60
    impact on social and economic world, 158
    liberalization of inter-state commerce, 160–1
    literature on, 158–9
    research examining, 159
    trade, statistical evidence of, 161–2
    voluntary compliance, 159
domestic courts
  collective action problems in, 218–19
  domestic publics role in, 215–16
  international court, comparison between, 214–15
  US Supreme Court, 218–19
domestic crisis and defection, 31
domestic law and international law, comparison between, 214–15
domestic publics and international courts
  diffuse legitimacy, 216–18
  indirect enforcement mechanism, 216

ECJ, factors influencing adjudication by
  EC's position on legal issue, 133–7, 153–4
    EC's briefs, 135, 137
    member-state briefs, balance of, 135, 136
    omitted variable bias, 134, 135
    plaintiff, 134–5
    probit models and, 136–7
    third-party briefs, 135–6, 137
  legal merits of case, 131–3, 153
    AG's position on, 132–3
    influence on rulings, 131–2
  measurement errors, 142–4
    random, 143–4
    systematic, 143
    third-party support for plaintiff, 142
  substantive significance, 144–6
  threats of override, 146–50, 154
    administrative cases, 149
    annulment actions, 149
    coalitions and, 148
    credibility of, 147–8
    effect of government briefs due, 148
    importance of sensitivity to, 147
    preliminary rulings, 150
    third-party briefs and, 147, 150
  variation in judicial procedures, 137–41, 154
    financial sanctions, 138–9, 141
    government as defendant, 139–40
    government as litigant, 140
    impact of government briefs, 137–8, 139
    responsive to government briefs, 141
    threat of noncompliance, 138, 139, 154–5
ECJ, theoretical model of, 65
  alternative argument, 68
  applications of, 82–3
  assumptions, 65, 68
  empirical predictions, 66–7
  explanation evaluation, 67
  hypothesis testing, 66
  preliminary reference system, 67–8
ECJ Database Project, 68–9
  coding at level of legal issue, 70–1
  database descriptive statistics, 71–6
  dataset, 69–71
  rulings from 1960–1999, 71
ECJ rulings, 22, 63, 64, 200–3, 204–5, 206–7
  against German government, 22
  and AG's opinion, agreement between
    see AG's opinion and ECJ rulings, agreement between
  and AG's opinion, comparison between, 94
  baseline analysis, 127–9
  database creation project
    see ECJ Database Project
  distribution of, 72
  preliminary rulings, 72–4
  third-party briefs, 74–5
  EC's impact on, 199
  EU institutions and, 75
  EU law interpretation, 76
  government noncompliance with, 66, 76, 78–82, 130, 194–6
  impact of, 84–5
  infringement procedure, 12
  inter-state trade and, 157
  intra-EU trade and, 158
  legal merits of case and, 86
  litigant identity for, 71–2
  market liberalization, 157
  member states' role in, 65–6
  narrower or broader set of, 125
  net government briefs and, correlation between, 129

Index

on legal issue in case, 125
policy change in response to, 186–7
policy implications, 76
probit analysis of plaintiff, 117, 123–4
probit models of, 127–8
procedural differences across, 194
promoting European integration, 196–7
third-party briefs and, relationship between, 83
third-party governments and, 19
ECJ rulings on intra-EU trade, judicial impact of, 197
 compliance problems and, 164–5
 heterogeneity in, 167
 hypothesis testing of
  see Conditional Effectiveness Hypothesis testing
 infringement rulings, 166
 intra-EU imports/GDP, 166–7, 176, 177–9, 180, 183, 184, 186
 preliminary references, 165–6
 third-party government support for, 187, 193–4
electoral system, 106
enforcement actions, 62, 63, 77, 133, 134, 135, 138
 noncompliance in, 78–9, 130
environmental standards, raising, 28–9
EU Commission, leadership of, 120
EU institutions
 annulment actions, 78
 bringing actions before ECJ, 62
EU laws
 ECJ preliminary ruling over, 62
 expansive interpretation of, 63
 flexibility in, 203–4
 member-state government compliance with, 60–1, 76
EU member states, 168
 costs of compliance for, 14
 intra-EU imports into
  see intra-EU imports
 political economic clout of, 126–7
European Atomic Energy Community (Euratom), 59
European Coal and Steel Community (ECSC), 59
European Commission (EC), 59
 bailout of Alstom, 23
 controls for position of, 136
 decisions on state aid, 77–8

ECJ's responsiveness to, 130
financial sanctions on member states, 138–9
impact on ECJ rulings, 199
position on legal issue, 133–7, 153–4
balance of member-state briefs, 135, 136
concern of omitted variable bias, 134, 135
EC's briefs, 135, 137
plaintiff, 134–5
probit models and, 136–7
third-party briefs, 135–6, 137
European Communities (EC) 59
European Council (EC), UK annulment action against, 80
European Court of Justice (ECJ), 21
 adjudication process, 64–5
 see also ECJ, factors influencing adjudication by
 as international court, 14
 compliance problems faced by, 14, 63–4
 decisions and third-party governments, 19
 dispute resolution by, 61
 judges, 61
 preliminary ruling system, 62, 67–8
 responsiveness to EC, 130
 role in EU performance, 65
 roles and responsibilities of, 14
 standing to bring suit before, 62
 supremacy doctrines, 209
 third-party briefs, 62–3, 67
 voluntary compliance assumptions, 67
European Economic Community (EEC)
 Common Agricultural Policy, 59
 common external trade policy, 59
 creation of, 58
 merger with ECSC and Euratom, 59
 role in barrier elimination, 58–9
European Union (EU)
 bicameral legislature of, 59
 European Court of Justice
  see European Court of Justice (ECJ)
 executive arm of, 59
 historical record of, 58
 judicial arm of, 59
 membership commitments, 14
 policy mandate of, 60
 policy objectives, 163
 success of, 59–60

European Union (EU), theoretical model
  of
 bringing suit before ECJ, 62
 collective action problem, 60–1
 compliance problems, 61
 ECJ rulings, 63
 enforcement problems, 63–4
 institutional role of ECJ, 61
 policy dilemmas, 60
 preliminary references, 62
 regulatory regime's policy domain, 60–1
 strategic dilemmas, 60
 third-party briefs, 62–3, 67

Federal Reserve chairman, appointment of, 120–1
financial sanctions, 138–9, 141
formal model
  assumptions, 51
  bringing case, 55
  continuation values of
   costs and benefits to parties, 51–2
   costs and benefits to third party, 52
   from on-path play, 51
   from punishment path play, 52
  cost of compliance, 52
  court ruling, 54, 56
  defendant's effort, 54
  filing briefs, 54
  government compliance with rulings, 52–3, 55
  international court influence on state behavior
   see international court influence on state behavior, formal model of
  issuing judgments, 54
  judgments, 52–3, 54
  off-equilibrium path strategies, 51
  on-equilibrium path strategies, 50–1
  ruling and judgment, 54, 56
formal modeling, 15–16
France
  air pollution policies, 28
  annulment actions, 77
  decision to bail out Alstom, 23

GATT membership, impact of, 162
GDP and intra-EU imports, 170–1
German Constitutional Court, 81
Germany, 22, 30
  enforcement actions against, 79

government briefs
  differential importance of, 126
  impact on ECJ rulings, 131–3
  threats of override, 148
  variation in judicial procedures, 137–8, 139, 141
government court relations, theory of, 81
government preferences and court influence, 49
governments
  back-channel negotiations, 32
  briefs filed against
   see briefs against defendant
  challenging, in court, 24–5
  consent based arrangements, 6
  defecting from regulatory regimes
   see common regulatory regimes, defecting from
  definition of, 5
  effort to persuade, 37, 42–3
  environmental standards, raising, 28–9
  international cooperation, 5–6, 7
  motivation for creating regulatory regimes, 25
  participation in regulatory regimes, 15–16
  policy changes and court rulings, 10
  power relations among, 5
  trade barriers, lowering, 27–8
governments, enforcement strategies of, 39
  components of, 40
  factors influencing, 41
  punishment conditioning on litigation process, 40–1
  punishment for defection, 40
  punishment for t periods, 41
Granholm v. Heald ruling, 160
  consequences for interstate trade, 160

highly legalized international courts, 21
  binding rulings, 9–10
  national court rulings and, 10
  home government briefs, 101
   AG's age and, 110
   AG's opinion and ECJ rulings, 102, 109, 114, 115, 118
   prime minister's party's survival, 109–14
   variable for forecasting models, 108

incumbent government, forecasting survival prospects of
 see cabinet survival, forecasting model for

Index

information exchange, 32
information transmission process, 13
infringement rulings, 82
  baseline analysis of, 175-6
  control of temporal shocks affecting, 173-4
  cross-national variation in, 173
  financial sanctions for noncompliance with, 138-9
  importance of, 189
  intra-EU imports and, 166
  intra-EU trade and, 166
  noncompliance with, 79
  pro-Commission, 171
  trade effect of, 167-8
international agreements, 1, 21
  adoption of, 1
  between two states, 31-2
  codified set of rules, 7
  compliance with, 5, 156
    consent-based arrangements, 6
    domestic political context, 6
  derogations and, 193
  design features of, 9
  efficient breach argument of, 23-4
  flexibility of, 9
  international courts
    see international courts
  multilateral international regulatory regimes, 2-3
  state behavior and
    consent-based arrangements, 6
    domestic political context, 6
    managerial model, 6
    realists' position on, 5-6
international agreements, liberal institutional perspective on, 7-8
  assumptions, 7
  collective action challenges, 7
  costs and benefits of cooperation, 8
  limitations of, 8
  shallow agreements, 8
international cooperation, 5, 23-4
  compliance with court decisions, 45
  convergence of interests, 5
  costs and benefits of, 8
  court's ability to enforce, 11, 13
  WTO Dispute Settlement Body, 11
international court influence, formal theory of
  actors' interests, 15-16
  applicability to regulatory regimes, 12
  assumptions, 16-18
  challenge regarding compliance, 12
  deductive argument, 16
  European Court of Justice
    see European Court of Justice (ECJ)
  formal modeling approach, 15-16
  generality of model, 12
  information transmission process, 13
  large-N statistical analysis, 18-19
  models of judicial politics, 13
  multinational generalization, 13
  WTO dispute resolution body, 15
international court influence on state behavior, formal model of, 23, 47-8, 49-50, 57
  assumptions, 48
  complete theory for, 24-6
  compliance with international law, 48
  dispute generation
    see dispute generation process, model of
  dispute resolution
    see dispute resolution process, model of
  environmental standards, 28-9
  game-theoretic models, 26
  government preferences, 49
  implications of, 57
  judicial process, 48-9
  key components of, 57
  levels of compliance, 49
  plausible explanation, 57
  punishment conditioning, 48
  social policies, 29
  trade barriers, 27-8
International Court of Justice (ICJ), 15
international court rulings
  compliance with
    international cooperation from, 45
    motivation for, 24
    WTO DSB ruling, 22
  effectiveness of, 58
  effect on trade liberalization, 190
    see also ECJ rulings on intra-EU trade, judicial impact of
  empirical implications, 24
  for defendant and plaintiff, 37, 39, 43
  implication of ignoring, 47
  judgment and, 54
  likelihood of compliance with, 193
  noncompliance with
    annulment actions, 79-80

international court rulings (cont.)
  direct actions, 138
  ECJ rulings, 76, 78–82, 130, 194–6
  enforcement actions, 78–9, 130
  infringement rulings, 79, 138–9
  preliminary rulings, 80–2, 130, 138
  result of misunderstandings and errors, 22–3
  third-party government involvement, 193
international courts
  activities, 3–4
  as fire alarm, 24, 32, 47
  as information clearinghouse, 24, 32, 47
  challenges faced by, 47
  design of
    adjudication process, innovations in, 209–10
    appointment and removal of judges, 208
    case generation process, 208–9
    less flexible legal regime, 210–11
    mandate for compliance, 210
  doctrinally innovative, 45
  domestic court and, comparison between, 214–15
  domestic publics role in
    diffuse legitimacy, 216–18
    indirect enforcement mechanism, 216
  effectiveness of, 3–4
  enforcement mechanism, 11
  enforcement powers of, 22
  European Court of Justice
    see European Court of Justice (ECJ)
  facilitating compliance with international law, 192
  facilitating cooperation, 46
  factors influencing adjudication by
    EC's position on legal issue, 133–7
    legal merits of case, 131–3
    measurement concerns, 142–4
    substantive significance, 144–6
    threats of override, 146–50
    variation in judicial procedures, 137–41
  highly legalized
    see highly legalized international courts
  impact on substantive outcomes, 189
  incomplete contract and, 45
  judges on, 64
  motivation for creating, 25, 33
  objectives of, 9

rational design perspective, 9–11, 192
regulatory regime enforcement, 32–3
repeat player, 130
international human rights regime, 12
international institutions
  effectiveness of, 194
  importance of, 1
  influence on state behavior, 5–6
international courts
  see international courts
rational design perspective, 9
  assumptions, 9
third-party review, 1–3
international laws, 1, 5, 192
  domestic law and, comparison between, 214–15
  implications for execution of, 212–13
international legal system, institutional innovations in, 211
  mandate for compliance, 210
  procedural rules of adjudication, 209–10
  shallower agreements, 210–11
international regulatory regimes, multilateral, 2–3, 21
international trade, 7
interstate commerce liberalization
  barriers to, 161
  Commerce Clause and, 160
  Granholm v. Heald ruling and, 160
  limits of judicial relief for, 160–1
interstate trade, ruling for
  dispute resolution mechanism, 162
  GATT membership, 162
  Granholm v. Heald ruling, 160
  states' statutory response to, 160
intra-EU imports, 20, 194
  ECJ rulings impact on, 166–7, 176, 177–9, 180, 183, 184, 186
  levels of, 169
  normalization by GDP, 170–1
  pro-liberalizing trade rulings and, 20
  references and rulings impact on, 166–7
intra-EU trade
  legal challenges to laws with implications for, 163
  liberalization of, 157

judicial decision making, legal principles in, 87
judicial politics, models of, 13

judicial procedures, variation in, 137–41, 154
 financial sanctions, 138–9, 141
 government as defendant, 139–40
 government as litigant, 140
 impact of government briefs, 137–8, 139
 responsive to government briefs, 141
 threat of noncompliance, 138, 139, 154–5

large-N statistical analysis, 18–19
law
 incomplete contracts, 212
 international
  see international laws
 regulatory, 212
 regulatory regime and, 212
legalistic adjudication mechanisms, 25
legal merits of case, 131–3, 153
 AG's position on, 132–3
 approach for controlling, 120, 129
  innovative identification strategy, 87–8
  legal characteristics quantification, 87
  political influences on AG's opinion:
   see AG's opinion, political influences on
  third-party, 88
 balance of, 64
 ECJ rulings reflecting, 86, 131–3
 influence on rulings, 131–2
 judicial decision making, 87
 third-party government briefs and, 86–7
legal system, activation of, 24–5
legitimacy cost, 39
life table, 121–2
litigants, 15
 annulments and preliminary rulings, 71–2
 bringing case, 36, 42

Maastricht Treaty of 1994, 138
majoritarian representation systems, 106
McCarroll v. Dixie Greyhound Lines, 161
measurement errors, 142–4
 random, 143–4
 systematic, 143
 third-party support for plaintiff, 142
member-state compliance, 60–1, 76
 annulment actions, 77–8, 149
 definition of, 76
 enforcement actions, 77
 preliminary reference system, 78

member-state governments
 AG's opinion, political influences on, 96
 amicus briefs, 126
 bringing actions before ECJ, 62
 plaintiff, annulment actions, 83
 plaintiff, preliminary rulings, 83
 political economic clout of, 126–7
 third-party briefs across, 74–5, 126

national bureaucratic efficiency, 173
national court rulings
 see domestic court rulings
net government briefs, 143, 146
 ECJ rulings and, 126, 129, 131, 143
 government litigant, 168
 plaintiff, 110, 116

observational equivalence problem, 45
off-equilibrium path strategies
 punishee, 51
 punisher, 51
on-equilibrium path strategies
 courts, 50–1
 governments, 50
 litigants, 50
override, threats of
 see threats of override

panel-corrected standard errors, estimation of, 169
Political Influence Hypothesis, 83
political preferences on dispute resolution, 15
Political Sensitivity Hypothesis, 19, 47, 58, 193
 difficultly with testing, 20
 statement, 125
Political Sensitivity Hypothesis, testing of
 baseline analysis, 127–9
 dependent variable, 125
 EC's position on legal issue, 133–7, 153–4
 factors influencing adjudication, 131
 independent variable, 125
 legal merits of case, 131–3, 153
 measurement errors, 142–4
 net government briefs and ECJ rulings, correlation between, 126, 129, 131
 noncompliance threats, 130
 political economic clout of member states, 126–7

Political Sensitivity Hypothesis (*cont.*)
  substantive significance, 144–6
  threats of override, 146–50, 154
  variation in judicial procedures, 137–41, 154
political survival forecasting models, 103–8
  based on observed past political experience, 104
  challenges associated with, 103
  hypothesis testing via, 108
  prime minister's party's survival, 104–8
  bargaining environment, 106
  basic measure, 121–2
  causal arguments, 104–5, 107
  Cox proportional hazard model, 122–3
  determinants of, 105, 106, 122
  electoral system types, 106
  home government briefs and AG opinions, 109–14
  hypothesized relationships analysis, 108, 119
  life table, 121–2
  macroeconomic conditions, 106
  sophisticated measure, 122–3
  stable coalition, 106
  survival analysis statistical models, 105–6, 107–8
  probit analysis, 110–11, 123–4
  survival question, 104
preferential trade agreements, performance of, 57–8
preliminary rulings, 62, 82
  baseline analysis of, 175–6
  control of temporal shocks affecting, 173–4
  cross-national variation in, 173
  domestic sources of variation in, 173
  importance of, 189
  intra-EU imports and, 166
  intra-EU trade and, 165–6
  litigant identity for, 71–2
  member state as plaintiff, 83
  member-state compliance, 78
  noncompliance with, 80–2, 130, 138
  national court studies, 81
  national policy and laws, 81–2
  pro-Commission, 171
  third-party government briefs in, 139, 140, 151
  threats of override, 150
  trade effect of, 167–8

prime minister party survival, historical data on, 121–2
prisoners' dilemma
  see collective action challenges
private parties
  annulment actions, 78
  bringing actions before ECJ, 62
  probit analysis, 110–11
  of AG's opinion supporting plaintiff, 110, 116, 123
  of ECJ ruling for plaintiff, 117, 123–4
pro-Commission infringement rulings
  trends in, 171–3
  with and without policy areas, correlation between, 171
pro-Commission preliminary rulings
  trends in, 171–3
  with and without policy areas, correlation between, 171
pro-liberalizing trade rulings and intra-EU imports, 20
proportional representation systems, prime minister's party's survival prospects in, 106
protectionist policies, demand for, 161
pro-trade rulings
  effectiveness of, 58
  likelihood of, 58
punishment strategies, 39
  components of, 40
  factors influencing, 41
  punishment conditioning on litigation process, 40–1
  punishment for defection, 40
  punishment for *t* periods, 41

quantitative restrictions, elimination of, 163

regulatory regimes
  see common regulatory regimes

search and seizure cases, legal characteristics of, 87
Single European Act (SEA), 167
social policies, 29
Spanish Constitutional Court, judges on, 120
standing tribunals, 21
  international regulatory regimes, 2–3
state aids, rulings invalidating, 79–80

Index

state behavior
 international agreements and
  consent-based arrangements, 6
  domestic political context, 6
  managerial model, 6
  realists' position on, 5–6
 international court influence on, formal model of
  see international court influence on state behavior, formal model of
 international institutions and, 5–6
 substantive significance, 144–6
Supreme Court justice votes, legal characteristics of, 87–8

third-party government briefs
 against defendant, 42, 46–7, 58, 64, 67
 Commission v. France (Case 265/95), 203, 204
 differential importance of, 126
 direct actions, 62–3, 139, 140, 151
 distribution across member states, 74–5
 ECJ rulings and, 83, 137–8, 139–40, 141
  government defendant, 139
  government litigant, 140, 151–3
  likelihood for plaintiff, 127
  threat of override, 150
 legal merits of case and, 86–8
 preliminary rulings, 139, 140, 151
 Schmidberger v. Republic of Austria (Case 112/00), 203, 204–5
third-party governments, 32, 125
 ECJ decisions and, 19, 20
 payoff, 34
 preferences for dispute resolution, 15
third-party review, 21
international regulatory regimes, 2–3
threats of override, 146–50, 154
 administrative cases, 149
 annulment actions, 149
 coalitions and, 148
 credibility of, 147–8
 effect of government briefs due, 148
 importance of sensitivity to, 147
 preliminary rulings, 150
 third-party briefs and, 147, 150
trade barriers, lowering, 27–8
 trading partner, 27–8
 unilaterally, 27
Trade Game, 28
Treaty of Rome, 163
Treaty on European Union, 138

US Supreme Court, 218–19
 Granholm v. Heald ruling, 160
United Kingdom (UK) annulment action against EC, 80
United States solicitor general (SG), 88
 as proxy for the legal merits, 88

voter preferences, shift in, 106

water quality, stringent requirements for, 28
World Trade Organization (WTO)
 standing tribunal, 21
WTO agreement
 escape clauses in, 9
WTO Dispute Settlement Body (DSB), 11
 challenges faced by, 15
 focus on trade issues, 15, 21–2
 formal theory testing on, 15
 game-theoretic models and, 26
 political preferences on dispute resolution, 15
 retaliatory penalties through, 192
 ruling against governments, 21–2
 ruling against US government, 22